AF814174

QUE Bee

From Doubts to Distinction
Your ICSE 2026 Exams Partner

GIST OF THE TEXTBOOK
Crisp & Complete Theory - No need to go back to textbooks!

ALL TYPES OF LATEST PATTERN QUESTIONS
Composition Writing & Other Writing Tasks, Unseen Passages of Comprehension, Functional Grammar.

Coverage of Exam Questions
Coverage of all exam questions with solutions

COUNCIL-STYLE ANSWERS
Write responses like an examiner expects

SAMPLE & SPECIMEN PAPER
Practice in real-exam mode. Perfect your timing, strategy and confidence.

arihant
SUCCESS AND NOTHING LESS

ARIHANT PRAKASHAN
(School Division Series)
All Rights Reserved

© PUBLISHER
No part of this publication may be re-produced, stored in a retrieval system or by any means, electronic, mechanical, photocopying, recording, scanning, web or otherwise without the written permission of the publisher. Arihant has obtained all the information in this book from the sources believed to be reliable and true. However, Arihant or its editors or authors or illustrators don't take any responsibility for the absolute accuracy of any information published and the damage or loss suffered thereupon.
All disputes subject to Meerut (UP) jurisdiction only.

ADMINISTRATIVE & PRODUCTION OFFICES
Regd. Office
'Ramchhaya' 4577/15, Agarwal Road, Darya Ganj, New Delhi -110002
Tele: 011- 47630600, 43518550; Fax: 011- 23280316

Head Office
Kalindi, TP Nagar, Meerut (UP) - 250002, Tel: 0121-7156203, 7156204

SALES & SUPPORT OFFICES
Agra, Ahmedabad, Bengaluru, Bareilly, Chennai, Delhi, Guwahati, Hyderabad, Jaipur, Jhansi, Kolkata, Lucknow, Nagpur & Pune.

PO No : TXT-XX-XXXXXXX-X-XX

Published By Arihant Publications (India) Ltd.

For further information about the books published by Arihant, log on to www.arihantbooks.com or e-mail at info@arihantbooks.com

Follow us on

PRICE ₹225.00

PRODUCTION TEAM

Publishing Manager
Keshav Mohan

Project Head
Manju

Cover Designer
Bilal Hashmi

Inner Designer
Ankit Tyagi

Page Layouting
Lalit Chaprana

Proof Reader
Harsh Agarwal

QUE Bee

ICSE
ENGLISH LANGUAGE (PAPER 1)
Class 9 & 10

No. of Questions in the Book

Chapters	Number of questions	Chapters	Number of questions
Descriptive Compositions	25	E-Mail Writing	19
Narrative Compositions	20	Unseen Passages	21
Argumentative Compositions	21	Tenses (Fillers)	23
Short Stories	21	Prepositions (Fillers)	21
Picture Compositions	21	Conjunction and Combination of Sentences (MCQs)	64
Letter Writing	31	Transformation of Sentences (MCQs)	137
Notice	17		

Created by

Mrs. Gitika Sharma

MA, M.Phill (English and Economics)

Special Faculty, St. Mary's Academy & Sophia Girls School, Meerut

Contributors

Parneet Kaur, Vaishali Jaiswal, Saba

From Learner to Leader

Step-Into the Spotlight

QUE Bee is more than just a book - it's a platform for young achievers like you to guide future toppers. If you've cracked the code to smart study or have insights that can make learning easier for others, this is your moment to shine!

What Can You Share?

- Your study techniques, time management tips, or motivation hacks
- Feedback or suggestions to make QUE Bee even better
- Real experiences that can guide other students through the exam maze

What's in It for You?

- Your name will be featured in our exclusive Student Panel in the next edition
- Win exciting & surprise rewards for impactful suggestions
- **Get published** - your photo, Ideas-or even interviews can be featured in the book
- **Become a student icon** - recognized and followed by peers across schools

Let your learning become someone else's ladder.
Be remembered. Be featured. Be the guide.

SCAN TO SHARE YOUR IDEA

Index

Latest
Course Structure

PAPER 2 - ENGLISH LITERATURE (Two hours) - 80 Marks

All questions will be compulsory.

QUESTION 1

Candidates will be required to write a composition of about 300– 350 words from a choice of subjects which will test their ability to: organise, describe, narrate, report, explain, persuade or argue, present ideas coherently with accuracy and precision, compare and contrast ideas and arrive at conclusions, present relevant arguments and use correct style and format. The topics will be varied and may be suggested by language or by other stimuli such as pictures. The topics will be so chosen so as to allow the candidates to draw on first-hand experience or to stimulate their imagination. The organisation of subject matter, syntax, punctuation, correctness of grammatical constructions and spelling will be expected to be appropriate to the mode of treatment required by the subject.

QUESTION 2

Candidates will have to write a letter from a choice of two subjects requiring either a formal or a friendly mode of treatment. Suggestions regarding the content of the letter may be given. The format of the letter with address, introduction, conclusion, etc., will form part of the assessment. Special attention must be paid to the format of the letter with emphasis on tone and vocabulary appropriate to the context.

QUESTION 3

Candidates will be given a specific situation and will be required to: (a) Write the text for a notice based on given directions. (b) Write an e-mail on the same content as the notice.

QUESTION 4

An unseen prose passage of about 500 words will be given. Uncommon items of vocabulary, or structure will be avoided. A question will be set to test vocabulary. Candidates will be required to show an understanding of the words/phrases in the context in which they have been used. A number of questions requiring short answers will also be asked on the passage. These questions will test the candidates' ability to comprehend the explicit content and organisation of the passage and to infer information, intention and attitude from it. The last question will consist of a summary that will test the candidates' ability to distinguish main ideas from supporting details and to extract salient points to re-write them in the form of a summary. Candidates will be given a clear indication of what they are to summarise and of the length of the summary.

QUESTION 5

There will be a number of short answer questions to test the candidates' knowledge of functional grammar, structure and usage. All the items in this question will be compulsory. They will consist of correct use of prepositions, conjunctions, verbs and structure of sentences

COMPOSITION WRITING

A composition is usually the way a writer assembles words and sentences to create a meaningful work. It is a highly structured and directional form of writing done for a specific purpose. It can use simple vocabulary, descriptive language or analytical structures to inform, persuade, entertain or convince the reader.

Types of Composition Writing

There are many types of compositions. However, in the ICSE Class 9 and 10 English Language Exam, we focus on a few types from which questions are generally asked.

- **Description** A description or descriptive writing, is an account that describes something or someone, listing significant details to provide a reader with a portrayal. In simple words, they are just representation of a person, place or thing in time. They provide the look and feel of objects, with as many details as you'd like.
- **Narration** A narration or narrative writing, is a personal account, a story that the writer tells his or her reader. It is either a true story or an imaginary. It can even be dramatic, in which case you can present each individual scene with actions and dialogue.
- **Argumentation** Also called argumentative writing or debates, an argumentation is basically an exercise in comparing and contrasting. It is the methodological presentation of either side of an argument using logical or formal reasoning. The end result is formulated to persuade why thing A is better than thing B or *Vice Versa.*

Format for Compositions

All of these forms of composition have a single format as discussed below

Introduction It draws the attention of the reader to the central concern of the piece of writing. It can start with an assertion, a statement or a question.

Body It is the main part of the essay. It includes the elaboration and expansion of all the ideas and thoughts to be discussed.

Conclusion It sums up your composition and thus must capture the essence of your writing.

Marking Criteria for Compositions

- The quality of the language and the vocabulary should be appropriate.
- The sentence structure, syntax, grammatical constructions, punctuation and spelling should be ensured to not lose marks.
- There should be a logical flow of thoughts such that the paragraphs form a comprehensive piece of writing.
- There should be no confusions in the written piece.

General Guidelines for Compostion Writing

- Remember to make your composition brief, interesting and complete.
- Follow a chronological order and do not be abrupt while putting forth your ideas and conclusion.
- Flavour your composition with rich vocabulary, idioms and phrases.
- Always plan your composition with a proper introduction, body and conclusion to organise your content.
- Use polite and courteous tone.
- Avoid any criticism of controversial issues.
- Always make sure to re-read your composition for any grammatical, punctuation or spelling mistakes.

DESCRIPTIVE COMPOSITION

A description is a type of writing that vividly describes a person, place, object, event or experience. It outlines the understanding of a person about the thing to be described. The language should be kept simple so that the information can be conveyed in an easy way.

Dos and Don'ts for Writing a Description

Do's	Don'ts
Structure the composition logically. (Start with a clear introduction, followed by well-developed paragraphs, and end with a strong conclusion)	Avoid straying from the main subject or theme of the composition.
Describe what you see, hear, smell, feel and taste as per the demand of the topic.	Avoid Informal language.
Writing in the active voice makes the composition more engaging.	Avoid too many adjectives. Also, avoid writing in a negative tone.

Sample of Description

Write a composition on the 'Christmas Carnival' organised by your school. How did the carnival bring the school community together, and what were some of the most exciting features?

The word 'carnival' itself brings forth tremendous excitement in the hearts of kids and adults alike. The word spells enjoyment and an occasion of fun with friends and family. Every alternate year, our school organises a carnival for students, their families and friends. This year, our school organised the carnival in the month of December and aptly called it the 'Christmas Carnival'.

This year, we had fifteen game stalls and seventeen food stalls. The junior and senior students were divided into groups and deployed at each stall in such an organised manner that they not only got an opportunity to shoulder the responsibility of the stall but also got time to visit other stalls and enjoy the carnival along with their friends. Amongst the game stalls, the most popular ones were Nine Pins, Ring the Duck, Shoot the Basket, Test of Strength, etc.

A large variety of fast food items were served at the various food stalls. There was a persistent rush at the Chaat stall, the Cakes stall and the Cookies stall. The coffee stall also turned out to be a huge favourite. As the evening progressed and the chill increased, everybody wanted to grab a cup of coffee.

As the carnival came to an end with the announcement of lucky draw prizes, everyone left with fond memories of a day filled with laughter and togetherness. The Christmas Carnival was a heartwarming event that strengthened the bonds within our school and created lasting memories for all who took part.

Teacher's Remarks

- Excellent description capturing the festive spirit and excitement
- Well-structured composition with a clear and engaging flow of ideas.
- Specific details about activities and stalls make the narrative lively and relatable.
- Expressive language effectively conveys the joyous mood of the event.
- Adding sensory details enhance the overall impact further.

EXAM ORIENTED QUESTIONS

Q.1 Describe what you see and hear as you move about the corridors and compound during your school break time. How does the scene change after the bell rings? **(ICSE 2025, 20 M)**

Ans. As soon as the bell rings for break time, the quiet classrooms suddenly come alive. Students rush out into the corridors, their footsteps echoing on the tiled floor. Some are laughing and chatting, while others hurry towards the canteen. The air is filled with the mixed sounds of voices, laughter and the clatter of shoes on the ground. Excitement is visible on every face as they enjoy their short break from studies.

In the school compound, small groups of students gather under trees or sit on benches. Some enjoy their lunch, while others share jokes and stories. A few students run across the playground, playing tag or football. Others prefer to relax and watch their friends play. The canteen is the busiest place, with students lining up to buy snacks. The smell of samosas and noodles fills the air, making everyone feel hungry. Some students quickly finish their food to have more time to play.

Teachers walk around, keeping an eye on the students. Some remind the students to keep the place clean, while others chat with their colleagues. Near the water taps, a group of students splash water on each other and laugh loudly. The whole school is full of energy and excitement. Even those who were tired during class now seem refreshed.

Then, the warning bell rings, and everything changes. Students quickly gather their things and start walking towards their classrooms. The noise begins to fade as friends say goodbye and hurry inside. Some students finish the last bites of their food, while others rush to the washroom before class. The playground, once full of movement, becomes empty.

When the final bell rings, silence takes over. The corridors are now quiet, with only a few latecomers running to their rooms. Teachers stand at the doors, waiting for students to settle down. Within minutes, the school returns to its usual calm, and the sound of lessons begins again.

Q.2 Describe the locality in which you live. Give details of what you see and hear as you walk around your locality? What do you especially like about the Place? **(ICSE Specimen 2025)**

Ans. I live in a charming locality that lies on the edge of a bustling city, offering a perfect blend of serenity and vibrancy. As I take a leisurely walk around my area, I am always struck by the harmony between nature and urban life. The streets are lined with tall leafy trees that provide a welcome shade, especially during the warm afternoons. Their branches sway gently in the breeze, creating soft rustling sounds that blend with the distant hum of traffic.

As I walk along the neatly paved roads, I notice rows of quaint houses with small gardens bursting with colorful flowers. The scent of jasmine and marigold fills the air, a fragrance that instantly uplifts the spirit. In the mornings, the streets are quiet, with sounds of the chirping of birds and the occasional car passing by.

I often see children playing in the parks, their laughter and joyful shouts adding to the lively atmosphere.

One of my favourite spots in the locality is the small pond at the corner of the street. Surrounded by willows, it reflects the clear blue sky and offers a peaceful retreat.

Another thing I love about my locality is the sense of community. Neighbours greet each other with warmth and the local markets are always bustling with activity. From fresh fruits and vegetables to handmade crafts, the markets offer a taste of the local culture. The friendly shopkeepers know everyone by name and there's a genuine sense of belonging.

What I particularly like about this place is the balance it strikes between tranquility and the energy of city life. It's a place where I can escape the noise of the world and yet still be connected to the pulse of the city. Living here feels like a perfect mix of peace and activity, making it an ideal place to call home.

Q.3 Describe how you spend your time on a holiday afternoon. Why do you think it is necessary to have these times of quietness and solitude? **(ICSE 2024)**

Ans. On a holiday afternoon, after the usual hustle and bustle of the week, I like to embrace the calm and quiet that comes with having a few hours to myself. With no schoolwork or family commitments to attend to, I find these moments to be a perfect opportunity for relaxation and reflection.

Usually, I start my afternoon by sitting in the cozy corner of my room, where the sunlight pours in through the window, casting a warm golden glow across the room. I love reading books, especially novels and stories that transport me to different worlds.

Reading is my escape from everyday pressures and I find it not only relaxing but also inspiring. Sometimes, I also listen to music - soft instrumental tunes that help clear my mind.

After a while, I might take a walk outside in the garden. The fresh air and the sight of blooming flowers always has a calming effect on me. The chirping of birds, the rustling of leaves and the soft hum of nature make me feel connected to the world around me. I often spend a few moments simply sitting on the porch, enjoying the quiet and letting my thoughts wander.

I also use my holiday afternoons to reflect on the past week what went well, what could have been better and what I learned. These quiet moments help me to clear my mind, recharge and gather my thoughts for the days ahead.

I believe that having these moments of solitude is essential. 'There is no companion as true solitude.' In today's busy world, we are constantly surrounded by noise, both external and internal, whether it's the demands of school, social media or personal goals. Quiet times allow us to slow down, think deeply and reconnect with ourselves. It is during these peaceful moments that we often gain clarity, creativity and a sense of balance. Without such times of reflection and rest, it would be easy to become overwhelmed by the constant rush of life.

Q.4 You are taking a leisurely stroll in a beautiful garden. Describe what you see around you, adding details about the sounds and the scents. (ICSE Specimen 2024)

Ans. I stepped into the garden and instantly, the busy world outside seemed to fade away. The moment I entered, the peaceful atmosphere embraced me. The garden was a perfect blend of colors, sounds and fragrances, creating a serene haven for anyone seeking solace.

Around me, tall trees swayed gently in the breeze, their leaves rustling softly like a whispered secret. The sunlight filtered through the branches, casting playful patterns of light and shadow on the grass below. The rich green of the grass seemed to stretch endlessly, dotted here and there with vibrant flowers in shades of red, yellow and purple. Roses, tulips and marigolds bloomed in full splendor, their petals glistening with dew, adding a burst of color to the landscape.

As I walked further, I noticed a small pond in the distance, its surface calm and reflective. I paused to listen to the soft murmur of water flowing from a nearby fountain, its gentle sound blending perfectly with the chirping of birds in the trees. The air was filled with the melodic hum of bees as they flitted from flower to flower, collecting nectar.

The scent of fresh earth was mixed with the sweet fragrance of jasmine flowers and the sharp, refreshing aroma of mint. Every breath I took felt like a rejuvenating elixir, cleansing my mind and body. The fragrance of blooming flowers seemed to hang in the air, sweet and intoxicating, while the scent of damp soil added a grounding touch.

I paused for a moment, closed my eyes and let the sounds and scents wash over me. The garden was not just a feast for the eyes, but a reminder of nature's simple beauty and the peace it could offer. It was a place where time seemed to slow down and I could truly appreciate the wonders of the world around me because Albert Einstein once said "Look deep, deep, into nature and then you will understand everything better."

Q.5 You are a regular visitor to your school library. Describe your library. Give details of the familiar sights. What do you see and feel as different students come in and check out the books? Why is this place so important? (ICSE 2023)

Ans. Books are called a man's best friends and best place to find them is a library. I am a bibliophile and I love books. You would often find me sitting in the library reading one of the detective mysteries there. Thus, it is safe to say that library is my favourite place to go to in the entire school and I relish my time there. The shelves are stacked with thousands of books that the school has accumulated over many decades. There are many kinds of fiction, non-fiction books and academic books available for students and teachers to choose from. I am personally fond of the fiction section, with books ranging from classics, horror, crime to fantasy fictions and much more. The library also has some interesting non-fiction categories, such as biographies. Mrs. Chawla, the librarian, can often be seen sitting behind her desk, waiting for students to return or issue books.

I often feel amazed by the whole idea of a library where students can come and take the books without worrying about having to buy them. Whenever I see the students selecting the books they want to read or take like with them, I find they have a sense of excitement and anticipation just like me.

I often feel like none of this would have been possible had the library not existed. It feels as if the knowledge of the entire world, everything that each of us would need to know to be successful in our lives awaits us in the library.

I often think of how the books that people check out can help them in their future and if they would look back and think of how this present moment changed their perception or sparked their interest in a particular thing. It all starts with one book.

The place is incredibly important for all the students as it gives them the freedom to read what they wish, a freedom that course books don't often provide. It also gives them the opportunity to learn and grow their knowledge of things outside the curriculum and get inspired by the lives of others through selected biographies. Moreover, Mrs. Chawla is incredibly kind and helps the students with finding books and often ignores the fines when the students tell them why they couldn't return the books on time.

Q.6 You are a regular traveller in your school bus. Describe what you see on your way home from school each after noon. Give details of the familiar sights and sounds you experience each day.
(ICSE Specimen 2023)

Ans. As soon as the bell rung, announcing the end of the day in school, voices of school children could be heard from every corner. I have been regularly using the bus service since nursery to Class 10th. Every year the bus number, driver and conductor keep on changing, though my route remains the same. Even children keep on changing every year. Travelling by school bus is sometimes interesting and at the same time, boring and tedious.

The bus I travel in, picks thirty students from the school and stops at ten places, picking and dropping children. In the morning, my mind feels fresh, enjoying morning scenes. Everything seems peaceful and even the roads remain clear. But the scenario is completely opposite when we return home in the afternoon. All my bus mates become very energetic during that time.

They talk and shout nonstop. Some even fight while others are busy relating their whole day's school experience with their friends.

Due to the peak hour, the streets are packed with people. This is increasing air and noise pollution and causing us to remain stuck in the suffocating traffic jams. While waiting at signals, both the students inside and the people outside make funny faces and wave to each other.

At times, we get hungry and thirsty, and we share our food with each other. While passing through the vegetable sellers, some of us ask the rates of vegetables to irritate them. Then, all of us laugh together. Sometimes, we even play games to entertain ourselves. Travelling from school in the afternoon is definitely a mixture of experiences and a lively time.

Q.7 Describe a time when all the lights in your locality went off. What were the sounds you heard as you sat in the darkness? How did you feel when the lights came on? **(ICSE 2022 Sem II)**

Ans. Have we ever wondered what happens at night? What kind of sounds can we hear in the night? I did and I was shocked to discover how nature is alive even at night when we humans are sleeping and resting.

It was a warm summer evening and my summer vacations were going on. I had just returned after many hours of playing cricket with my friends in the locality and was enjoying the cool air of the AC when suddenly the lights went off.

All of us initially thought that it would come in an hour or so as was the norm. But we all were wrong. The lights would not come back until 4 am and till then we had live without any chilled air, sweating and finding way to beat the heat. The first hour was fine but after that it was a terrible torture.

My parents had lit many wax candles near us so that we could see but the heat was killing us. So, we all made paper fans to dispel the heat. The time was passing really slowly and everyone in my house decided to try to sleep. I also went to my room but could not sleep. Sitting idle by the bed, I realised that the night was not so silent. One could hear even the faintest sounds of movement in the night. I heard the slick movements of the lizards outside the windows and the rustles created by the winds. The '*thap thap*' of the guard's stick could also be heard clearly. I could even hear the tick-tock of the clock.

The night and the sounds made me wonderstruck. For a moment, I forgot all about heat I was feeling and tried to listen as many sounds as could. I don't know how but I fell asleep while doing so. And when I woke up, the electricity was back.

Q.8 If you were granted a special wish what would you choose? Say why you would make this choice and how it will be useful to you and your loved ones.
(ICSE 2022 Sem II)

Ans. If I were granted a special wish, I would choose the ability to heal be it physical, emotional or mental ailments. The world around us is filled with suffering and I often feel powerless when I see loved ones struggling or when I hear about tragedies in the wider world. This wish, I believe, would not only transform my life but also bring immense relief to those around me.

Imagine being able to ease the pain of someone battling a life-threatening illness or soothe the mind of someone overwhelmed by anxiety. I could bring comfort to my grandparents, whose aching joints often make their days difficult. I could offer a sense of hope to friends who feel burdened by stress. Watching someone smile with relief after being healed would be a reward beyond words.

This ability would also allow me to help people far beyond my immediate circle. I could volunteer at hospitals, visit disaster-stricken areas or provide solace to those enduring unimaginable hardships.

In a world where medical resources are often limited and mental health is stigmatised, having the power to heal could bridge gaps and make a real difference.

For me, this wish would hold personal significance as well. I would no longer feel helpless when faced with suffering. It would give me a purpose-a chance to use my gift to create a ripple of kindness and hope in a world that often seems divided. In choosing this wish, I envision not only a healthier and happier life for my loved ones but also a legacy of compassion and service. After all, the greatest gift one can offer is the ability to ease another's pain and help them find joy again.

Q.9 Describe an area in your city or hometown which is famous for its street food. Give details of the familiar sights and sounds you would experience on this street. **(ICSE Specimen 2022 Sem II)**

Ans. A city does not comprise only of the infrastructure or the people residing there but it also comprises its food, festivals, styles, traditions and customs of the city. Every Indian city has its own charm.

For instance, the existence of Kolkata is itself an art. Not only due to the appreciation and thriving of the literal sense of art and culture but there's also more to it. Each and every location has its own style and type of food, which is also influenced by the creed and sect of the people living in majority in that area.

I belong to Kolkata, Old Lake Town region which is very peaceful yet thriving locality. The planned locality was earlier not very developed. There were only street food stalls and small local stores. But now it is full of important food. It has become a leisure hub having many famous local as well as international fast food chains and a shopping mall. The street food stalls still exists in full swing.

One can find many local sweetmeat shops with tasty *sondesh* of many varieties and mishti doi served in mud pots. One can also find small stops to eat the spicy and tangy puchka, churmur and jhaalmudi. It is not uncommon for these stalls and shops to be brimming with customers.

One cannot forget the many varieties of rolls sold here. The stalls selling these rolls are always surrounded by people waiting for their turn to get their delicious rolls. The streets are completely busy with people thronging around hawkers haggling to buy their wares. One can also find stores selling biryanis, macher jhol and many other dishes.

Apart from iconic sweets to popular street snacks, the area also offers other cuisines, including mughlai, chinese and South Indian food, catering to different tastes. Whether indulging in spicy Kolkata biryani or savoring a plate of fish curry and rice, food in lake town reflects the city's rich culinary heritage and evolving modern flavours.

Q.10 Which do you prefer-morning, afternoon, evening or night? Describe your favourite time of the day. What are the sights, sounds, smells and feelings that you associate with your favourite time of the day? Why do you like this part of the day better than the others? **(ICSE 2020)**

Note Choose one part of the day and justify your choice.

Ans. **Morning**

My favourite time of the day is the morning. I like mornings the most because they are quiet, fresh, and full of new energy. When I wake up early, I feel calm and peaceful. The world looks new, and it feels like anything is possible.

In the morning, the sky is painted with soft and beautiful colours. Sometimes, it turns pink, orange or golden. I love watching the Sun rise slowly from behind the trees or buildings. Birds start singing, and their sweet sounds make me feel happy and relaxed. Everything around me feels still, as if the world is gently waking up from sleep.

The air is cool and fresh in the morning. I enjoy taking deep breaths and walking outside for a few minutes. The smell of wet Earth after watering plants or the scent of flowers in the garden is very soothing. Sometimes, I can smell tea or breakfast being made in the kitchen, which makes me feel warm and cozy inside.

Mornings also help me think clearly. My mind is fresh and focused. It is the best time to study or plan my day. I can concentrate better because there are no distractions. The world is quiet, and I feel I have more time to do things calmly.

I like mornings more than afternoons or evenings because the day has not yet become busy or noisy. In the afternoon, it gets too hot and tiring. In the evening, there is traffic, noise, and too much rush. Nighttime is peaceful too, but by then, I am already tired from the whole day.

Morning gives me hope and a chance to start fresh. It is like a new beginning every single day. I feel motivated to do my best and face all challenges. It is also a time when I can enjoy some quiet moments with myself in peace.

This is why morning is my favourite time of the day. It brings me joy, peace, and a fresh start, and I feel thankful for that every day.

Afternoon

Everyone has a part of the day they like the most. For me, it is the afternoon. Many people prefer the morning or evening, but I enjoy the calm and quiet of the afternoon. It is a time when everything slows down a little, and I can relax, think and enjoy small moments.

In the afternoon, the Sun is high in the sky, and everything around looks bright and golden. The trees shine under the sunlight, and the streets look peaceful. There is less noise compared to the busy morning or evening hours. The sounds I hear are soft - maybe the hum of a fan, birds chirping in the distance, or sometimes the sound of a distant vehicle passing by.

The smell of food is often in the air during this time. In many homes, lunch is being cooked, and the smell of spices or freshly made chapatis fills the surroundings. It reminds me of comfort, warmth and home. If I've already eaten lunch, I often feel a little sleepy and relaxed, which adds to the peaceful feeling of the afternoon.

I like this time because it is perfect for reading, drawing or just sitting quietly. Sometimes, I take a short nap, and it helps me feel fresh for the rest of the day. The afternoon gives me a break from the rush and noise that mornings and evenings usually have.

I like the afternoon more than the night because I don't feel tired. I prefer it over the morning because I'm not in a hurry to get ready for school or other things. Evenings are often busy with homework or other activities. But in the afternoon, there is a pause. It is calm, warm and quiet.

That is why afternoon is my favourite time of the day. It helps me slow down and enjoy the simple things around me.

Evening

Out of all the times in a day, I like the evening the most. It is the time when the day starts to slow down, and everything feels more peaceful. After a long day of school or work, evening brings a break. It feels like a reward after working hard throughout the day.

One of the best things about evening is the sunset. The sky looks beautiful with colours like orange, pink, red, and purple. Sometimes, I just sit and look at the sky as the sun goes down. It makes me feel calm and happy. The soft, golden light at this time is neither too bright like the afternoon sun nor too dark like the night. It feels just right.

The sounds of the evening are also nice. Birds fly back to their nests, and you can hear them chirping. Sometimes, the wind blows gently, making the leaves rustle. People return home from work, and the roads slowly become quieter. It feels peaceful.

There are also lovely smells in the evening. Sometimes, the smell of flowers becomes stronger. In my neighbourhood, I can smell food being cooked as families prepare dinner. The smell of fresh food and spices reminds me of home and comfort.

Evening is the time I can relax. I usually sit with my family or go for a walk. I also like to read a book or listen to music during this time. It helps me forget the stress of the day. I like evening more than morning because I am not in a rush. I like it more than afternoon because it is not too hot. I prefer it over night because evening still has some light and energy.

To me, evening is the perfect balance between light and dark, noise and silence, activity and rest. It is the time when I feel most at peace, and that's why it is my favourite time of the day.

Night

Everyone has a time of the day they love the most. Some enjoy the busy mornings, while others like the warm afternoons or peaceful evenings. But for me, the best time of the day is night. I like the calm and quiet that comes after a long, busy day. Night makes me feel peaceful and safe.

At night, the world slows down. The roads become less crowded, and the noise of the day fades away. The sky turns dark, and the stars start to shine. I love looking at the moon and stars. They make the sky look magical. Sometimes, I sit on my balcony and just enjoy the cool breeze and the silence.

The sounds of the night are soft and soothing. I can hear the chirping of crickets and sometimes the distant barking of a dog. Unlike the loud noises of the day, these sounds are gentle. They help me relax.

The smell of night is also special. After the Sun sets, the air smells fresh and cool. If it has rained, the scent of wet Earth fills the air, which I really like. It reminds me of peace and nature.

I enjoy the feeling of being alone with my thoughts at night. It is the best time to read a book, write in my diary or just think. There are fewer distractions, so I can focus better. I often feel more creative and calm during this time.

Night is also a time for rest. After working or studying all day, I look forward to sleeping well. My mind and body both get a chance to relax and recharge.

I like night better than other parts of the day because it is quiet, calm, and gives me time to be with myself. It is a beautiful ending to each day. That is why night is my favourite time of the day.

Q.11 Your class had to conduct a Morning Assembly. Write an account of how you prepared for it, what your role was and what you gained from the experience.

(ICSE 2019)

Ans. I am the class monitor of Class X in our school. One week before Teachers' Day, our school Principal informed me that my class will conduct the Morning Assembly on Teachers' Day. That day, I asked my classmates to wait in the classroom during the short morning break and announced this decision by the Principal. I also informed two classmates that they would look after the public address system and lighting arrangements.

The remaining students of our class (35 in number) would ensure that all the school students were seated in their respective places well before the Principal arrives. I was to act as the Principal.

The programme decided was that after I made the announcements for the day, one student would speak on a topic of interest for five minutes. We chose a highly vocal girl, Rashmi, to speak on the importance of Teachers' Day. For the next two days, we rehearsed our roles in the auditorium.

I made some improvements in what Rashmi had prepared. I also asked her to speak slower than her normal speed as students of junior classes should also understand what she said. The two boys in charge of the sound and light arrangements also checked that all the equipments were in working condition one day before the important day.

The day finally arrived. My classmates came 15 minutes earlier than normal and ensured that all students were seated. When the bell rang for the start of the Assembly, I came out from behind the curtain and walked up to the podium. Simultaneously, all the students stood up. After we had greeted each other, we sang Vande Mataram.

Then, I told the students to sit down and made two announcements. After that Rashmi spoke very enthusiastically on her topic. The rehearsals had paid off handsomely in her case. After singing the National Anthem, I announced the end of the Assembly.

From the experience of conducting the Morning Assembly, I have learned that successfully organising any important event requires proper and detailed planning. I also learnt that it is important to conduct rehearsals to iron out any flaws before the actual event.

Q.12 Summers are becoming hotter with each passing year. Write a description of one such very hot day. What did you see and hear as you walked outside? How were birds and animals affected? (ICSE 2019)

Ans. I was spending the summer holidays in my small native village. It was the beginning of June when I had to go out to the post office in the nearby village for some work. The morning was very stuffy. There was not a single cloud in the sky or any breeze to dry my sweat as I walked three-kilometre distance on the cart track. As the Sun rose higher and higher, it shone more strongly. Although I was wearing a cap, I felt the Sun's heat. I walked on the ground that seemed as hot as a furnace.

Then, hot winds began to blow and the dust started swirling around me. I saw that the condition of birds and animals was as bad as mine. The birds were trying to seek shelter in the trunk of leafless trees. I saw some black buffaloes that had lain down in a pond which still had some water. The trees and bushes looked withered.

The grass was yellowed and totally dry. The cart track was deserted, as all people were indoors. I did not meet anyone during the 30 minutes I walked to the post office.

By the time, I finished the work at the post office, it was 2 p.m. I was dreading the trek back home. However, I was lucky to find a small dhaba in this village where I could eat lunch and relax till the evening in the shade. As I had nothing to do back at home, I decided to go back later. After eating a delicious lunch, I dozed off while sitting under the fan in the dhaba.

The heat continued till evening. When I woke up, I found that the Sun was about to set. After having tea at the dhaba, I started the walk back home. People had begun to move about. The silence of the village was broken by the shouts of some hawkers and it seemed like. The village was coming to life. I hastened my steps and reached back home. The first thing I did was take a bath and change into fresh clothes. I was feeling comfortable again.

Q.13 You had been waiting outside the examination hall. Describe what you saw and the sounds you heard when you arrived at the place. What were your feelings? Describe how the scene changed once you entered the hall and the examination started. (ICSE 2018)

Ans. Examinations sap the examinees of energy and make them sleepless for nights. But then, it has not so far been possible to devise a better way of judging their ability. So, they are a necessary evil which all students have to face. Students have to work hard for months. As the crucial day arrives, they reach the examination hall in tension.

I had a similar experience during my Board examination. A few minutes before the start of the first paper, I saw a strange scene outside the examination hall. An eerie silence prevailed there. The examinees were carrying their books and notes in their hands which they had already mugged up and were now trying to revise. Most of the examinees were not inclined to talk to anybody. But a few, sitting or standing in groups of two or three, were seen discussing some points. I did not form a group, rather stood alone to wait for the Supervisor to turn up.

Even the dullest students appeared to be great scholars outside the examination hall. They were reading their books most attentively. Some of them may have been thinking of devising some means of copying or how to behave if they were caught copying.

Most of the students reached the examination hall well before time. They looked at the notice-board to find out their room and even tried to locate their seats. As soon as the bell rang, all the students entered the hall.

A few examinees reached the hall late and entered in a state of great excitement. The supervisor was lenient and accommodated them. Soon, everyone was seated in silence. The only sound was that of the supervisor who was getting ready to distribute the papers and announcing the rules of the exam. No one talked or tried to recall anything, rather everyone prayed and prepared to do their best.

Q.14 There has been heavy rain in your city/town. You went to school but found that it was closed because of the rain. Describe the sights and sounds near the school and narrate how you finally reached home and spent the rest of the day. (ICSE 2017)

Ans. It had been raining very heavily since last night with lightning and sound of thunder terrifying us. In the morning, the streets and roads were flooded but still I got ready for school. I took a raincoat and left.

While walking, I saw that there was water everywhere. At some places, it was knee deep. Fewer people could be seen on the roads. The roads had disappeared under the water and one could cross it only by walking through it.

I saw no student of my school on the way except Mr. Sharma. He teaches Maths at our school and rarely takes any leave. Though the rain had stopped, water drops were falling from the tree leaves as if it was still raining. The sky had become dark again with heavy clouds suggesting that it could rain at any moment, so I was walking at an escalated speed.

When I reached the school, I saw a large notice stating that the school was closed for the day due to water entering some of the classrooms. The school grounds were also flooded. A few other students had braved the weather and made it to school in spite of the odds.

I decided to go back home since the weather looked uncertain. As I was leaving, I saw Rishi, a friend of mine, entering the school campus. I greeted him and shared the news with him. We live nearby so we decided to go together. he told me that the road he took wasn't flooded, so we took that path.

On the way, I saw a few huts which were in a very bad condition. The tin sheets on top of a few had fallen down. They were being put back in place by people. Nearby, a couple of trees were struck by lightning and had fallen on the footpath. The road, however, was cleaner than the one I took and thus, I reached home in little time.

My mother was waiting for me. She told me to change into clean clothes as soon as she saw my wet trousers. I was given a hot cup of milk and told to study at home. Soon, it started drizzling again. Looking out the window, I wondered how the rain had troubled people and prayed it would stop soon.

Q.15 You walk home from school one afternoon to find the door unlocked and on entering you are shocked to see the house in total disarray. You call out but get no answer. Describe in detail what you saw, the reason behind your house being in total disarray and how you found your family. Mention also, how the experience ended and what impact it had on your life. (ICSE 2016)

Ans. I returned home from school in the afternoon. When I reached home, I found the door unlocked. I went inside and was shocked to see the house in total disorder.

I called my mother, who would usually be home at that time, but nobody answered. When I entered the drawing room, the whole furniture was turned up side down.

Every bag and almirah was emptied, throwing everything on the floor. It seemed that the whole house was searched for something. What was more disturbing and strange was that nothing was stolen; even the i-phones and i-pods were on the desks, along with my mother's wallet.

As I was worried about my mother and younger brother, I enquired all my mother's friends and our relatives.

She was at one of her friends' house. Hearing about the incident, my mother arrived home in ten minutes and was equally horrified to see the house in such a condition.

My mother informed me that she had gone to meet her friend who had won a lottery. She might have not locked the house properly in a hurry. Later, after much investigation, it was found that some small children, who were playing outside, were being chased by some monkeys.

In panic, the children, seeing the door unlocked, entered the house to hide but the monkeys followed them.

A long hide and seek game ensued between the children and the monkeys. The monkeys were responsible for throwing everything out of the closets and the furniture was turned upside down by the children.

Somehow, the children managed to hide themselves in the store adjacent to our bedroom. Monkeys left and went outside the house. We all breathed a sigh of relief that there was no theft or robbery. It took at least two hours to settle the house again in order.

It was really an unforgettable day in my life as I got really scared looking at the condition of my house and not one member of my family member present there. But, I thanked God that my mother's mistake resulted in something positive and saved small children from being harmed by the monkeys.

Q.16 Describe in detail the view from your bedroom window. Does your room overlook a park? A busy street? What are the sights, sounds and smells that you would typically see, hear and experience at different times of the day? (ICSE 2015)

Ans. My bedroom is the zone of maximum comfort for me. The mere sight of my bed, study table, almirahs, etc. dispels all my fatigue and freshens me up. The view from the window is very beautiful. My window overlooks a park. The park has tall and wide trees which attract a variety of birds like parrots and white pigeons. The grass and bushes are neatly trimmed and the little plants bear flowers in many colours. There is a jogging track too built inside the park. Indeed, just one look outside the window has such a soothing effect on me, which is beyond description.

In the morning after waking up, I see people running and jogging on the track. I also hear the sounds and hoots of birds. Besides, the breeze of dawn coupled with the aroma of trees, prepares me to kickstart my day on a positive note. I, however, enjoy the evening view the most.

When I return home in the evening, the sweet smell of the trees and the sight of little kids playing in the park rejuvenate my soul. The rays of the setting Sun are scattered all over the sky giving it the most radiant look. The birds are seen returning to their homes and there is a pleasant and calm aura all around.

I gaze at all the trivialities and activities that are visible from my window while taking my evening snacks and tea. Sometimes, my sister joins me and we chat and discuss the various things and people around us. We also miss the regular visitors if they do not turn up.

The comfort that one draws at one's home is unmatched by all the luxuries of expensive hotels and buildings. The little corner called the bedroom is the coziest place.

Therefore, the window of my room and the view of the park are seemingly little things but together they make up an integral part of my daily routine.

Q.17 You were on a school trip and were on your way back to the hotel late one night when your school bus, full of children, broke down in a lonely area. Describe what you saw and experienced as you looked around. How was the problem solved?

Ans. We had been looking forward to our school trip from the very first day in Class X. Every year, school plans tours for every class and it is always a special affair. This year, we went to Nainital for three nights and four days. We left for Nainital late in the night. We reached our hotel in the morning and after breakfast, our teachers advised us to take some rest.

After some rest, we got ready and gathered for lunch. After having a hearty lunch, we left for local sight seeing and shopping in the local markets. In evening, our teachers gathered us for dinner. We dined at a local restaurant which was celebrated for its taste and variety.

It was dark when we left for our hotel. Singing songs, we had hardly reached half way when suddenly the bus broke down. It was 11 pm and we were in a deserted place. The driver left the bus to find a garage so that he could get it fixed. It was totally dark and cold too. The hills and trees outstretched on both the sides.

It was an eerie feeling.

Our teachers were also worried but they kept their calm and instructed us to remain quiet and not to make any noise, least we drew attention of anti-social elements. At a distance of 200 metres, we saw some light for there were lamps burning. We all moved towards it with hope in our hearts. We saw a group of friends who were camping there.

They were singing, dancing and enjoying themselves around the bonfire. When we approached them, they were shocked and questionably looked at us. They asked us a lot of questions. We told them our predicament. They asked all the students to use their tents. We all had such a nice time dancing, singing and sharing some of our school experiences with them. It became the most memorable trip ever.

Then, noodles were prepared and everyone enjoyed their late night maggi around the bonfire. We were awake until the first rays of the sun indicated that it was morning. The bus was redeemed and so we all bid our goodbyes to the lovely people who helped us and made our trip an exciting adventure to be cherished life-long.

Q.18 People play a very important role in our lives. Describe in vivid detail, any one person and show how he/she has been a very special influence in your life.

Ans. When reflecting on personal influences in my life, no one has had a greater impact than my father. He is a role model for me. He always stands by my side. Whenever I fall down, he encourages me to stand up by myself. I have always admired his open mind, compassion and sense of understanding. He is a very reserved man but has a great sense of humour and always knows how to put a smile on my face.

One good lesson my dad has taught me is that you most likely won't have the answer to everything but that is what life is for–to learn from your mistakes and find the answers you are looking for. From him, I also learned the value of standing up for oneself.

My father has always taught me right behaviour. I still remember the day when my father sat next to me and convincingly said, "Hey son! The most important thing that will help you become a successful person is your honesty. Never lie to anyone and never lie to yourself."

He slowly explained the value of honesty and explained how every bad situation in the world began with a lie. I always look back on his words whenever I am in trouble.

In every aspect of my life, my father continuously pushes me towards excellence. Whenever I feel like giving up, or have a question or a concern, I know I can always call on him for advise. He has taught me to consider everyone a part of my family and to love people by sharing and giving. From him, I have learned that sometimes you have to put other's needs ahead of your own but only to a certain extent.

His strength seems to be unbreakable during hard times. He is extremely determined to accomplish anything he sets his mind and heart on. I hold great esteem for how he stands up for what he believes in and never back down. I am what I am because of him and whatever I will achieve in my life will be credited to him.

Q.19 The waiting room at a railway station presents a wonderful opportunity to observe human behaviour. Describe an experience when you were early for a train and had to spend some time in the waiting room with different kinds of people.

Ans. If you ever want to observe human behaviour closely, I think one of the best places to do so is the waiting room of a railway station that accommodates a huge variation of our modern day society. I was enroute Delhi to Kolkata and due to an unfortunate misunderstanding, was forced to switch trains at Lucknow. The time gap was two hours between both train hence, I had no other option but to take refuge at the waiting room of the railway station.

As I entered the waiting room, a foul smell tickled my nostrils but I soon became accustomed to it.

The announcement of the arrival of a train made some seats vacant and I quickly occupied one and made myself comfortable. Opposite to me, a family of five was busy haggling over some petty issue. Apparently, the wife had forgotten to complete some household chores before leaving and the husband was reprimanding her for the same.

Their three children, the eldest being not more than eight years old, were chasing each other around the waiting room and the mother was screeching her head off trying to control them.

On another bench, sat an elderly couple who were hardly talking to each other. They seemed to be too lost in a world of their own, probably weighed down by the worries of this relentless world. Suddenly, the old lady said something which brought a smile to the otherwise serious face of the gentleman and he keenly began to observe the three little ones playing with each other.

Another young newly married couple sat in the farthermost corner of the room talking in hushed voices to each other. Fortunately, the next announcement was for their train and they were replaced by a contingent of women hockey players who were returning from a match. By their upbeat mood and excitement, one could easily guage that they had won their match and were now eager to get back home.

It was indeed a very interesting two hour wait. Isn't it strange that when a person sits idle, he notices a variety of human behaviour which normally a troubled mind would have overlooked? Such was the case with me and believe me, I enjoyed every moment of it till the arrival of my train was announced.

Q.20 You are an audience at the famous Coldplay concert happening in your city. Suddenly, trouble erupts in the auditorium and you witness a riot among the crowd. Give a vivid description of the scene. What was your experience?

Ans. The Coldplay concert started as a magical evening. The air was filled with the soulful chords of Fix You, and thousands of us swayed in unison, lost in the music. The stage was a dazzling display of lights, shimmering confetti and Chris Martin's magnetic energy. But then, without warning, the harmony shattered.

At first, it was just a faint disturbance-murmurs from a section of the crowd near the stage. A man shouted sharply, cutting through the music. Heads turned, confusion spread and the evening's perfect rhythm faltered. Suddenly, like a spark in dry leaves, chaos erupted. A scuffle broke out between two groups and the reason was unclear. People pushed and shoved, trying to move away. The sharp sound of a bottle smashing on the floor caused panic. Screams mingled with Coldplay's melodies, which now felt distant and surreal.

The orderly rows of fans dissolved into a chaotic mass. A man stumbled, bleeding from his forehead, while a terrified woman clung to her friend. The flashing stage lights only added to the confusion. One moment, there were anxious faces; the next, security officers rushed in to calm the situation.

Chris Martin and the band stopped playing, their expressions showing shock and concern. 'Calm down, everyone!' Chris shouted into the microphone, but his words were drowned out by the chaos. Security personnel formed barriers to separate the agitators from the rest of the crowd. The air was thick with fear, the smell of sweat and spilled drinks overpowering. People began moving toward the exits, jostling and shouting as they tried to escape.

Eventually, the riot subsided when the police arrived and restored order. The once–joyful auditorium was now a mess–upturned chairs, scattered belongings and broken glass on the floor. I stood frozen, heart pounding, unable to process how a night of celebration had turned into such chaos. As I left, the echoes of Coldplay's unfinished song stayed with me, a haunting reminder of how quickly joy can turn to disorder.

Q.21 You have returned to your city after spending five years in a foreign country. The city has changed during your absence. Describe the changes that have affected the life of people in the city. Give your personal views regarding the changes.

Ans. I spent five years outside my home country, so coming back amid all the changes was a sensory overload. It was so bewildering to see how the city I left behind looked almost unrecognisable. I remember trying to spot familiar landmarks outside the train window, but all I could feel was nostalgia mixed with wonder.

Major buildings in the city came off as a bit bizarre, but the unchanged aspects of the city offered some comfort.

I remember the modest structures that used to surround the streets, now multiplied into modern skyscrapers. The narrow, congested lanes in the city were transformed into clean widened roads, which along with the electric buses, were a testament to the efficiency the new metro network offered. All of these changes helped tame the chaotic unruly traffic the city suffered from.

The LED streetlights that illuminated the streets now complimented the parks full of colourful flowers that were previously barren and neglected. Not only did the greenery offer families a place to enjoy their evenings, but the designated cycle lanes helped encourage them to lead a healthier lifestyle.

Every corner of the city was in contact with the technology. There were smart kiosks everywhere in the marketplaces that served information and a plethora of other services at the touch of a button. The markets on the other hand had transformed into organised, clean, modern houses of retail stores and shops which paired beautifully with the old style. Even my favourite street food vendor accepted digital payments!

While I was impressed by these changes, a part of me missed the slower, simpler pace of the old city. The warmth of neighbours chatting at every corner and the leisurely life I grew up with seemed somewhat overshadowed by this new, fast-paced lifestyle.

Yet, I couldn't deny that these changes had improved the quality of life. Pollution levels had dropped, public spaces were cleaner and people seemed more connected to their surroundings.

As I stood on a terrace overlooking my transformed city, I felt pride and hope. Though it had changed, it retained its soul. This balance between progress and tradition gave me confidence that my city was evolving into a better place while still holding on to its roots.

Q.22 Recently, your elder sister moved to Sikkim for her higher studies. You visited her during your school summer break. While you were there, you explored the beauty of the place. Describe your experience.

Ans. This summer, I had the chance to visit my elder sister in Sikkim, where she had moved for her higher studies. It was my first trip to this mystical state, and I was mesmerised by its beauty. Sikkim was like a painting come alive, with its breathtaking landscapes, vibrant culture and serene atmosphere.

As our car climbed the winding mountain roads, I was greeted by lush green valleys and snow-capped peaks in the distance. The crisp mountain air was a welcome change from the summer heat of the plains. Every bend in the road revealed a new postcard-perfect view-cascading waterfalls, terraced fields and quaint villages nestled against the hillsides.

One of the highlights of my trip was a visit to the famous Tsomgo Lake. Surrounded by rugged mountains, the lake's turquoise waters reflected the sky like a mirror. Yak rides by the lake added to the charm of the experience. Later, we visited the Rumtek Monastery, an architectural marvel.

The colourful prayer flags fluttering in the wind and the soothing chants of the monks created an atmosphere of peace and spirituality.

Exploring Gangtok, the capital city, was equally delightful. The MG Marg, with its vibrant shops and cosy cafes, had a unique charm. I particularly enjoyed sipping a warm cup of butter tea while taking in the lively atmosphere. The people of Sikkim, with their warm smiles and gentle nature, made me feel at home.

One morning, we woke early to witness the sunrise over Kanchenjunga. The golden rays hitting the snow-covered peak left me awestruck, a sight so beautiful it felt otherworldly. Sikkim's commitment to sustainability also stood out. Clean streets, no plastic waste and lush greenery everywhere made me realise how much could be achieved with community effort.

As I returned home, I carried with me not just pictures but memories of a land so beautiful and serene that it felt like a dream. My summer in Sikkim wasn't just a vacation-it was a journey into nature's heart and a reminder of the wonders our country holds.

Q.23 Recently, you visited the 'Bandhavgarh National Park'. Describe your visit.

Ans. During autumn break, my family planned to visit Bandhavgarh National Park, which is situated in the Umaria district of Madhya Pradesh. My father planned everything and had booked two rooms in a resort situated near the park. We went by our own car as it is more convenient for family outings. We started our journey early morning around 5 am and stopped only for breakfast and lunch.

At around 6:15 pm, we reached the resort. We decided to rest for the night and go around the park the next day. Bandhavgarh has one of the highest density of Bengal Tigers known in the world and is a famous natural hub for white tigers. Our very first three-hour drive in Bandhavgarh Tiger Reserve had converted us into total tiger devotees.

The next day, we saw a large male tiger, named Charger, the undisputed hero of Bandhavgarh. This chance sighting of the tiger became the highlight of our entire trip. We realised that our guide, Dewan, was a terrific tiger tracker. His mind worked very sharply, like that of a tiger.

It was he who helped us spot Charger. It was a massive creature, royal in stature, assured of itself, walking with a relaxed attitude and a full stomach. Charger demonstrated his masculinity as he marked his territory at regular intervals. Over the next two days, we happened to see Charger twice again.

On the last day, on an elephant's back, we were taken very close to yet another tigress and her two full grown cubs.

Four days, ten individual tigers, sixteen sightings, we could not ask for more. Bandhavgarh had more to it than just tigers. During the safari drive, we got opportunities to watch three species of vultures, lesser adjutant and woolly-necked storks, the resident brown fish owl, green pigeons, peacocks and peahens of all shapes and sizes and the famous malabar pied hornbills. The total number of bird species recorded in the area is nearly 25. It was an experience of a life-time and worth the effort. I will cherish those memories for a long time to come.

Q.24 **You planned an adventure with some friends while you were in Delhi for a competition. You went out at night to explore a seemingly spooky place. You experienced something strange which later turned out to be a facade. Describe your experience.**

Ans. Last winter, while in Delhi for a debate competition, my friends and I decided to make our trip memorable by exploring an abandoned haveli (mansion) rumoured to be haunted. The whispers about strange happenings piqued our curiosity and we ventured there late at night.

The haveli stood in eerie silence, its crumbling walls and ivy-covered facade glowing under the pale moonlight. Its broken windows resembled hollow eyes and the creaky gate groaned as we stepped inside. The air felt damp and heavy, carrying a faint smell of decay.

As we moved deeper, the silence gave way to unsettling sounds. The floorboards groaned beneath us and faint whispers seemed to echo in the darkness. Our torchlight flickered and a shadow darted across the wall. Just then, we heard a loud bang, as if a door had slammed shut on its own.

Fear began to creep in when we saw a white, ghostly figure appear at the end of the corridor. It moved toward us slowly, its shape hazy in the dim light. We froze, unable to run, as the figure came closer.

Suddenly, the tension broke with the sound of laughter.

A group of teenagers appeared, holding up a white sheet.

To our astonishment, they revealed it was a prank! They had overheard our plans and decided to scare us. The eerie noises had been created using hidden speakers and the 'ghost' was simply a clever setup.

Relief flooded over us and soon we were laughing along with them. What had started as a terrifying adventure became a story we would fondly recall. Though the haveli wasn't haunted, the thrill of facing our fears made the experience unforgettable.

As we left the haveli, the streets of Old Delhi seemed less spooky and more alive with possibilities. The night taught us that even in the scariest situations, there is often more humour than horror waiting to be discovered.

Q.25 **A village fair is very different from a city one. It is usually held annually and is connected with a religious festival or harvest. The purpose of such fairs is usually trade and to exhibit and sell village handicrafts. Describe one such fair.**

Ans. A village fair is very different from one in a city. The village folk seek entertainment in fairs and festivals. It is usually held annually and connected with a religious festival or harvest festival. The purpose of such fairs is usually trade and to exhibit and sell village handicrafts. The shopkeepers open temporary stalls in such fairs. The magicians and jugglers also entertain people and make money.

Punjab is a land of vibrant people who celebrate festivals and other occasions with great zeal and enthusiasm. Baisakhi is one such occasion as it marks the beginning of the harvesting of crops, signifying reaping the fruit of their labour. Last year, I went to visit my maternal uncle in Punjab. I was overjoyed to see the fair which was spread over a large tract of open land.

The stalls were tastefully decorated with ribbons and buntings. Young people all decked up in beautiful bright clothes were being irresistibly drawn towards the stalls where ornaments of all colours were displayed.

The greatest attraction of the fair was the wrestling bouts being held in a big open ground surrounded by the spectators. Big prizes had been announced for the wrestlers winning over their respective rivals.

There was a vast variety of sights that attracted the attention of the visitors. A motor cyclist was running his vehicle on the walls of a pucca pit.

A magician was showing his tricks. There was also a snake charmer, a monkey show and a bear dance. Children were especially interested in buying balloons and toys.

The shopkeepers who had put up their stalls of eatables were having a hay day. Pakoras and jalebis could not be missed by anybody as they are the favourite with the Punjabis.

However, the greatest attraction of the fair was 'Bhangra', the folk dance of Punjab, which was being performed enthusiastically by a few young boys. The cattle fair was a sight not to be missed since the best breeds of cattle-the cows, bulls, horses, buffaloes, etc. were brought for sale. In this way, fairs show the rich cultural heritage of a state to the people in the stands.

NARRATIVE COMPOSITION

A narrative composition is a written description of an event that took place in one's life. It is presented to its readers in the form of a story or an essay, providing them with the necessary details in proper order so that the message is conveyed thoroughly. A narration is usually based on the real life experience or incident.

Dos and Don'ts for Narrative Composition

Do's	Don'ts
Structure the composition logically.	Avoid introducing too many aspects.
Narrate your experiences keeping in mind the small details.	Avoid leaving the reader with unanswered questions.
Incorporate vivid descriptions of settings, emotions and actions to create a clear mental picture for the reader.	Avoid informations that seems to distract from the focus.

Sample of Narrative Composition

You are of forgetful nature. Once you bought a lottery ticket and kept it safely. Later you were informed that you have won the first prize on your lottery ticket. But where was the lottery ticket? Narrate how you managed to find out the lottery ticket.

I have always been known for my forgetful nature, a trait that often leads me into awkward situations. However, I never imagined that my forgetfulness would result in something as intense as the search for a lottery ticket that held the first prize. A few weeks ago, I bought a lottery ticket from a local agent after much persuasion. I wasn't particularly keen on lotteries, but I decided to buy the ticket for the sake of trying my luck. The agent assured me that I should keep it safe and I made a mental note to do so.

One afternoon, I received news that I had won the first prize of ₹ 5 crore in the Maharashtra State Lottery. The moment I heard this, I was both excited and alarmed, for I had absolutely no recollection of where I had placed the lottery ticket. The news of my win quickly turned into a dilemma. I checked all my pockets, my bag, and even the counter of my shop, but the ticket was nowhere to be found.

I quickly left my shop and headed home, hoping to recall where I had stored the ticket. As soon as I reached home, I began searching through my cupboard. I checked every drawer and every possible nook and cranny in my study but the ticket was nowhere to be found.

Panicked and desperate, I called my wife, asking her to return home immediately. She arrived soon and joined me in the search. We turned the house upside down, looking through every possible place where I could have kept the ticket.

Just as I was about to give up, my wife suddenly remembered that she had given the ticket to our son to keep it safe. We immediately called him at his office, and he confirmed the ticket was safe with him. He rushed home, and when he handed it over to me, a wave of relief washed over me.

In the end, this experience taught me an important lesson. Forgetfulness can sometimes lead to stressful situations but with patience and help from those around you, even the most challenging problems can be solved.

EXAM ORIENTED QUESTIONS

Q.1 Your friends once played a harmless prank on you. Give an account of what happened, you response to the prank and what you learnt from the experience. **(ICSE 2025, 20 M)**

Ans. One evening, my friends and I were sitting in the park, talking and laughing. It was a normal day and I had no idea that they were planning to play a prank on me.

Suddenly, my friend Rahul pointed towards a tree and said, "Look! There's a snake!" I froze in fear. I have always been scared of snakes. My heart started beating fast and I quickly moved away. My other friends also pretended to be scared. They ran in different directions, making me even more frightened.

Rahul then shouted, "It's coming towards you!" That was enough for me-I turned around and ran as fast as I could. I didn't stop until I reached the park gate. My friends burst into laughter. Confused, I turned back and saw them holding a rubber snake in their hands. That's when I realised they had tricked me!

At first, I felt embarrassed. But soon, I started laughing too. I had to admit, they got me really well. It was just a harmless joke and they didn't mean to hurt me. Later, we all sat together, and they promised not to scare me like that again. We talked about other funny pranks we had seen or experienced before.

This experience taught me an important lesson. Sometimes, we take things too seriously, but it's okay to laugh at ourselves. I also understood that friends may play pranks, but they do it for fun, not to make us feel bad. However, I also learned that we should be careful while playing pranks so that no one gets truly hurt or scared.

That day, I realised that friendship is about fun, laughter and understanding. Even though I was scared at first, in the end, it became a funny memory that we still talk about and laugh about today. It showed me that the best friendships are filled with joy, trust and unforgettable moments.

Q.2 Your teacher has asked you to form a group and work on a particular project. Write an account of how you work together and each of you learned through this experience. **(ICSE Specimen 2025)**

Ans. Our teacher assigned us a project in which we were to form a group and work together. The task was to create a presentation on 'The Impact of Social Media on Society'. At first, I was a bit unsure about working in a group but soon, I realised that the experience would be a great learning opportunity.

We were a group of four members– Riya, Aman, Neha and myself. We began by dividing the work based on our strengths. Riya, who is good at researching, was in charge of gathering information. Aman, who is skilled at creating visuals, handled the design and presentation slides. Neha, being a confident speaker, took responsibility for presenting the final product. I, on the other hand, was in charge of compiling the information and organising the content for the presentation.

At first, we faced some challenges. Since everyone had different schedules, it was difficult to find time to meet. However, we decided to use online tools to collaborate, share ideas and drafts on Google Docs.

This way, we could work independently but still stay connected. Over time, we learned how to communicate effectively and respect each other's opinions. Even though there were disagreements about the design of the slides, we discussed our views openly and found a middle ground that suited everyone.

Through this project, I learned the importance of teamwork and flexibility. Working together taught me to trust my teammates and value their strengths. I also realised that good communication is key to overcoming challenges. Riya learned how to manage time effectively, as she had to balance research with other responsibilities.

Aman discovered that creativity is not just about design but also about how information is presented. Neha gained confidence in public speaking and learned how to engage an audience.

In conclusion, this group project not only helped us gain knowledge about the topic but also improved our collaboration skills.

We each grew individually and as a team and the experience made me realise the value of working together towards a common goal.

Q.3 Narrate an incident from your experience in which your parents had entrusted you with a difficult task. Give details of the task, how you carried it out and your feelings at the end. **(ICSE 2024)**

Ans. Last year, my parents entrusted me with a task that seemed simple at first but turned out to be much more difficult than I had imagined. It was my mother's birthday, and my father, who was busy with work, asked me to organise a small surprise party at home. The task was to invite the relatives, order the food, decorate the house and ensure that everything went smoothly without my mother suspecting anything. I immediately felt excited and confident at the start. I created a guest list and sent out invitations to our relatives. Then, I started making arrangements for the food, choosing a caterer who could deliver the dishes my mother loves. However, as the day of the event approached, things began to get complicated.

First, the caterer called to inform me that there was a mix-up with the order and some dishes would be delayed. Then, my younger brother, who was supposed to help with the decorations, spilled paint all over the living room carpet. I was starting to feel overwhelmed, but I knew I couldn't disappoint my parents, especially my mother.

I quickly rearranged things. I called a local restaurant for backup food and spent the next few hours cleaning up the mess with my brother. I also improvised with the decorations, using some handmade banners and flowers from the garden.

As the evening approached, I began to feel the pressure but I kept reminding myself that I had to stay calm. When my mother entered the house and saw all the guests waiting for her, her face lit up with surprise and joy. The party was a huge success. Everyone praised the food, the decorations and the atmosphere.

At the end of the evening, I felt an immense sense of pride and relief. The task had been difficult but I had managed to pull it off. I realised that with patience, problem-solving and hard work, I could handle even the most challenging situations. It was a moment of personal growth, and I was glad my parents had trusted me with such an important task.

Q.4 Have you ever forgiven someone when it was hard to do so? Explain what helped you to forgive them, and the positive impact it had. What did you learn from the experience? **(ICSE Specimen 2024)**

Ans. A few months ago, I faced a situation where forgiving someone was incredibly difficult but in the end, it proved to be a crucial and transformative experience for me. It involved a close friend, Karan, who had hurt me deeply.

We had been friends for years, sharing secrets, laughter and support. However, one day, during an important school project, Karan made a mistake that affected our entire group. He had forgotten to submit our final report, which led to a poor grade for all of us.

I was furious because I had worked hard on the project, and I felt that his carelessness had ruined everything. What hurt the most was that Karan didn't even apologise initially and acted as if nothing was wrong.

For days, I struggled with anger and frustration. I didn't want to speak to him and I distanced myself from our friendship. Yet, deep down, I knew holding onto the grudge wasn't healthy for me. It took a while, but I realised that forgiveness wasn't about condoning his actions but about freeing myself from the negativity that was consuming me. I reminded myself of the good times we had shared and how much I valued our friendship.

What helped me forgive Karan was understanding that everyone makes mistakes and he, too, must have felt guilty about what happened. I decided to talk to him, expressing how his actions had made me feel and how important our friendship was to me. To my surprise, Karan apologised sincerely, acknowledging his mistake and how bad he felt about it. This conversation opened the door to healing and I realised that forgiving him didn't mean I was weak - it meant I was strong enough to let go of the pain.

The positive impact of forgiveness was immediate.

Not only did I feel a sense of relief and peace but our friendship also grew stronger because we learned to communicate better. I realised that forgiveness can rebuild relationships and improve emotional well-being.

From this experience, I learned that forgiveness isn't always easy but it's an essential step toward personal growth and healthier relationships. Holding onto anger only hurts us in the long run. By letting go of grudges, we allow ourselves the opportunity to heal and move forward. I also understood what Gandhiji said "The weak can never forgive. Forgiveness is the attribute of the strong."

Q.5 Imagine a situation where you get an opportunity to change one thing in your school. What would it be? Why do you want to change it? How would you bring about the change? **(ICSE 2023)**

Ans. Modifications and updations have become the norm of the era. We can always find things for improvement and change. Hence, if I get the opportunity to change one thing about my school, I would change the way of communication which leads to the wastage of paper. There are times where I feel that my school is too reliant on using paper even for small things.

For instance, the school library still puts up the issue slips on the books to keep record of issuing history and find out when a book is due to be returned.

They also use the issuance register book for recordkeeping. The teachers also use attendance registers for marking attendance in the classroom. Further, any message to be passed within the school premises is written on a paper and then passed.

I personally feel that in the modern day and age where certain alternatives are available, we should try and minimise our usage of paper. Global warming is a serious issue and trees are helpful in protecting our environment from the climate change.

The environmental effects of paper production include deforestation, the overuse of energy and water as well as air pollution and waste problems. Given the situation, it is important to consider methods that are more environment -friendly.

I would like to digitise all the recordkeeping in the school, including the library and class attendance.

This could be easily done with the help of any smart-device, such as a tablet or laptop. I would also like to encourage the school to switch to recycling the used paper and using recycled notebook for work. Students should also be given the option to email their assignments and homework.

If my school can reduce the unnecessary use of paper, it can contribute in protection of our environment and its resources.

Q.6 Imagine a situation where your mother has been unwell and you had to help her. Explain what you did to help. What did you learn from the experience. **(ICSE Specimen 2023)**

Ans. "Mother is the name for the God in the lips and hearts of little children." We might not realise it but mothers play a very vital role in a family, be it keeping the family together or helping everyone with their work. We might often fail to understand how hard they work for us. I got an opportunity to realise her responsibilities when she fell sick. It was during my Class IX mid-term examinations just around the corner.

She couldn't go to work or do household chores at all. It was then that my father and I took over her responsibilities.

My father took leave from office during those days.

Our daily routine included my father cooking breakfast for us in the morning, with me getting up early in the morning to revise for some time and mop and clean the house. Then, I would get ready and after giving medicines to my mom I would go to school.

After coming back from school, I would help my father in preparing lunch, following which we ate together. In the evening, I used to talk to her and help her with whatever she needed. Then, I made sure that she was taking her medicines on time. My mother did not want me distracted from my studies right before my examinations. So, I didn't forget to do that. She had become so weak. And she would have trouble relaxing at night. Sometimes, I used to give her a head massage so she would get better sleep.

She did not get any better in the first two days, so I took her to the doctor. I did laundry, putting all the clothes in the washing machine and then putting it out for drying. She started getting better on the third day and by the fifth day, she was completely fine, carrying out with the household chores and her job.

This incident taught me to be more helpful and now I make sure to contribute, by doing all my work myself and being more organised and cleaning my room myself. I am trying to be less dependent on her so that she gets time to rest. We realise that she has her own individuality and she deserves some time alone. On holidays, I try to help my mom with nearly everything.

Q.7 It is very important for young people to spend time quietly or alone for a short while every day. If you were given an hour to spend on your own, how will you spend it? What will you learn from the process? **(ICSE Specimen 2022 Sem II)**

Ans. In this pro-social world, we are strongly influenced in favour of being with people, or at least constantly interacting with others, be it through social media or other electronic means. We are always going somewhere, doing something or at least chatting to someone about going somewhere or doing something. In this constant interaction setup, we often forget to spend some alone time thinking it to have many negative impacts.

There is an increasing amount of evidence suggesting that a certain amount of quality time alone is critical to well-being of an individual. In fact, research finds that there are many positive impacts of some alone time.

It allows one to learn more about oneself and become self aware. It empowers one to become comfortable with oneself. This confidence, in turn, will project in the future decisions one will make. It boosts creativity.

It gives one an opportunity to plan life. It improves your mental wellbeing, makes one happier, experience lower levels of stress and less likely to suffer from depression.

Hence, if I were given an hour to spend on my own every day, I would either start journaling or learn to play violin. Journaling would help me reflect on how I had spent the day, the people I met, the words we shared and the activities we engaged in. I'd like to understand how my activities and the people I encounter affect me and my viewpoint. I'll consider whether I could have done or said something better or whether I could have said or done nothing at all.

It will assist me in comprehending my errors: whether or not I could have avoided them and if so, how? How could I get out of it if I even made it? How could I make it less likely that I'd do it again?

Because we learn from our experiences and conversely, we are constructed from our experiences: both joyful and painful. I believe that some time in solitude can help you become a more thoughtful, compassionate human.

Q.8 Have you ever said or done something that changed the life of another person? Give an account of your words or actions that led to this change and describe how the experience made you feel. **(ICSE 2020)**

Ans. Most things that change a person's perception happens to be an experience that they have gone through and learned from. And of all these experiences, there are some rare instances when an individual becomes the agent or the cause of bringing change in someone's life.

Recently, I had the opportunity to become a medium of bringing such a change in somebody's life. It so happened that I accidentally bumped into a very old friend of mine.

It look us some moments to recognise each other as both of us had changed a lot but when we did, we exclaimed with joy.

She had left the city because of her father's transfer and had come back to attend a family function. We decided to sit in a coffee shop and spend some time with each other while discussing our lives. She was very happy because her father had been recently promoted and they were prospering financially. I was so happy to see her enjoying life.

We had been sitting there for an hour, when we realised that it was getting dark. When the bill came, she insisted upon paying my share as a treat for her father's promotion. I hesitated at first but then gave in. She paid the bill and gave the remaining amount as a tip to the waiter. I was a little surprised but didn't say anything. Just as we stepped out of the coffee shop, it started raining. Since both of us had to go in the same direction, we decided to take a rickshaw.

However, because of the rain, we couldn't find any. Suddenly, a rickshaw pulled in front of us. We asked if he would take us to Pandav Nagar.

He agreed and said that he would charge fifty rupees.

I was about to get on the rickshaw when my friend told the old man that she only give him thirty rupees. I was surprised to hear this. It had been three years since she left the city and the prices had increased. What the old man was charging was fair enough.

But my friend kept on arguing. And it was at that moment that I said, 'Isn't it strange that we tend to spend extravagantly in places where we have to show off our prosperity, but when it comes to pay a fair price to a hardworking man, we start negotiating?"

My friend immediately realised that I was referring to her gracious tip in the coffee house. She felt ashamed and quietly got on the rickshaw. The old man safely dropped us home and happily took the money.

I saw that my friend had understood the real meaning of happiness when she saw the gleam in the eye of the old man as he held the fifty rupees note in his hand. This episode made my friend a little more humble and compassionate.

Q.9 Imagine that you have changed your school recently. Narrate your experiences on your first day in the new school. How did you feel at the end of the day.

(ICSE Specimen 2019)

Ans. The first day at a new school can always be scary and nerve-wrecking. Starting a new school can seem stressful as we have to give a first good impression to one and all and also make new friends. However, a new school calls for new experiences and new friends which is exactly what I had thought when I was to go to my new XYZ School.

I was in 11th grade when my parents had recently bought a new house in a nice quite neighbourhood.

I was ecstatic as I always wanted to move to a new house. I was happy but at the same time realised that I had to switch schools and make new friends.

The prospect of entering a new school sacred me a little but I bore with it.

It was finally the first day of school; I was excited yet nervous. I hoped I would be able to make new friends. The school itself was very elegantly constructed with black and white theme, a large playground, swimming pool, badminton and basketball court and large classrooms. When I reached the reception, my class teacher was already waiting for me to guide me to the class. My class had 35 students who were looking at me as if I was an alien.

I lost all the confidence that I had gathered before entering the school. After gathering as much courage as I could, I introduced myself and took my seat beside a boy.

The class went on normally with no one talking to anyone else and only focusing on studying till it was lunch. I thought I was going to have lunch alone but was surprised when everyone came and huddled together beside me. One-by-one they introduced themselves and started talking to me as if they had known me for years. I was shocked and soon found myself becoming friends with them. All my nervousness had dispelled now for I had friends and teachers- the few that I have met- seemed to like me.

At the end of the day, I was happy and satisfied that it was a great first day at my new school.

Q.10 Narrate an incident from your own experiences when you helped in preparing a meal. Explain what you did and what you gained from the experience. (ICSE 2018)

Ans. When I was in Class 9 and it was the summer holidays, I thought I would help prepare a meal. It was early morning, my mother had gone for grocery shopping, my sister was asleep, and no one else was at home.

I decided to help in preparing breakfast by making an omelette. I had seen mother making it many times, so how difficult could it be?

I took two eggs, two tomatoes and a large onion. I chopped the onion on the work surface just as I had seen chefs do it. Then came the tomatoes. I washed them and started chopping them. Suddenly, I cut my finger in hurry. There was no bleeding but it was just as painful.

It took me two or three attempts to crack open the eggs and drop them into the whipping bowl. The spices were next. Mother always kept the spices on the top shelf in the kitchen. I couldn't reach them, so I got a stool and climbed on to get the chilli powder and salt. I put all the ingredients in the bowl with the eggs and whisked them. I lighted the stove, put the big frying pan on it and poured some oil in it. However, some oil spilled on the floor too.

Till the pouring of the batter into the pan, everything was going perfect. Then, I wondered what was used for turning the egg upside down in the pan. Soon, I was running all over the kitchen, searching all the shelves and drawers to find the spatula; all the while the omelette was sizzling in the pan.

Finally, I found the spatula and made a rush to turn over the omelette. I managed to do that without breaking or spilling it out of the pan, only to see a very nicely browned, or rather burnt, side up.

While I was busy taking it out in a plate, someone came up behind me. It was mother. I was dumbstruck. She was angry at seeing the kitchen in a mess, the drawers all open and some salt and chilli powder on the stove and countertop. She found a fitting punishment for me: I had to eat the burnt omelette. Sitting on the table and eating the omelette, I realised it didn't taste as bad as it looked. My first cooking experience had turned out to be a minor disaster.

Q.11 Narrate an incident from your own experience when you helped a friend who was in trouble. Explain what happened. What did you do to make the situation better? **(ICSE 2017)**

Ans. I still remember what happened when we had gone for a picnic. Everything was going fine when suddenly, my friend Kaushal got a call from his sister that his parents had met with an accident. Kaushal was devastated and did not know what to do. As he belonged to a lower middle class family, he did not have enough money to hire a taxi and reach home fast. I assured Kaushal not to worry and left the picnic in the middle.

I took out whatever money I had in my savings account, called a taxi and left for the spot where his parents had met with accident. Kaushal is the eldest in his family, he has two younger sisters.

He was unable to take any decision as the unexpected tragedy had left him too shocked to react. Kaushal had a very few relatives and most of them were unwilling to render any help. I called up all my friends and requested them for help. Kaushal's parents were admitted in a hospital and the surgery could take place only after the required amount had been deposited. I called my father and explained him the situation.

As he was a doctor, he reached the hospital and talked to other doctors about Kaushal's parents. Meanwhile all my friends gave away not only their pocket money but also reserved money and an amount of ₹ 25000/- was arranged. I bought some snacks and juice for Kaushal and for his sisters who were crying miserably. The next two days were very crucial. Kaushal's father needed some blood which was voluntarily donated by my parents and the parents of my friends who had come there at the hospital.

I didn't leave Kaushal alone even for a minute. My mother took his sisters to our home as there was nobody to look after them. After the surgery was done, Kaushal's parents were out of danger and Kaushal relaxed a little.

In those days of need, I spent most of my time with Kaushal, reassuring him that everything was going to be alright. Kaushal, till today, remembers this help. He had returned the money but he says he can never pay back the cooperation and help given by me, my family and our friends. Kaushal's whole family treats me like their own son and loves me dearly. I feel very proud of myself. Most importantly, all know "Friend is a blessing of heaven."

Q.12 Write about a time when you were late for an important function. What lesson on punctuality did you learn? **(ICSE Specimen 2017)**

Ans. It was the day of my cousin's wedding, a grand occasion my entire family had been looking forward to for months. The ceremony was to begin at 10 a.m., and I was tasked with carrying the wedding rings-a huge responsibility. I was both excited and nervous about. Little did I know that this day would teach me a lifelong lesson about punctuality.

The morning started chaotically. I underestimated how much time I had and stayed up late the previous night scrolling through social media. As a result, I overslept and woke up to my mother's frantic calls at 9 a.m. I quickly got dressed and grabbed a quick breakfast, thinking I could still make it on time. However, I hadn't considered that it was a Saturday morning, and the roads would be clogged with traffic.

As the car crawled through the congested streets, panic began to set in. My cousin kept calling to check on my whereabouts and the frustration in her voice made me feel worse. By the time I reached the venue, the ceremony had already begun and everyone was glaring at me. Worse still, the rings, which were supposed to symbolise the bond of the couple, were delayed because of my carelessness. My cousin's disappointment was evident and I felt a wave of guilt wash over me.

After the ceremony, my uncle pulled me aside. Instead of scolding me, he said, "Punctuality isn't just about being on time; it's about respecting other people's time." His words stuck with me. I realised that my tardiness had disrupted not just the schedule but also the mood of such an important event.

From that day forward, I made a conscious effort to value time. I began waking up earlier, planning ahead and setting reminders. This incident, though embarrassing, instilled in me the importance of punctuality. I learnt that being on time reflects one's responsibility and consideration for others. This quality, I strive to uphold to this day.

Q.13 Narrate an incident from your own experience when you expected to do very well, but for some reason were unable to do so. Explain what happened and why it happened. What lesson did you learn from it? **(ICSE 2016)**

Ans. Lately, I learnt a lesson for life which I am never going to forget. I live in a locality with independent houses. Recently, a man shifted to a house closer to mine. He became quite friendly with my children and often used to give them sweets and toys.

He became friendly with my parents too. Suddenly, he stopped coming to the park. He did not meet anyone for many days. One day, my sister Kavya and I were playing cricket when the ball went into our new neighbour's house.

We were very sure that our neighbour would allow us to pick up the ball. We rang the bell which was answered after a long time. We asked him, if he could give us our ball but that man very sternly said 'No' and slammed the door behind him. We were really surprised at his behaviour. He was so friendly but his sudden change of behaviour perplexed me.

Suddenly, one idea struck me when I saw the water tank behind his house. We wanted to get our ball so we climbed the water tank and jumped inside his house. The door was open. Nobody was there. We went inside and tried to look for the ball under the bed.

I saw the ball. Hurriedly, I took the ball and along with it came a gold bar. We took out both the ball and the gold bar and climbed up the water tank again. Reaching my house, I found my father watching a news on TV.

I couldn't believe my ears when the news reader read that 20 gold bars were stolen from a jewellery shop.

They showed a picture of the gold bars and it was exactly like the one we had found. I quickly told the whole story to my father who immediately called the police. The police came and searched our neighbour's house. To our surprise, gold bars were recovered and he was arrested. The police informed my parents that the man was a thief and a smuggler. He wanted to carry on illegal activities under his pleasant facade.

I realised that this person should not have been trusted and I should have thought over the reason that why he was trying to be so friendly with his neighbours. I learnt the lesson that we should never trust a stranger.

Q.14 You had booked a ticket on an early morning train. However, you woke up late and missed it. You then decided to run to catch a bus to the next station where you hoped to catch up with the train. Narrate the entire event, how you felt, the effort you made and how you finally caught the train. What did you learn from this stressful experience? **(ICSE 2015)**

Ans. The alarm bell buzzed at 3:00 am to wake me up from my sleep so that I could catch my train which was to leave for Udaipur at 5:00 am. However, I put the alarm off and went back to sleep.

Around 3:45 am, my phone rang. I reluctantly answered, half asleep. On the other end of the call was my cousin who enquired whether I had got ready to leave the house for the station. Her question "What time will you reach the station?" made me wake up at once. I looked at the watch and rebuked myself for sleeping extra, when ideally I should have been getting ready. I told her that I would reach the station at 4:30 am and hurriedly put the phone down. I got up from my bed and rushed to the bathroom. By 4:10 am, I reached the cab stand. However, there was no cab to be found.

In a state of panic, I called up my friend who stayed nearby. Thankfully, he answered my call and rushed to help me. He drove as fast as he could and we reached the station exactly five minutes before the scheduled time. However, to my utter shock, I was on the wrong platform.

I hurried to the platform where my train was waiting. Unfortunately, by the time I reached the platform, the train was rolling on its wheels.

My cousin was shouting at me from inside the train and asked me to run. I ran as fast as I could but missed it.

I couldn't believe what had happened. I did not know what to do. Other passengers were looking at me and some were mocking at my carelessness. However, an old couple came and suggested me to catch a bus to the next station where I might catch up with the train.

I hurried to the bus stand which was nearby. Thankfully, the bus was about to leave. I found myself a seat and prayed to reach in time. To my relief, the bus dropped me an hour prior to the scheduled timing of the train. I bought water, drank some and splashed the rest on my face.

This stressful experience taught a very important lesson to me of punctuality. Time and tide wait for none. It's better to be early than late.

Q.15 You planned a trip with your friends wherein you experienced the famous Nilgiri mountain train. Narrate your experience.

Ans. The previous summer, following months of fantastic dreaming, my best friends and I decided to explore Nilgiris. We wanted to see the legendary Nilgiri Mountain Railway, which, aside from being declared by UNESCO as a stretch of World Heritage Site, ranks very high with the grace and simplicity with which it touches the eyes and soul. It all seemed to be just about an unexpected trip – one that turned out to be the most memorable, if not the only part of our journey.

Upon arrival at Mettupalayam station quite at dawn, our eyes met a quaint blue-and-cream train ready for dispatch in the track. The air of bygone years prevailed, the vehicle with an ancient breath of a steam locomotive. The air was filled with the thrill of voyagers, the hissing of steam engines, and the rhythmical movement of the train. We settled down on the fantastic wooden seats of this ancient train, looking forward with eagerness through the window glass.

The journey was truly magical. The train moved slowly, letting us to submerge in the watching of the tremendous beauty around. The tracks led throughout a luscious tea garden, encroaching dense green forests and touching ever-so-steep mountain peak slopes. Every turn disclosed something new, for instance, the rivulet falling noisily and angrily on greenish-black stones or a misty valley with no end and then was the charm of the hooting of whistles resounding throughout the hills.

Halfway through the journey, we crossed a few viaducts and tunnels, the longest of which plunged into complete darkness for a few giddy moments. We crowded into such darkness and shouted with delight, laughing to hear the reverberations fleeing our voices. The journey was a continuous source of joy. The vendors hopped on here and there at the various stations, offering piping-hot cups of tea and delicious snacks to set the mood and add to the fun atmosphere.

By the time we reached the historic end of the journey, Ooty, it was like waking up from a dream. The excitement was a merger of the experience of the sheer natural beauty, history, and the joy of being with friends. During the train trip, memories were stored up and realised that we should take life slow with fulfillment, one moment at a time.

Q.16 Write about your most weird dream and mention the unusual things that happened in your dreams.

Ans. The night was cold, a thick fog hung outside my window. I was trying to catch some sleep which was eluding me. My mother had just put me to bed wishing me sweet dreams but it seemed that sleep was miles away from me.

I paced up and down, clutching the shawl to myself and switched on the television to see if there was any interesting programme on it. The movie 'Mars Attacks' was being aired of which I had read good reviews. It was an exciting movie about strange unpredictable creatures from Mars landing on Earth. The movie kept me spellbound. After it was over, I stretched myself on the bed and fell fast asleep.

After some time, I got disturbed by a knock at my door. I woke up to see, before me, a strange looking boy with two antenna like objects sticking out of his head over a hairy body. His owl like eyes resembled the characters I had just seen in the movie. I screamed in fright but he said something in a strange language.

He turned on a small device which helped me to understand what he was saying and *vice-versa*. I learnt that he indeed had come from Mars. He extended his thin wing hand for friendship but I was scared of him and chose to do *namaste* instead.

He talked about life on Mars, telling me that it is much bigger than our planet Earth. They do not eat, rather they survive on noble gases that are in abundance there. However, unable to take it any longer, I politely requested him to let me sleep, for I had to wake up early to attend school. He reacted with haste. Snatching the translator from my hand, he pointed his gun at me and in a flash I was in flames. I screamed with all my might "Help, Help, this boy from Mars has killed me."

I suddenly felt a splash of cold water on my face. Opening my eyes, I saw my mother looking down at me. How relieved I was to realise that it was all but a dream.

Q.17 While you came back from holidays with your parents, you saw that the renowned Sanjay Leela Bhansali is shooting a few scenes from his upcoming movie in your society. You saw an advertisement for a short cameo role in the film. You appeared and got selected. Narrate your experience and feelings.

Ans. Back from an enjoyable family vacation, with my parents, I was quite taken aback to realise our very sedate society awakened by an unusual sound. Imagine my surprise to find that a film crew had taken over the entire central park, and, if it wasn't Ms. Fame, then it was none other than that very renowned Sanjay Leela Bhansali who had agreed to shoot scenes for his next great one! The whole area was the scene of activities, lights, cameras and of course, the members of the entire crew giving instructions. I almost rubbished my eyes.

Moving closer, I noticed a flier pasted on the noticeboard "Casting Call for a Short Cameo Role - Auditions Today!" My heart missed a beat. I adored Mr. Bhansali's films and nursed a secret dream about all aspects of the cinematic world. Encouraged by my parents, I thought of giving it a shot.

The auditions were nerve-wracking. There were scores of hopefuls in the queue from pros to shy dreamers like me. By the time it was my turn, my knees had turned to jelly but the casting director, who was lovely, warmed up to me and calmed down my nerves. They asked me to do a simple scene-two lines of dialogue with the supporting artist. I put my soul into it and imagined myself in great splendour as in a Bhansali film.

And then I had been short–listed! I had to act a little role, very crucial one–a village girl delivering a message to the protagonist. The day of the shoot found me in a typical outfit entering the beautifully designed set.

Gazing across a short, glorious distance into Mr. Bhansali's brilliant face, I marveled at his impressively calm, though every inch commanding, demeanour. When 'action' was cried, there came forth an 'I know' sort of assurance though it was less expected. It was a baby shot; despite this, I put all my efforts forth in shooting it. The crew clapped, and Mr. Bhansali himself nodded his head in my favour. I was very excited!

This experience has changed and inspired me. It has shown me that dreams can come true in the most unexpected ways.

Q.18 **Once you had a nerve-wracking experience when you were locked in a room with a big cobra. Narrate the incident and how you came out of that situation.**

Ans. It was a sweltering summer afternoon when I had the most nerve-wracking experience of my life. My parents had gone to visit relatives, leaving me alone at home. Bored, I decided to clean the storage room, a place
I rarely ventured into. Little did I know that this innocent task would lead to a terrifying encounter.

As I rummaged through dusty boxes and old furniture,
I suddenly felt a faint movement behind me. I turned and there it was a massive cobra slithering out from beneath a pile of old newspapers. Its hood flared and it fixed its unblinking eyes at me. My heart stopped. I froze, unsure of what to do.

Panic set in when I realised I had unknowingly locked the door from the inside. I was trapped, with no way to escape. The cobra hissed, its forked tongue flicking the air. My mind raced. I had read somewhere that sudden movements could provoke a snake, so I stood as still as a statue, barely breathing.

Minutes felt like hours as I stared at the cobra, silently praying for a way out. I remembered that cobras usually avoid confrontation unless threatened. Gathering every ounce of courage, I slowly backed away, inching towards the window. I gently pushed it open, trying not to make a sound, and squeezed myself through the narrow gap.

Once outside, I bolted to my neighbour's house and called for help. They summoned a snake rescuer, who arrived promptly and carefully removed the cobra from the room. Watching it being carried away, I finally let out the breath I had been holding.

The incident left me shaken but taught me an important lesson about staying calm under pressure. I still shudder at the thought of that cobra but I am grateful I managed to escape without harm. That day, I truly understood the meaning of facing fear head-on.

Q.19 **Write a narrative comparing life to riding a roller coaster.**

Ans. I have never really liked roller coasters. The first and only time when I rode a roller coaster, I was fifteen and naively excited. I lacked the foresight to remove my glasses before boarding, a silly mistake. Stupidly, my friends did not warn me about it either. However, like a lamb brought to slaughter, I was calm, innocently curious about what would come next.

Soon, I was at the very top with the entire amusement park spread below my feet. As I was confronted with the vertical descent below, all spidery dark metal curving sharply down and away, my stomach started twisting uncomfortably. The realisation that this was definitely not where I wanted to be became a solid block of panic tearing at my chest as the coaster paused for a moment and then sliced downward and curved into a corkscrew, straining to throw us off.

I wanted to scream, I really did, but the whole of my mental capacity was focused on somehow preventing my glasses from slipping off my face using sheer willpower. Somehow, the ride was over and I made it off and onto the nearest bench, sanity without my glasses my glasses fell off on the downward descent. I breathed a sigh of relief that I survived.

The experience taught me that like any well-designed coaster, life has its twists and turns and steep drops but it also has ups. Agony is inevitable but it does not last forever and we are stronger and wiser having lived through it, even if only by a little bit.

Q.20 Recall a remarkable event of social importance in your city or locality. Give a little of its background, the event as it occurred and its impact on the lives of people.

Ans. Last year, something extraordinary happened in my city, something that left a lasting impact on all of us. The streets were dirty, the parks littered, and there was a growing sense of helplessness about the state of our neighbourhood. That's when an initiative called 'Mission Clean Green' was launched a cleanliness drive to restore our locality and bring the community together.

The event was planned for a Sunday morning and though I wasn't sure how many people would show up, I decided to be there. To my surprise, the park was buzzing with energy. There were students, shopkeepers, retired uncles, and even little children holding brooms and garbage bags. It was heartwarming to see people of all ages come together, united by a common goal.

I teamed up with a group of friends, and we were assigned the job of cleaning a particularly messy stretch of road. At first, it felt overwhelming. The garbage seemed endless-plastic wrappers, broken bottles, and all sorts of discarded junk. But as we got to work, it became less about the mess and more about the effort we were making. Strangers became friends, offering water and encouragement as we went along.

The best part? By lunchtime, the transformation was unbelievable. The streets looked cleaner, the park was spotless, and colourful murals had been painted on the walls with messages about protecting the environment. I still remember the look of satisfaction on everyone's faces as we stood back and admired what we had achieved together.

The impact of that day was more than just a cleaner neighbourhood. People started caring more about segregating waste, using fewer plastics and encouraging others to do the same. The drive didn't just clean our surroundings; it changed our attitudes.

Even now, when I walk through the park or those freshly painted streets, I feel a sense of pride. It showed me that small actions, when combined, can truly create a big difference.

ARGUMENTATIVE COMPOSITION

An argumentative composition is an argument on a subject on which people have different opinions. It is used as a means of putting your points forward to convince the audience about a particular point of view. In this type of composition, the person is free to express his/her views by writing either in favour of or against the topic. In argumentative/debate composition, the person arrives at a conclusion through reason to persuade the listeners of the speaker's point of view.

The following expressions can be included to enhance your debate to make it more emphatic

- I support the motion whole heartedly
- I strongly oppose the motion
- In my opinion
- I'd like to present my views
- I totally disagree with the view
- Let me explain my point
- I reject/submit/sympathise/agree
- It may sound strange but

Do's and Don'ts for Writing an Argumentative Essay

Do's	Don'ts
Clear Structure (Start with a strong introduction, present your arguments logically and conclude)	Do not make sweeping statements that can be easily contradicted.
Stick to the subject of the debate and avoid deviating from the main issue.	Avoid using insulting or overly harsh language.
Support arguments with evidence.	Do not make claims without evidence.
Use simple sentence structure with clear meaning.	Avoid using overly complicated vocabulary or intricate sentence structures.

Sample of Debate

"AI is changing the world for better." Express your views for or against the statement.

For the Motion

Artificial Intelligence (AI) has made its way into almost every corner of our lives, transforming the way we work, learn, and even stay healthy. Its impact is hard to ignore, especially when it's making things faster, smarter and more accessible for everyone.

Take healthcare, for instance. AI is helping doctors detect diseases early. Imagine how many lives have been saved because an AI system flagged something a doctor might've missed in a scan. Even during the COVID-19 pandemic, AI models predicted infection rates and helped distribute vaccines efficiently. Innovations like robotic surgeries are improving patient care and giving people in remote areas access to health advice they couldn't get before.

In education, AI is making a difference too. Think about how apps and platforms can personalise learning-whether you're a fast learner or need extra help, there's something for everyone. It's no longer about being in a big classroom; it's about learning at your pace, anywhere in the world.

AI is also helping us tackle global problems. Climate change is one of the biggest challenges we face and AI is making renewable energy more efficient, tracking deforestation and helping scientists predict climate trends. It's a powerful tool for protecting our planet.

Even industries are evolving. Farmers now use AI to grow crops with fewer resources, self-driving cars are reducing accidents and businesses are becoming more efficient. Sure, there are concerns about job losses, but AI is also creating new opportunities in fields like data science and robotics.

In the end, AI is like a tool-it's what we do with it that matters. When used responsibly, it's helping us create a world that's smarter, healthier and more sustainable. It's not just technology; it's a partner in making life better.

Against the Motion

Artificial Intelligence (AI) might seem like a miracle but it's not all sunshine and roses. In fact, there are many reasons to worry about how it's affecting the world.

The first big issue is jobs. Imagine how someone working in a factory or as a cashier might feel when they hear their job could be replaced by a machine. It's happening everywhere. Even creative jobs-like artists, writers or musicians-are being impacted. While AI creates new tech jobs, not everyone can just switch careers overnight, leaving many people struggling.

Then there's the problem of fairness. AI might sound neutral, but it's only as good as the data it's trained on. If that data has biases, the AI inherits them. For example, hiring tools powered by AI have been shown to favour certain genders or backgrounds. That's unfair and often invisible to the people affected.

AI can also be dangerous when misused. Think about deepfakes-fake videos that look real but spread lies or harm someone's reputation. Cyberattacks are also getting smarter because hackers are using AI to break into systems, putting personal and national security at risk.

One of the scariest concerns is AI in warfare. Autonomous weapons powered by AI are being developed and the idea of machines making life-or-death decisions is chilling. What if something goes wrong? Who's responsible?

Lastly, over-relying on AI could make us lose touch with our own skills. If machines handle everything, from writing to problem-solving, where does that leave our creativity and critical thinking?

So, while AI has its bright side, it's not without its shadows. If we don't regulate it carefully, it could do more harm than good, leaving us to wonder if we let it take over too much too soon.

***Note** In Argumentative Composition, the student can express his/her views either in favour or in against of the topic.*

EXAM ORIENTED QUESTIONS

Q.1 "More collaboration, less competition is the need of the hour." Express your view either for or against this statement. **(ICSE 2025, 20 M)**

Ans. **For the Motion**

In today's world, people focus too much on competition. Everyone wants to be the best but this often leads to stress and unhealthy rivalry. Instead of competing, we should work together and support each other. More collaboration and less competition can create a better society.

First, collaboration helps in learning and growth. When people work together, they share ideas and knowledge. This leads to better solutions and faster progress. In workplaces, teams achieve more when they cooperate instead of competing. In schools, students can understand concepts better when they help each other.

Second, competition creates pressure and stress. Many students and employees feel anxious because they always have to prove themselves. This can harm their mental health. Instead of focusing on beating others, people should focus on improving their skills through teamwork.

Moreover, collaboration leads to a peaceful and friendly environment. When people work together, they build strong relationships. It reduces jealousy and promotes kindness. Society benefits when people help each other instead of trying to win all the time.

In the modern world, innovation happens through teamwork. Scientists, doctors and engineers work together to solve big problems. If they only competed, they would not make such great discoveries. Even in business, companies succeed when they form partnerships and share ideas.

Some people believe that competition pushes people to do better. However, too much competition can create selfishness and dishonesty. People may focus only on winning instead of learning and growing together. A balance is needed, but in today's world, collaboration should be encouraged more.

In conclusion, working together is better than competing. Collaboration leads to learning, reduces stress and creates a friendly environment. To build a better future, we must support and uplift each other instead of always trying to be better than others.

Against the motion

Competition is an important part of life. It motivates people to work harder, improve their skills and achieve success. While collaboration is useful, focusing only on teamwork and reducing competition may not always be the best approach.

First, competition encourages progress. When people compete, they try to do better than others. This leads to new inventions, better services and higher-quality products. For example, in business, companies compete to provide the best products, which benefits customers. Without competition, progress may slow down.

Second, competition builds confidence and resilience. In schools, students work hard to score well in exams because they compete with their classmates. This makes them disciplined, focused and goal-oriented. If competition is reduced, many may lose interest in improving themselves.

Moreover, competition prepares people for real-life challenges. In the professional world, people compete for jobs, promotions, and recognition. Those who work hard and prove their skills succeed. If there is no competition, people may not feel the need to develop their talents.

Some argue that collaboration is better because it promotes teamwork and reduces stress. While this is true, collaboration works best when people have already developed their skills through competition. Without competition, collaboration alone may lead to laziness and a lack of innovation.

In conclusion, while collaboration is important, competition should not be reduced. A balance between the two is needed. Healthy competition pushes people to do their best, while collaboration helps in sharing knowledge and working towards a common goal. Instead of removing competition, we should encourage fair and positive competition that benefits everyone.

Q.2 "Peer Pressure is a force for good." Express your views either for and against this statement. **(ICSE Specimen 2025)**

Ans. **For the Motion**

Peer pressure can motivate students to adopt healthy habits and engage in productive activities.

For example, when students are part of a group that values studying hard, exercising regularly or staying away from harmful substances like alcohol and drugs, they are more likely to follow these positive habits. The desire to fit in with their peers can push them to engage in activities that lead to personal and academic success.

Peer pressure can create a healthy competitive environment where students are motivated to perform better in academics, sports and other activities. When students see their peers working hard and achieving success, it can push them to strive for the same level of excellence. This can lead to improvement in their skills and encourage them to set higher goals.

When students are encouraged by their peers to take on challenges and engage in new activities, it can boost their self-confidence. Positive peer pressure helps students step out of their comfort zones and try new things, whether it's joining a new club, participating in a public speaking event or volunteering for a leadership role. Successfully completing these challenges can improve their sense of self-worth and contribute to their personal development.

Peer pressure, when positive, can create a sense of belonging within a group. Being part of a supportive group encourages students to adopt behaviours that are aligned with group values, such as kindness, respect and responsibility. This connection can provide emotional support and help students feel valued and accepted, which is important for their emotional well-being.

Healthy peer pressure helps in socialisation. It encourages people to engage in activities to not only build character but also create a sense of responsibility and belonging. Being surrounded by motivated, goal oriented peers can push an individual to work harder and achieve their personal goals.

Against the Motion

Peer pressure often leads students to engage in unhealthy or dangerous activities just to fit in with their friends. This includes experimenting with drugs, alcohol or smoking, skipping classes or engaging in risky behaviours like bullying. Instead of making choices based on their values, children can give in to peer pressure. They do so to avoid being ridiculed or rejected by their friends.

Peer pressure often pushes students to conform to the group's expectations, which can cause them to suppress their own unique values and personal identity.

Students may start doing things they don't believe in, just to fit in, whether it's changing their appearance, adopting certain habits or acting in ways that are against their personality.

Constant peer pressure to fit in or meet expectations can lead to anxiety, stress and depression. Students who feel they can't live up to the standards set by their peers may experience a decline in self-esteem and confidence. This mental strain can affect their academic performance and overall well-being.

Peer pressure can create unhealthy competition, where students are more focused on outdoing others rather than personal improvement. This can lead to jealousy, rivalry, and a feeling of inadequacy, especially when students constantly compare themselves to others. Such competition can also lead to stress, burnout and negative emotional impacts.

Sometimes, peer pressure can lead to poor decisions that have a long lasting consequences. Fear of rejection is a fear of teens in particular who are highly sensitive to social acceptance. Society, social media and peer groups often set unrealistic standards about what people should look like or how they should behave.

Q.3 **Express your views either for or against the statement. 'Junk food should be banned.'** **(ICSE 2024)**

Ans. **For the Motion**

Junk food is known to be high in sugar, salt and unhealthy fats, which are linked to many serious health issues like obesity, heart disease, diabetes and high blood pressure. Young people, especially children, are increasingly consuming junk food, which puts them at risk of developing these health problems at an early age. These diseases not only affect people's lives but also increase medical costs, putting a burden on society.

Junk food is highly addictive. It contains chemicals, artificial flavours and preservatives that make it tasty and easy to consume in large amounts. This leads to unhealthy eating habits. People, especially children and teenagers, are often unaware of the dangers of eating too much junk food. Over time, this can lead to lifelong habits that are hard to break and can result in long-term health problems.

The world is facing an obesity epidemic and junk food is one of the main reasons for it. With its high calorie content and low nutritional value, junk food contributes to weight gain. Obesity leads to many other health problems, including joint pain, diabetes and heart conditions. By banning junk food, we can take a big step towards reducing obesity rates and promoting healthier lifestyles.

Children are especially vulnerable to the negative effects of junk food. Junk food advertisements target kids, encouraging them to eat unhealthy foods from a young age. This can lead to children becoming addicted to unhealthy food choices, affecting their growth, development and overall well-being. A ban on junk food would protect children from these harmful influences and promote better eating habits.

The production and packing of junk food often results in significant environmental damage. The excessive use of plastic packaging, along with unsustainable agricultural practices to produce processed food, contributes to pollution and environmental degradation. A ban could encourage sustainable practices.

Against the Motion

The junk food industry is an important part of the global economy, providing millions of jobs worldwide. From fast food chains to snack manufacturers, many people rely on this sector for employment. If junk food were banned, it could result in job losses, especially in the food and restaurant industries. This would hurt many workers and could lead to economic problems, particularly in low-income communities where junk food is often the most affordable option.

The real issue with junk food is overconsumption, not the food itself. Junk food is not harmful when eaten occasionally. If people are educated about the importance of moderation and balanced diets, they can make better choices.

Banning junk food might only create a sense of restriction and lead to more cravings, making the problem worse. Instead of banning junk food, we should encourage people to eat it in moderation.

Everyone has the right to make their own choices about what they eat. If we start banning junk food, we may be infringing on people's personal freedoms. Just as adults have the right to make other lifestyle choices, they should also have the freedom to enjoy food, even if it's not always the healthiest option. Instead of banning junk food, we should focus on educating people about healthy eating habits.

Junk food has become part of modern life and is often tied to social events and cultural practices. For example, families often enjoy fast food together or people may treat themselves to snacks while watching movies. Banning junk food would take away this aspect of enjoyment. Life should have room for indulgence and junk food in small amounts can be a harmless part of socialising.

Rather than banning junk food outright, more effective solutions could focus on educating people about the risks of consuming too much junk food and promoting healthier alternatives. Governments could introduce policies to regulate advertising, labeling and portion sizes to make healthier choices easier without restricting individual freedoms.

Q.4 "Competition hampers the overall development of students." Express your views either for or against this statement. **(ICSE Specimen 2024)**

Ans. **For the Motion**

Competition often places immense pressure on students to perform better than their peers, which can lead to high levels of stress and anxiety. This pressure can cause feelings of inadequacy and failure in students who may not perform as well as others.

The constant need to outdo others can lead to emotional burnout, which affects not just academic performance but also overall well-being.

In a competitive environment, the focus is primarily on achieving academic success. This often comes at the cost of other important skills such as creativity, teamwork, emotional intelligence and leadership. Students may feel forced to prioritise grades over personal growth, extracurricular activities and the development of social skills. As a result, their overall development is limited to a narrow academic focus.

In competitive environments, failure is often viewed as something negative and shameful. This can lead to students developing a fear of failure, which can prevent them from taking risks or exploring new interests. Instead of seeing failure as an opportunity to learn and grow, students may start avoiding challenges altogether. This mindset can stifle curiosity and creativity, two essential components for holistic development.

While healthy competition can drive students to improve, excessive competition can foster unhealthy rivalries. Students may become overly focused on beating others rather than learning and growing for themselves. This can also create a toxic atmosphere where collaboration is discouraged and students are more concerned with their own success than with helping their peers. This leads to a lack of cooperation and teamwork skills.

When the emphasis is on individual achievement, collaboration and teamwork take a back seat. Students may feel isolated, as they are constantly focused on outshining their peers. This undermines the importance of cooperation, a key skill for personal and professional growth in the future.

Against the Motion

Competition drives students to perform better and push their limits. It motivates them to put in their best effort, work harder and constantly strive for improvement. Healthy competition encourages students to reach their full potential and perform at their best, both academically and in extracurricular activities. This motivates them to set higher goals and work diligently towards achieving them.

Competing with others helps students develop important life skills like time management, problem-solving and decision-making. These skills are crucial for success in the real world, whether in higher education, the workplace or personal life.

Students also learn valuable lessons about dealing with setbacks and perseverance, which help them grow stronger emotionally and mentally. When competition is structured in a healthy and constructive way, it can foster a sense of healthy rivalry. This means students learn how to handle both victory and defeat with grace. Losing a competition doesn't mean failure; instead, students learn how to cope with disappointment and improve their future performance. This teaches resilience, which is an essential part of personal development.

In the real world, competition is a part of nearly every aspect of life-whether it's in the workplace, sports or personal ambitions. Students need to learn how to handle competition in a controlled, supportive environment before they face it in the adult world. By participating in competitive activities, students develop skills that will help them succeed in future challenges and prepare them for the competitive nature of society.

Competitions teach students valuable life skills that are necessary for success in the real world. These include teamwork, time management, organisation and leadership. Students involved in competitive activites and lead teams learn skills that will serve them well in their careers.

Q.5 **"Every school must have a playing ground." Argue either for or against the above statement.**

(Competency Based Que.)

Ans. **For the Motion**

We all know that a good education opens the doors to society but it alone doesn't guarantee success in life. Success requires much more than just theoretical knowledge or specialised skills taught in classrooms. To succeed, we also need important life skills like teamwork, communication and collaboration skills that are often developed through games and sports. This is why I strongly agree with the motion, 'Every school must have a playground'.

First, a playground provides a much-needed break from the routine of classroom learning. Continuous studying can lead to a loss of focus and a short period of physical activity during recess or games helps students refresh their minds. This makes learning more effective and enjoyable.

In fact, many people believe that more valuable lessons are learned on the playground than in the classroom. In the playground, students learn important skills like cooperation, teamwork, leadership and time management. If you think about it, the playground is like a mini version of life itself.

The experiences and lessons we gain there are priceless and last a lifetime. Sports and games teach us how to be good friends, how to cooperate with others and how to deal with success and failure. In short, they teach us the virtue of tolerance and how to adjust with others. On the playground, students learn how to be part of a team, how to work together and how to deal with winning and losing gracefully.

Moreover, young people have a lot of energy. If this energy is used in sports, it can help lay the foundation for a healthy society, where discipline, cooperation and team spirit are valued. In many ways, the lessons we learn from sports are just as important as those we learn in the classroom.

Playing ground is essential for the physical well–being of students. Regular participation in sports and physical activities helps children develop strong bones, muscles and cardiovascular health. It also plays a crucial role in combating sedentary lifestyles, which are a growing concern among young people today.

Thank you.

Against the Motion

Learning is one of the most important activities for human beings. It is through learning that we gain new knowledge and skills and it's essential for the development of society. Schools are formal institutions where students focus on learning a wide range of subjects and this requires their full attention and dedication.

I do not believe that every school must have a playground. There are two main reasons for this. First, having a playground at school can be a distraction. Students may get more interested in playing than in studying. After spending time playing, their energy levels drop and they may find it difficult to focus on their studies. This can hamper their learning process.

Second, playgrounds sometimes become places where dangerous activities like bullying or ragging can take place. Rather than serving as a space for healthy play, they can turn into areas of conflict and aggression, which is harmful to students' mental and emotional well-being.

For these reasons, I believe schools should focus on creating an environment that prioritises education and concentration. While sports are important, they should be organised outside regular school hours or in designated sports clubs, rather than being a core part of the school infrastructure.

Many schools, especially in urban areas, face space constraints. Not all schools have tha available land or financial resources to build a dedicated playing ground. In such cases, it might be more practical for schools to focus on providing quality education and other resources, rather than diverting funds to sports facilities that may not be feasible.

Q.6 **"School examinations do not test intelligence." Express your views for or against this statement.**

(ICSE 2023)

Ans. **For the Motion**

Evaluation is the key to testing one's academic knowledge and not intelligence. We all know that evaluations or pen-paper examinations have been accepted by everyone as one of the best ways to tests a student's knowledge, understanding and learning. But does it test the practical skills that are required in the world? Does it test a student's presence of mind or precisely state the positives of one's personality?

The answer is no. Hence, I stand in favour of the motion that school examinations do not test intelligence. While success in school examinations may reflect the knowledge and hard-work of a student, it may not necessarily reflect their intelligence levels or their potential. It only tests the factual knowledge that the student learn from books and in classes.

We all agree that each individual is unique in their own way and there is not one particular pattern of defining intelligence. The school examinations, however, do have a particular pattern and those who fit the mould tend to succeed in it. History is full of examples of such individuals who didn't particularly fit in the pattern of school or examinations but went on to become great individuals in their fields.

The great Mathematician, Srinivasa Ramanujan, was so fond of Mathematics that he failed most other subjects. Albert Einstein generally didn't like lectures or tests. It would not have been possible for either of them to be considered intelligent had they been judged based on their examination results only. The complexity and intelligence of their minds is reflected in their groundbreaking theories and research work. It was only when they were allowed to think freely instead of being restricted by the education system that they could achieve their true potential.

It is also important to understand that academic success isn't the only form of human intelligence. Some students are great at other activities like sports or art. These activities involve just as much effort and intelligence as conventional academics and examinations. For example, the strategies involved in playing sports, the detailing required to complete a painting or the imagination required to write a novel are all different forms of intelligence. Hence, the human intelligence cannot be limited to just school examination.

Against the Motion

Evaluation is an essential criteria that tells us the level of learning possessed by a child. We all learn a variety of subjects in our school. But how do we check if the child has understood and learnt the basic ideas or concepts that are crucial to life. The answer is examinations. Therefore, I stand against the motion that 'school examinations do not test intelligence.'

While I agree that examination does not completely test a student's intelligence, it cannot state that intelligence and examination have no relation. We know that some students work really hard and do not often get the best results, while some can get top results by working less than others.
This kind of a situation shows us that intelligence does have a role in examination.

It is also important to take into consideration that many universities and schools provide scholarship on the basis of the examination results. Some universities also consider the examination scores of a student before accepting them. This helps us understand that examinations can be extremely helpful for teachers to assess the students.

Especially because there are generally many students at the same level, it may not be possible for a teacher to individually assess each student. Examinations can help them to find out the students that are able to understand the subject and those who need more help to improve.

It is generally believed that school is helpful to lay the foundation for the things that we do in our future lives. Examinations are important in this regard as they help the students to test how much they learnt from what was taught to them. This can reflect the knowledge, dedication and work put in by a student to their studies and acts as a crucial indicator of their general level of intelligence. Thus, good examination result is a reward that a student receives in return for their effort and speaks volumes about their intelligence.

Q.7 "Democracy cannot survive without education." Express your views for or against this statement.
(ICSE Specimen 2023, ICSE 2019)

Ans. For the Motion

Thomas Jefferson said, "An educated citizenry is a vital requisite for our survival as a free people." In a democracy which is believed to be the best way for realising human rights, one cannot survive without education. Democracy is a form of government in which all the power lies in the hands of the citizens and the representatives chosen by them. But, its true realisation can only come with proper education.

The total adult literacy rate around the world in 2010 was 84.1%. This means that there were nearly 785 million illiterate adults in the world. This kind of ignorance and lack of knowledge can be very harmful, especially considering the number.

For instance, let us take a look at plebiscites. It asks the voters only one question that can be answered only with a 'yes' or 'no'. Will every voter be aware of the possible consequences of their choice for the whole nation? How can they make informed decision? It is only possible to make a serious decision like this when every single voter is properly educated.

Education should be provided right from childhood because without it, a person's ignorance and vices would cost the nation dearly, creating a need to correct them later on in life. On the contrary, if children are educated, they would imbibe virtues which would enable them to contribute as responsible citizens to their nation. They would be able to make correct choices for the country.

Along with providing children with the right information, it will also teach them honesty and integrity and for a democracy to prosper, it needs people with truth and integrity in all the departments.

Thus, the key to a rich, progressive country is not democracy in itself but proper and informative education. An ignorant crowd, if given the right to choose from a number of options, can inflict more damage to the state than a well-educated monarch or dictator.

Against the Motion

Imagine the ancient Greek democracy which only considered its citizens to be Athenian men of age, thus excluding everyone who was not Athenian. Now, compare it with today's democracy, where everyone has a right to vote and get represented as a candidate to fight in the elections.

During those days, great thinkers like Aristotle and Plato thought about educating the masses by educating their mind and in this way, giving them power through education. For this, they had to democratise the government.

Democracy is a process which took time to reach its goal of equality and even now we have not achieved it, though we are closer to it. For this purpose, we have to be educated enough to understand the political structure of our government.

I do agree with this fact. But, this does not apply to the Indian Democracy, where political literacy matters but education might not.

How can we judge a politician by their educational qualifications? There have been many great leaders who were uneducated but did fantastic work for the country and the Indian people has succeeded in recognising them. Take, for instance, the current Prime Minister of India.

Mr. Modi, though not highly educated, has proven to be a great and capable leader. He is the person India chose for three consecutive elections to be the nation's Prime Minister.

He has proven to be a far-sighted visionary who has worked to improve the Indian economic growth globally. And, he was chosen by the masses of India. Several people, both educated and uneducated, vote to choose him as the leader of the country. They did so because they realised his potential, through his past works and his tenure as the Chief Minister of Gujarat.

So, according to me, though education helps in making wise decisions, democracy itself can survive without education. If a person is hard working, simple, honest, devoted to his service and has a far-sighted vision of future, then democracy also will outshine without education.

Q.8 "More learning happens outside the classroom than inside it." Express your views either for or against this statement. **(ICSE 2022 Sem II)**

Ans. **For the Motion**

Learning cannot be simply equated to marks, grades, degree or job. It is a life-long process. It does not ensure success in our lives. To be successful, we must experience the world outside the classroom as school days are just a small chapter in our lives. We learn the realities of life only when we enter the society. Thus, I agree with the motion 'More learning happens outside the classroom than inside it'.

Learning is the primary as well as one of the most important things we do in life. It starts pretty much when we're born. In fact, many say learning begins even earlier. An unborn baby listens to the outside sounds and gets used to the different patterns of intonation. This is when we first start learning a language. As soon as a child is born, he/she spends time doing nothing but learning.

A child learns from family and the society as well as school books. While school books teach formal and factual things, it is the world outside that teaches a child the best ways of life.

Education in a classroom is like petrol to a car, whereas education outside is like the engine which propels the car forward through the boulevard of life. Hands-on learning and community involvement often allow young minds to expand their horizons and explore topics that are not offered in school.

Learning outside the classroom can help raise achievement, improve classroom behaviour and improve the engagement of students, including those who are hard to engage in the classroom environment. In a classroom scenario, the routine is fixed and predictable which spare the students from changes needed to adapt oneself into the world.

A student can read about a culture or watch a video about the ocean but it does not have the same impact as seeing the sculptures and paintings live or enjoying the marvels at an aquarium. This can hold especially true when it comes to learning and experiencing science.

So, in my opinion learning outside the school helps us a lot in our learning style. Although, people learn in different ways, I'm sure that they will learn much faster when they experience from outside world. Schools are just the microcosm of the real world, as the real world is bigger and more diverse.

Against the Motion

Learning is arguably the most important activity that human beings engage in. It is through learning that we are able to acquire new knowledge and skills. It can therefore be said that learning is integral for the development of the society.

Due to the importance of learning, many societies have come up with formal institutes where learning takes place. These institutes include schools where students attend and gain information on a wide variety of subjects.

Students can interact with one another when they learn in a classroom setting. All students are learning and teaching others at the same time. All of the experience outside starts with the classroom. Students can build on each other's ideas and produce better final results. In addition to this, students are more motivated to learn when other individuals who are also engaged in the same learning surround them. But when children learn outside the classroom, they may remain deprived of this experience and end up learning alone. Learning outside the classroom can surely give them new experiences but those experiences can be both positive and negative for which students may not be prepared to handle.

Classroom learning leads to better learning outcomes for the student because of direct contact with the teacher. Teachers are a very important part of the learning process since they act as informative guides and make children disciplined. Interaction with the teacher also increases the concentration level of the individual. Students have to learn on their own outside the classroom. No one is there to guide them and make them learn the importance of discipline in life to become successful.

Learning requires a significant amount of time to be dedicated to the activity. Classroom learning is well-structured and the teacher has a program of what the students should learn. This is not the case with learning outside the classroom. There are no prepared schedules and life teaches lessons in its way. Although we gain a lot of knowledge outside the classroom, this knowledge can only be implemented due to what we learn inside the classroom. Therefore, classroom learning can provide in-depth knowledge on how to be prepared for life.

Q.9 "Parents can never be friends with their children." Express your views either for or against this statement. **(ICSE Specimen 2022 Sem II)**

Ans. **For the Motion**

The first authority figures in our lives are our parents. The primary goal of their lives is to help us grow into the finest versions of ourselves while simultaneously guiding us to accomplish the same for ourselves.

The parent-child relationship is a special one.

A positive parent-child bond plays a crucial role in raising confident and resilient children. A parent's role is to discipline and guide children. So, while being friends with your child may seem very attractive, numerous studies state that it's really not the best idea for either parent or child.

Parenting is one of the most difficult tasks in the world. It takes a herculean effort to give birth to human beings and mould them so that they are ready for the world. They will always try to provide their child with the best of everything, even if it means sacrificing their own happiness. However, many a times in making sure that their little one is getting the best and becoming the best, parents become an overbearing authority who children are scared of.

A parent-child relationship is unequal because parents are in a position of authority, more knowledgeable and exert more influence than the child. As a result, parents often forget that children have their own personality. They perceive their child to be an extension of their own personality and then anticipate their child to grow up to be how they want them to. They impose their own unfulfilled aspirations and ambitions on their children. They forget that their children have the right to their own set of likes, dislikes, ambitions and goals, which they should support as long as the goals are real, honest and positive. Consequently, children are often afraid of being criticised, harmed or misunderstood if they confide in their parents. All of these imply that they are not always able to be friends with their children.

Against the Motion

The idea that "parents can never be friends with their children" doesn't hold up in today's world. If anything, parents can be some of the best friends their children will ever have. Friendship doesn't mean giving up authority-it means being understanding, approachable and supportive.

When parents act as friends, they create a bond of trust and openness. Imagine a child who feels comfortable sharing their fears, struggles or dreams with their parent. That's what a friendly parent can achieve-becoming a safe space where their child feels understood, not judged. Often, kids confide in their parents more than in friends, knowing they'll receive wisdom and unconditional support.

Being friendly doesn't mean letting go of rules or discipline. It means guiding with empathy instead of control. Think about how much easier it is to follow advice when it comes from someone who listens and understands your point of view. A parent who builds trust this way naturally earns their child's respect.

Today's challenges-like peer pressure, mental health struggles, or social media stress-are difficult for kids to navigate alone. A parent who's also a friend can make a world of difference. For instance, if a child is being bullied or feels overwhelmed by exams, they're far more likely to reach out to a parent who's been supportive rather than critical.

Friendship between parents and children doesn't blur roles. It's about building mutual respect. Parents can still be role models while remaining approachable and relatable. This kind of relationship creates stronger family bonds, where children know they're loved and supported no matter what.

In the end, parents who are friends help their children grow into confident, emotionally secure individuals. Friendship strengthens their relationship-it doesn't take away from it. It's not just possible for parents to be friends with their children; it's one of the most beautiful relationships they can have.

Q.10 "A family without pets is an incomplete family." Express your views either for or against this statement. **(ICSE 2020)**

Or "Every home should adopt a pet animal." Express your views either for or against this statement. **(ICSE Specimen 2017)**

Ans. **For the Motion**

We all have seen many movies which have moved us with a representation of great bonds of love between a family and its pets. In fact, many of us might have come across families who share great love with its pets.

If you talk to such families, you would realise that a family is incomplete without a pet. Hence, I fully agree that a family without pets is an incomplete family.

Pets provide companionship and help to reduce our loneliness. Sometimes playing with pet reduces our stress level and makes us emotionally well. Hence, the presence of a pet in the family ensures a great physical, emotional and mental well-being of its members.

Having a pet delivers a great sense of responsibility to the child. Feeding and caring for pet encourages childhood responsibility. Children with pets display improved impulse control, social skill and self-esteem. Kids with a pet go outside more frequently to go for walks, run and play in the park.

Research shows children who live in homes with a dog can possibly have fewer ear infections, respiratory tract infections and require fewer antibiotics. The exposure to animals at a young age stimulates the immune system. Children who grow up in homes with pets have less risk of developing common allergies and asthama. Thus, pet owners require fewer doctor's visit.

Pets also teach kindness and compassion. Pets are a perfect stepping stone for teaching children empathy and how to take care of another living being.

A pet offers unconditional support when anyone in the family is sad, angry or upset. We can always trust our pets as they would never betrays us. Pets like dog give safety to our family and lots of entertainment to family members. There are lots of benefits of owning a pet. Pets teach adults as well as children valuable life lessons which have great significance in our life.

Against the Motion

In the modern times, we all have hectic schedules with no time even for ourselves. Looking after a pet in such conditions becomes an ordeal. Most parents are professionals and the children are busy with their schools and other activities. Nobody has time to play with pets or look after them. Pets have to spend long hours without any companion at homes. This makes them anxious and irritated. To solve this problem, some families appoint servants to look after pets.

But these paid persons are not kind enough to the pets. Sometime pets like cats and dogs carry infections diseases. It is not good for the child below 10 years of age. Thus, parents have to be cautions while selecting pets for their family. A pet can also not be a good choice for your family if you do not choose right kind of pet.

Families with young children should be very careful about getting a pet. If the child is too young, sometimes he/she may be hurt by the animal accidentally. Finally, we should remember that bringing a pet home means also having to adjust with them. Pets like cat, dog or bird can make a lot of noise in the middle of the night. We have to prepare ourselves to take these challenges positively, when we decide it's time for a pet.

Q.11 "Closed Circuit Television (CCTV) must be installed in every classroom." Give your views either for or against this statement. **(ICSE 2019)**

Ans. **For the Motion**

We have all heard or read stories of children being ill-treated by unsympathetic teachers at schools around the world. These incidents happen, as they are reported regularly in the media.

Accordingly, everyone has their own opinion on whether a school should have CCTV cameras installed or not. I wholeheartedly agree with the idea that a CCTV should be installed in every classroom.

There are many advantages of installing CCTV cameras which can be monitored by the Principal. The first one is that this move will deter bad behaviour, both by the students as well as the teacher. If the students know they are being watched, they might be better behaved. This might prevent bullying and intimidation.

Further, teachers and students can be protected from false accusations later on. If there was an incident regarding safety (for instance, a fight, bullying, etc.), the recordings can be used as evidence. With closed circuit cameras we would easily know what is happening and can take suitable actions quickly.

Teachers can also use past recordings for improving classroom management and work on their problem areas. The Principal can evaluate a teacher's effectiveness by analysing the video footage.

The most important thing is the trust generated in parents' minds when they come to know that every classroom is being thoroughly monitored. Parents will feel more secure if they know that the classrooms are being constantly monitored.

Parents of new pupil being admitted to the school will be put to ease when they discover that the classrooms have cameras. So, it encourages them to send their children to one school over another.

For all these reasons, I believe CCTV in the classrooms at our school can be a good thing. Parents can come in, see the footage and any problem situation can be settled faster than it could have been previously without the cameras.

Against the Motion

I disagree with the view that CCTVs must be installed in every classroom.

The biggest problem with installing CCTV cameras in classrooms is that teachers and students would feel uncomfortable. Teachers would be afraid of using innovative methods of teaching due to the fear of being misunderstood by the Principal. They would be afraid to take up any classroom activity other than the accepted thing, as they may fear that it may be used against them.

This could lead to a 'guilty until proven innocent' attitude. It will create an authoritarian atmosphere and students may come to school with a sense of apprehension. Another important issue which goes against installing CCTV cameras is that of intrusion of privacy of the students and teachers. Teachers and students would be worried whether there are any hidden cameras installed in places other than classrooms which could invade their personal privacy.

A further issue is regarding the cost to the school of such systems compared to the benefit they will give. The whole system will need not only the cameras.

The associated equipment includes a Digital Video Recorder (DVR) to record information from the cameras, a switcher to view scenes from different cameras, power supply for the system and the extensive cabling involved. With such a large expenditure, the school Principal and Management will definitely want a commensurate return in improved learning, better security and ultimately, better results of the students. It means that the Principal will be overworked unless he hires an assistant to help him with the monitoring. This will again bring up the matter of intrusion of privacy, as the assistant will not be of the same stature as the Principal.

Thus, if we do a cost-benefit analysis of installing CCTV cameras in classrooms, it is doubtful whether the benefits will outweigh the costs.

In conclusion, while safety is crucial, installing CCTV cameras in every classroom compromises privacy, trust and the learning atmosphere. Alternative approaches that prioritise ethical behaviour and mutual respect are more conductive to a positive and secure educational environment.

Q.12 "Money is important for happiness." Express your views either for or against this statement. **(ICSE 2018)**

Ans.

For the Motion

Everybody in the world needs money for not only their basic needs but also for other needs. Hence, there is no harm in earning money as per one's capacity and need. Swami Vivekananda once said that earning money is a duty for the family men. But need is a relative term. There is no limit to need. 'Give me more', has become the philosophy of this age.

These never-ending demands makes many people money-earning machines and forever unhappy. Happiness comes from fulfillment of physical, emotional and mental needs. These are fulfilled by the three equal and independent parts of wealth: economic, social, intellectual. Money is the main component of the economic part of wealth. Hence, money is one of the important resources that is needed for happiness.

Indian philosophy has always taught us how to be satisfied with limited resources. A man needs some minimum amount of wealth for survival and to lead a dignified life. So we should be satisfied with whatever money, amenities, power and resources which are available to us as per our highest capacity. There is no trouble in trying our best for success and upliftment. But when the final outcome is decided, we should satisfactorily accept that we have done our best.

We should also remember that many people have less money or resources than us. They have less food, clothes and other basic needs for survival and for leading a dignified life. But they are still happy. They are grateful to God and are always obliged to him for what wealth they possess. They never blame anybody or compare themselves with anybody. They are content and satisfied with what they have. However, if they did not even have this much of wealth, they may have faced various issues in life which could bring unhappiness. They may lose the opportunity to fulfill their aspirations and always regret this matter later on in life. An example is a typical rural farmer who cannot progress in life due to his inability to get loans from financial institutions, as he cannot furnish collateral to guarantee the loan. Thus, lack of such wealth will cause permanent unhappiness.

Against the Motion

Most individuals are of the view that a good amount of wealth results in happiness, while some believe that being very rich has its own curse. I completely agree that excess money always brings with it many unforeseen problems as well.

Money and its vicious power to attract humans to fulfill their various wishes, at any cost, has always been debated. Earning sufficient money for one's basic needs and amenities, as well as to fulfill their family obligations and provide them with suitable comforts of a modern life are indeed justifiable.

However, the issue arises that more wealth leads to a feeling of greed and a sense of invincibility amongst family and peers. As a result, a sense of suspicion, envy and jealousy creeps in within social relationships and takes a heavy toll on family matters as well.

For instance, the recent war of words in public between two wealthy brothers, due to differences of opinion for sharing and taking control of the vast business empire left over by their father. Such instances, due to fear of personal financial loss, leads to a permanent damage in relationships and splits between members of a family.

Secondly, gaining more financial clout, and enjoying the material luxuries the world has to offer, comes with its own set of sacrifices. Many high-earning corporate CEOs and senior level management at big companies struggle with their daily hectic work schedules and get overburdened by the responsibilities, with the only aim of maximising the profit at any cost. This results into them not being able to devote enough time to their family and friends, as well as also deteriorates their physical and mental well-being, and later lead to life-threatening diseases.

A recent survey showed that more than 40 per cent of top executives in India are suffering from high-blood pressure and stress related issues. In conclusion, I believe that having too much money not only leads to issues in personal and family relationships, but also deprives one of a healthy and peaceful way of life that can be enjoyed with just sufficient money.

Q.13 "School days are the happiest days of our lives." Express your views either for or against this statement. **(ICSE 2017)**

Ans. **For the Motion**

Yes, I agree with the statement that school days are the happiest days of our lives. We are surrounded by our own group of friends and enjoy every moment of school time. Be it Sports or Yoga, Maths or English period, there is always giggles and laughter over matters which may not be laughable for others. We are free from worries which adults face and enjoy life as it comes. These are happy carefree days. Friends are plentiful and life is all about fun, fun and more fun.

Moreover pretending to be sick, playing pranks on the teachers and not doing homework are some of the naughtiest things, we remember of our school days. In our school days, we have no tension of earning money as whatever we need, is provided by our parents or we are given money to buy that thing.

A healthy competition among the students also makes school life fun. No matter what kind of competition it is, it inculcates the spirit of determination and self -confidence without gorging the feelings of enmity for anyone.

School days are happy not only in the context of fun but also in the context of learning. We learn important lessons of life– like respecting our elders, sharing our things with our friends, helping one another and many other.

We do make mischief and get punished, but it does not go in vain. As with them, we learn that bad actions always bring bad results.

During school days, holidays are best realised. For us, they are like a gift from God himself as we do not have to get up early and get ready like a machine. We can have fun – playing cricket or football in the morning or watching our favourite programme on TV. The picnic spots that we visit in our school trips are the most memorable ones and cannot be forgotten throughout our lives because they are the trips where we do not have to arrange anything and the company of our best school buddies and teachers adds the happiness.

During school days, we get different experiences with different teachers. As our class changes, our teachers change too. Some of these new teachers are good and some are strict. They may be strict or ignorant, but always remain our well wishers and make our school days happier ones.

Hence, the time spent in school is the golden period of one's life as one does not need to pay heed to the worldly problems rather one needs to realise that each moment of this time should be enjoyed to the fullest.

Against the Motion

I do not agree with the statement that the school days are the happiest days in our lives. To support my point, I will give you the following reasons.

My first point is the unnecessary competition that we have to face during school days. We have to compete for everything from occupying a seat in our school bus to securing the top position in the class. We are supposed to give our best performance and get the best regardless of our own choices. This makes our life stressful and worrisome.

Secondly, we get less time for recreational and physical activities. No sooner do we go out to play than our mothers call us back home on the pretence of upcoming exams or some other activity in school. And if, we do not perform as expected by our parents and teachers, we are made to feel guilty and are made to feel that we are nothing, turning our days into nightmare.

Thirdly, we face discrimination on the grounds of performance in the exams. When it comes to scoring marks in exams, everybody becomes our tormentor – our parents, our teachers, tutors and even our siblings who want nothing from us but the highest marks in exams.

Their behaviour toward us changes according to the marks we score. More marks affectionate behaviour, less marks rudest behaviour as if we have committed a crime.

Some children in class behave like hooligans who are always ready to fight. They create such an atmosphere in the class as one feels unsecured. Even the teachers do not pay heed to their mischief. The tension of homework is always looming as all the teachers give a lot of homework which has to be completed on the same day and on being it to be incomplete, the students have to face punishment.

The holidays are not free. The students are given homework that consumes all their time. Some of the teachers are of the habit of using abusive language and beatings. Each passing day at school is full of stress that does not let a child live free rather he feels confined. Thus, I do not agree with the statement.

Q.14 "The use of mobile phones must be allowed in schools." Express your views either for or against the statement. **(ICSE 2016)**

Ans. **For the Motion**

Shakespeare has very wisely said: "There is nothing either good or bad, but thinking makes it so." Similarly, mobile phones in themselves are neither good nor bad; however, the way we use them categorises them into good or bad. I strongly feel that mobile phones do not harm a student and should be allowed in schools. Hence, I will speak for the motion.

Cell phones or mobile phones have become an important part of our daily lives. Today, it is difficult to imagine our life without a cell phone as most of our work is done using them. They provide an easy access to information which is a boon for brilliant students. Knowledge that was earlier limited to books and libraries is now at the finger tips.

With mobile phones, you can communicate with anyone from anywhere at any time. Thus, a student can easily connect with his/her parent at any time of the day from anywhere. Day-by-day, these devices are getting smaller in size and lighter in weight. Such features make them easy to carry around. They do not just help us in making calls but also allow self-learning with thousands of application promoting learning.

Thus, it is better to make the students use the cellphones constructively. Cellphones can make the children organise, can improve their safety as they will be able to contact people in medical and safety related incidents. If we trust our children with computers, we must trust them with cellphones also.

Against the Motion

We all are living in 21st century which is the age of science and technology. All the scientists of the world are constantly inventing new technology to ease our life and make it comfortable. Mobile phones or smart phones are invented to give us comfort and to keep us updated with the knowledge of the world, at a fingertip away.

However, these devices have become a source of major distraction for the students. Young boys and girls seem to have become inordinately addicted to them, always scrolling though social media sites and continuously texting. They are thoughtlessly and uselessly wasting their precious time on them, neglecting their studies.

Children get hooked to the gaming apps and social media sites. They become passive and kill their creativity. They spend less time in playing sports, exercise and outdoor activities. Mobile phones have become a means of flaunting one's social status quo. Overuse of mobile has posed serious health issues.

Radiation caused by network towers as well as mobile phones, affect not only eye sight but also causes difficulty in concentration, fatigue, headaches and sleep disturbance that can further trigger health complications. Owing to late night use of mobile phones, the youngsters skimp on sleep which has made them aggressive and irritated.

Another major disadvantage of the increasing use of mobile is the spread of undesirable information. Not only is such information confusing but they are also not age appropriate.

At this age, mind is usally tender and gets influenced easily. Cellphones can be seen as a means used by students for cheating during examinations. They can simply text anyone and ask for assistance. Moreover, mobile phones spoil the healthy and learning school decorum. Schools are meant for imparting education, knowledge and life skills. Thus, the cellphones should not be allowed inside the school ground.

If teachers have to make a call, they can use school landline or if a kid needs to call his/her parents, he/she would be allowed to use the landline. The children must be guided and counselled by the teachers and parents about how to use cellphones judiciously. School authorities must monitor children. Discussions can be done to make the children aware of the advantages and disadvantages of using mobile phones in schools.

Q.15 "All girls or all boys schools provide a better learning environment than co-educational schools." Express your views either for or against the statement. **(ICSE 2015)**

Ans. **For the Motion**

We all know that it is our duty to ensure that our children feel a sense of security and freedom at school. In this light I agree with the statement that all-girls or all-boys schools provide a better learning environment than co-educational schools.

It has been observed that all-girls or all-boys schools can provide a more structured learning environment for both boys and girls. Boys and girls differ in the way they act and learn. They have different interests and abilities. They need an educational environment tailored to meet their unique needs. In general, boys are more physically active, assertive and comfortable learning in a more chaotic environment than girls. Girls prefer a quiet, focused and orderly classroom.

In all-girls or all-boys schools, the curriculum and course offerings provide advanced work in areas of the children's greatest interests and natural abilities. Moreover, single-sex schools encourage children to take risks in expressing themselves as they learn without the fear of embarrasssing themselves in front of the opposite sex.

A study conducted states that single-sex schools develop greater self-confidence and broader interests especially among adolescents. Girls report that they feel more comfortable, they can interact more with teachers and develop move favourable attitudes towards subjects such as Maths and Science.

In addition, single-sex schools for boys allow adequate time for male maturation and benefit the boys by giving them more structure and discipline due to their tendencies of restlessness and aggression.

Furthermore, separating girls and boys fosters an environment of non-stereotyping and encourages learning. It also promotes interest for boys in humanities courses and they feel more at ease because they do not feel the peer related societal pressures. It benefits girls as co-educational schools foster obsession over hair and clothes and tend to make them distracted. The students in all-girls or all-boys schools also feel the freedom to attend classes usually associated with the opposite sex.

Thus, in my opinion, all-girls and all-boys schools provide a better learning environment than co-educational schools.

Against the Motion

Whether to admit their children into all-girls or all-boys schools or co-educational schools has always been a debate that parents are disturbed with. It seems to be a dilemma, but I would say there is absolutely no difficulty in making this choice.

Coming from a co-ed school, I stand against the statement that "All-girls or all-boys schools provide a better learning environment than co-educational schools". Education in the general sense is a form of learning in which the knowledge, skills, values and beliefs are transferred from the teacher to his students. The modes of education do not vary as per the sex of the students. Thus, education cannot be divided on the lines of sex.

Not only have the students of co-educational schools done academically well but also, it has been seen that they are more confident beings than the students of same sex schools. When girls sit along with boys in the same classroom, it helps develop cordial relations among students and instils in them mutual harmony and brotherhood. Moreover, co-educational schools offer a diverse curriculum that is available to all students, de-emphasising gender-linked stereotypes related to course work. Co-educational schools encourage all children to explore a broad range of career opportunities. Today is especially an age when men and women work together and compete with each other in offices, homes, etc. Thus, co-education teaches or prepares them to interact with the other sex in the future. Boys and girls learn to respect one another and cooperate as equals.

There is no way to avoid contact with the opposite gender, and it is essential to learn the proper way to interact with others so that one can develop healthy relationships with people around. An all-girls or an all-boys school cannot provide such an environment to its students within the campus. This may lead to the development of a negative response to the approach of the opposite gender. It is the accumulated experience from interacting with the opposite gender and observing others interact with the opposite sex that enables one to be apt and able in communicating with others, whether male or female. This is certainly an important advantage of studying in a co-ed school.

Last but not least, students studying in a co-ed school can enjoy the advantage of building a set of balanced moral values, more easily than those studying in a single-sex school.

Q.16 "Boarding schools are far better than day schools for the all-round education of a child". Express your views either for or against this statement.

Ans. **For the Motion**

Students in a boarding school show better progress and are supposed to be more disciplined. Furthermore, there are many special help programmes available there such as mentor-mentee programme in a boarding school. The purpose of this mentor-mentee system is to provide guidance to students about academic matters and to foster a close and constructive professional relationship between students and the staff of the faculty.

While all lecturers in the faculty are potentially academic advisors to all students who seek their advice, each teacher who is a mentor, is assigned particular responsibility to a small group of students which are the mentees. In day schools, programmes like this are not present.

Moreover, by staying in a boarding school, children will learn to be independent and deal with difficult situations on their own. This is because students, who are in boarding schools, are mostly far apart from their parents. They usually have to make their own decisions, unlike day school students who always depend on their parents. This will help them grow as an individual and bring out the best in them.

Boarding school can also produce individuals who are very creative. This is because they can make students do things that day school students cannot do such as dorm decoration. They need to decorate the dorm with some challenging themes. Moreover, small class size, diverse curriculum and individual attention from faculty and advisors give boarding students many distinct advantages so that students can focus on their education well.

At the same time, the teachers can give more attention to individuals who do not understand a topic as the number of students in the class is less. Boarding school reduces compartmentalisation, because academic studies are blended with other activities, such as sports. This natural juxtaposition increases the appeal of both pursuits.

In conclusion, I want to emphasise that boarding schools are better than the normal day schools because it produces individuals who can tackle the real world where their attitude and discipline, determine their success.

Against the Motion

I am here to express my views against the motion 'Boarding schools are far better than day schools for the all-round education of a child'.

In my opinion, day schools are better than boarding schools. Many day schools offer co-educational facilities and this is an important requirement in terms of today's world. Interacting with the opposite sex in the early years, will enable children to be comfortable in the presence of the opposite sex when they reach a stage where they might have to work alongside them in an official environment.

Although, there may be a few boarding schools that offer co-education, day schools clearly outnumber the boarding schools doing this and co-education in day schools is a much more accepted and existent structure, especially in India.

Day schools are a preferred option as they are much less expensive than a boarding school. Tuition fee in day schools is cheaper. Most good quality day schools are relatively cheaper than boarding schools and this is another reason why parents opt for day schools over boarding schools.

Day schools allow parents to admit students in private tuition of their choice as well, in case their children need extra coaching.

Most boarding schools in India have fees that is a bit exorbitant and unless parents are willing to fund a new experience and style of education for their children, most average Indian parents prefer day schools. Day schools are a better option for those parents who wish to have close supervision over their children.

Day schools also enable constant parent-teacher contact and this helps the parents monitor the progress of their children in terms of both academic and extracurricular activities. This is also an important aspect of a day school. Parents can provide moral guidance if they are in constant contact with their children and this is possible only if the children are admitted in a day school.

Moreover, if children are used to the comforts of home, they might find it difficult to survive in a boarding school. Day schools enable the children to relax a bit more than boarding schools. In a boarding school, students are required to take part in many events and many students find it difficult to deal with this schedule.

Furthermore, in case of any sickness or injury, parents can be with their children immediately if they are admitted in a day school.

Q.17 A working woman is a dynamic personality. She knows the intricacies of lives. She can instil the values better. Summing all these, draft a debate on 'Working women are better mothers.'

Ans. **For the Motion**

'The hand that rocks the cradle is the hand that rules the world'. It is very true that mothers play an important role in the growth and development of the future generation. These days, there is a fight between two kinds of mother, working and non-working. Mothers are constantly fighting and debating to figure out who is the better parent. In my opinion, an educated and a working woman will have a more positive impact on the child and hence, is more capable of moulding the destiny of the future generation.

Now, when the women are moving shoulder to shoulder with men and moving ahead in life, debating if they are better mothers is like emotionally blackmailing and making them weak.

It is also as if accusing them of neglecting their responsibility of bringing up their children well. They should not be made to feel small for wanting and working to move forward in their professional life. In the age of equality, women are increasingly encouraged to 'have it all' by balancing their career, children and marriage in order to be seen successful. And still, they are accused.

It's like maintaining a double face. On one hand, people talk about the necessity of a woman to actively participate in the country's economic growth. As a result, when she steps out there is a constant criticism of her on not being able to balance her home and office.

It is also not necessary that the women who stay at home prove to be perfect or better mothers. Children whose mothers who stay at home are more pampered whereas a working mother's children are more disciplined. Also, working mothers are able to guide their children better by providing them with the right amount and kind of exposure.

I think it is not right to constrain and limit women to house-keeping and child-rearing and waste the abundant potential which is within them.

We should not, thus, be stuck in tedious arguments about whether women, especially mothers, should or should not work. What is noteworthy is that it is the happiness of a woman we should really be talking about.

Against the Motion

The idea that working women are better mothers is subjective and overlooks many important factors. While working mothers contribute to their families and society, it is unfair to say they are better than stay-at-home mothers.

If a woman is working outside the home, she can only feed her baby once or twice a day and that is not enough for the well-being of the child.

A child learns by example and so the first school of the child is the home and his first teacher is the mother.

If a woman works outside the home, how would she have the energy to nurture the cognitive ability of the child?

She may not be there at meal-times and the child would have to be kept in the care of a maid. This would not ensure that her child gets proper nourishment in his all important formative years.

When a woman is at home, she has enough time to spend with her children not because she has less work to do but because, being at home, she is there for the child whenever needed. The children gets time to share their problems, happiness, fun and curiosity with their mother. She teaches them manners, traditions and customs. A child's best friend is its mother but if she is too busy taking care of both the home and her job, how would she have the time and energy to be there for the child?

A working woman has to leave her child when it is barely an year old. She remains constantly worried about her child. A child cannot be looked after properly in her absence. As a result, baby-sitters are hired, who often turn out to be a facade.

Moreover, a woman who works outside, suffers from the guilt of not being able to spend enough time with her child. This affects her relationship with the child. She either over-indulges with the child to compensate the lost time or becomes very strict because she does not want the child to get spoilt.

Hence, I would like to conclude that non-working women make better mothers than working women. If a woman stays at home and looks after children, it is definitely more beneficial for both to her own well-being and that of her children.

Q.18 Assistance is necessary for the growing buds. But, this assistance should not be purely commercial in nature. In the light of this statement, justify 'private tuitions being necessary evil'.

Ans. **For the Motion**

I am here to express my views in favour of the motion 'Private tuitions are a necessary evil'.

Private tuition is a part of the learning process that has become a backbone and a big part of our education system. Private tuitions have existed for decades and will always exist because we have a system of education which is coupled with competition.

Without that additional coaching, it is not easy for a student to compete with their classmates. Very often what they get in class is highly inadequate for them to clear the competitive exams. To be successful, they are compelled to seek extra coaching outside school hours to stay in the race to pass the finishing line.

Today, the syllabus taught in class is not sufficient for those who are in quest for knowledge or who are on the competitive track. Very often, the teacher finds themselves in front of an uncooperative class who deliberately puts a spoke in their wheel and makes their work a real ordeal. A teacher, in spite of all the skills and competence, if does not get the cooperation of the class, is utterly unable to make progress and is never able to deliver good.

Therefore, those who are in search of knowledge, are compelled to recourse to private tuition. Moreover, private tuition helps in improving the performance of the child. It can be complementary when the lessons done in the class have not been fully understood by the student.

Generally, a classroom is not conductive to individual teaching. The teacher-pupil interaction highly spoken of is not possible in the class due to large class-size.

A teacher normally tries to avoid a dull student. So, such a student may fail to catch the eye of the teacher. In such cases, private tuition may be helpful. The pupil may not only be taught, but also made to work at exercises which they would normally avoid in class.

If the tuition teacher is earnest, the pupils can progress and improve gradually.

Some of the topics that are not covered in the class or which require supplementary reading could very well be done in the tuition hour. Additional exercises could be done, better reading is possible which may lead to better understanding. Thus, private tuitions are necessary as they provide the needful things to the students.

Against the Motion

I am here to express my views against the motion 'Private tuitions are a necessary evil'.

In earlier days, tuition was not necessary as education was not so emphasised. But, now-a-days, many students prefer to go to tuition because they believe that it helps achieve success in examination. They may sign up for tuition either because they are forced by their parents or just out of their own willingness.

Some students decide on studying on their own. However, deciding on taking tuition have respective pros and cons on student's achievement and life.

Private tuition makes a child depend more on the teachers and the notes they give rather than on himself. Children, who take tuitions, give stereotype answers because they don't use their own mind to produce answers rather they become machines of learning answers.

Private tuition can be a financial burden to parents who are not wealthy. Taking tuitions is very expensive as well and not everyone can afford to send their children for extra private tuition.

According to research, those children, who take tuitions, don't study seriously in the class because they feel that they can learn and grasp the topics while taking tuitions. This way they disturb the whole class and also waste the time of serious minded students. Now a days, we see that teachers are more inclined in giving private tuitions as it has become a source of extra income for them but this is completely against the noble profession of teaching.

Teacher should make a target to set the maximum output in the class/school so that the tuition trend fades away and every child can get an equal opportunity to learn from his teachers. Moreover, tutors provide additional homework on top of those given by the teachers in school. Sometimes, tutors do arrive at the wrong timing. For instance, students are not in the mood to learn or have gone through a hard day in school and are, therefore, mentally tired. Despite such a bad timing, the tuition sessions may still have to carry on, which make it unfruitful.

Some students treat their tutors as a walking dictionary, expecting them to furnish answers to the homework given by school without thinking through the solutions by themselves over time. This can make them mentally lazy.

Thus, in my opinion private tuitions are not mandatory.

Q.19 "No other subject taught in school is as important as Moral Science." Express your views either for or against this statement.

Ans. **For the Motion**

I am here to express my views in favour of the motion "No other subject taught in school is as important as Moral Science."

In today's rat race, values are eroding faster. Children go to schools daily thinking how to scale heights they will reach, how rich education can make them. In today's cut throat competition, even the parents instruct their wards that they should excel academically. Childhood is an impressionable age. The mind is like soft wax, so whatever one is taught at a tender age leaves a deep impression.

Therefore, Moral Science must be made a compulsory subject in school curriculum. It is also a science of human soul and a mirror to one's inward mind and one's ethics. Moral science inculcates values in mankind and value education is vital.

Schools should shoulder the responsibility of imparting moral values to them. In order to make them self-reliant, confident and responsible citizens, they need to be imparted with value based education, which only Moral Science can do. After all, today's child is tomorrow's citizen.

Moral Science is not a religion based subject. Rather it eliminates fanaticism, superstition and violence. It preaches 'Love All, Serve All', a value which lacks in the modern world. It helps a child to pay heed to their conscience and not to be led away by worldly show. However, theoretical knowledge is not enough. Teachers should make their life exemplary to their students. The lives of great patriots or spiritual leaders must be brought to the forefront.

Only moral science can stem the tide of rapid value erosion and motivate the students towards a healthier life. A child is then trained emotionally, mentally and physically how to be a responsible citizen or a good son or daughter. They can resist wrong peer pressure, intolerance, and through right conduct lead forward their nation.

One becomes more understanding, patient, pious, decent and wise. One learns to do things without any selfish motives. Pleasure is derived in doing things for others as one feels that one is doing it for welfare.

Therefore, there can be no doubt about the fact that no other subject taught in school is as important as Moral Science. Let the light of spirituality shine through the eyes of the little ones.

Against the Motion

I am here to express my views against the motion "No other subject taught in school is as important as Moral Science."

I would rather emphasise the point that knowledge is power and this power comes through learning not merely moral Science but all subjects prescribed in schools. Thorough study of all the subjects will unravel the vast potentialities that can enrich our life and resolve many mysteries about the universe. A well sounded education is necessary to prepare students for the real world. Mathematics and Science develop logical thinking and problem-solving skills, which are crucial in everyday decision-making. Language studies enhances communication abilities, helping individuals express themselves effectively. History and social sciences teach students about past events, cultures and governance, which shape their understanding of society. Without these subjects, students would lack the knowledge and skills needed for professional and personal success.

Whereas not much effort is required to learn ethics and morality, much mental labour is involved in learning subjects dealing with different branches of learning. Moral

Science teaches us about what is morally good or bad which can be learnt spontaneously and instinctively by observing the behaviour of the elders we come across daily. The great advancement in technology in conquering time and space has been possible because much more emphasis is being laid on the study of science. Now, environmental study is being given more importance and it is made a compulsory subject at all levels of school education.

The harmonious development of a student's personality can only be possible with equal emphasis on the study of all subjects and not becoming isolated by simply meditating on God, Life and Death. Let such things be special subjects of religion and metaphysics to be taken up only by those exclusively interested in this particular branch. The more we learn about other subjects, the richer will be our knowledge.

Q.20 **"The computer will soon replace the book." Express your views either for or against this statement.**

Ans. **For the Motion**

I am here to express my views in favour of the motion, "The computer will soon replace the book".

Computers have already taken a major role as an information resource today. Computer technologies such as hypertext and the internet remove the geographical constrains of print media and allow for a new method of distributing and reading documents. Books will always be affordable and concrete sources of information but the next ten years will bring computers that are faster to access, convenient to use and hold more information than books. With the internet, one piece of information is accessible from millions of computers around the world. A researcher may need to travel no further than his/her computer to find a document in a virtual library 3000 miles away.

In the next 20 years, print media may not be able to keep up with the exponential growth of information because the density of information on a computer is far greater than that of a book. The internet already holds more data than any physical library. A typical computer hard drive can hold around 2000 novels.

In addition to their seemingly unlimited storage capacity, computers also provide much faster access to information, e.g. looking upwards in a dictionary might take a few minutes while computers can give the definition for any word and pronounce it for you immediately. The computer's speed and space will make it a necessary technology as we move into a new millennium.

The future will bring even greater advantages to the computer over the book. Soon, computers will have screens that are crisper and more comfortable to view than a printed book. With new technology, computer screens will no longer strain the eyes and it will become feasible. Technology will soon produce a computer that is as compact, durable and comfortable to read as a book but that could contain thousands of books in electronic form. Although computers will never completely supplement books, we may soon rely on them more than books. Computers will meet our needs of information storage and distribution and will be a convenient way to hold more information in less space than today's book.

Against the Motion

I am here to express my views against the motion "The computer will soon replace the book."

Computers any day, are far more expensive than books. Unlike books, they need to be powered through batteries. One cannot lie in bed and read them leisurely. Furthermore, any spillage can cause irreparable damage to them.

Computers can get infected by viruses and are not completely dependable but a book in a shelf is very dependable. It doesn't strain your eyes as computers do.

Moreover, with the help of computers, students simply copy-paste and the matter is complete. The pride of a library and collecting the first edition as well as autographed books of an author will have no relevance. A book reveals the nature of a person but with a computer no one can know who is an avid reader and who is not.

A book somehow has a sense of belongingness. The printed book can easily be read and stored. Students can write their notes and refer to them at any point of time. Computer troubles its users, while a book is perfect source for relaxation. The joy of placing your hands on a book and reading through its pages is ecstatic and can never be for replaced by computer. One can even sleep with a book on one's bedside and wake up in the morning to continue reading.

No one is going to put computers into the hands of kindergarten students and moreover, not everyone can afford to have a computer. Thus, let's forget about such an idea and live realistically. Books may have their limitation but they can never be superseded by computers. No one wants to lose the joy of reading a book and at the end announcing to himself that, 'It is finished'.

Q.21 **A concern for environment is a concern for everyone. In the light of this statement, write an argumentative composition on the topic, "EV vehicles are better than those which run on fuel."**

Ans. **For the Motion**

I stand here in favour of the motion "EV vehicles are better than those which run on fuel."

'Electric vehicles (EVs) are a game-changer in the world of transportation. They're not just a trendy innovation —they're better for the planet and for us. The biggest reason EVs stand out is that they're environment friendly.

Unlike petrol or diesel cars that pump harmful gases into the air, EVs don't have any tailpipe emissions. Cleaner air means healthier lungs and a step towards slowing down climate change, which is something we desperately need right now.

Yes, buying an EV might feel expensive at first, but think long-term—it's worth it. Electricity is cheaper than fuel, and because EVs have fewer moving parts, they need less maintenance. Governments are even giving discounts and perks to people who choose electric cars, which makes them more affordable.

Another win? EVs are super quiet. Imagine cities with less noise pollution—doesn't that sound peaceful? Plus, EVs often come with cool features like smart connectivity, regenerative braking, and advanced safety tech.

And here's the best part- if we start using renewable energy like solar or wind to charge EVs, we can make driving completely green. That's a future we should all want—a world with clean air, quiet streets, and sustainable energy.

In short, EVs aren't just better than fuel cars—they're a step towards a healthier, more sustainable world. If we care about the environment and the generations to come, switching to electric vehicles is the right thing to do.

Against the Motion

I stand here against the motion "EV vehicles are better than those which run on fuel."

While EVs might seem like the perfect solution to our problems, they're not as flawless as people make them out to be. For starters, let's talk about those batteries.

Making EV batteries requires mining for materials like lithium and cobalt, which harms the environment and often involves questionable labour practices. Plus, what happens to the batteries when they're no longer usable? Managing that waste is a big issue we still haven't solved.

Another major problem is charging. Unlike fuel-powered cars that can refuel quickly almost anywhere, EVs need charging stations, which aren't as common. And even when you find one, charging takes much longer than filling a tank. This makes EVs less practical, especially for long trips.

Then there's the electricity used to charge EVs. In many places, it still comes from coal or other non-renewable sources, which means EVs aren't as green as they're claimed to be. If your power source isn't clean, how can your car truly be eco-friendly?

Let's not forget the cost. EVs are expensive to buy, and while they might save money on fuel, replacing their batteries can be ridiculously pricey. This puts them out of reach for a lot of people, especially in countries where incomes are lower.

Fuel-powered vehicles are more versatile and reliable. They perform better in extreme weather conditions, have higher towing capacities, and are more suitable for industries like logistics, construction and emergency services, where power and endurance are essential.

In the end, while EVs have their benefits, they also come with a lot of challenges. Maybe the solution isn't choosing one over the other but finding a way to balance both technologies. That might be a smarter and more realistic approach for the future.

04

SHORT STORY

Story writing is a creative but difficult art of composition. It requires a lot of innovative thinking, planning and mastery of narrative skills and language. A short story is a narrative of moderate length that revolves around a single incident involving one or more characters. It must have a proper beginning, middle and an end. A story needs to be well-planned and written in an interesting manner.

Do's and Don'ts for Writing a Short Story

Do's	Don'ts
Capture the reader's attention immediately by an interesting opening line.	Avoid unnecessary length.
Ensure your story has a central message or idea.	Don't over-explain or introduce irrelevant subplots.
Keep the story simple, focusing on a central conflict with a clear resolution.	Avoid predictable or overused ideas and phrases.

Sample of Short Story

Write an original short story that begins with the words: "It wasn't going to be easy she knew... but somehow she had to confront him. She took a deep breath and walked into the room ...."

Confessions

It wasn't going to be easy she knew but somehow she had to confront him. She took a deep breath and walked into the room. She came across a dark corridor and saw the room as the light came. He was sitting right in front reading the newspaper. She was nervous as she knew why she was called. She also hesitated but somehow she ignored the lump in her throat and called for him. Dad! Hearing her voice, he turned towards her and kept the newspaper aside.

He turned his chair. His eyes were somewhat bulging out as though they were supported by the spring. He asked her about her school report card. She kept looking down as she did not have the courage to look him in the eye. He waited for her response but when there was no answer. He lost his calm and shouted with anger.

It made the poor girl rattle with fear. Scared, she dropped her report card on the floor hoping her result would pacify her father. She hoped her father would not scold her for her marks. Her father picked up the report card. As he opened it, he saw that his daughter scored all the marks in the nineties. A smile came upon his angry face.

He suddenly went towards her and hugged her. She was aghast at her father's behaviour. Although out of words, she felt the love of her father for her. This was all she ever desired after her mother's death.

Teacher's Remarks ....

- The emotional challenges introduced in the story make it more interesting.
- Characterisation of the father adds to the tension in the scene.
- Building tension makes the reader empathise with her.
- The ending shows the girl's realisation of her father's love providing emotional closure.

EXAM ORIENTED QUESTIONS

Q.1 Write an original short story in which a poor tailor wins an award which changes his/her life. **(ICSE 2025, 20 M)**

Ans. Ravi was a poor tailor who lived in a small town. He had a tiny shop where he stitched clothes for the people in his neighbourhood. He worked hard every day but he barely earned enough to buy food for his family. Even though his life was tough, Ravi never complained. He loved his work and always tried to make beautiful clothes. His dream was to become a famous tailor one day but he did not know how to achieve it.

One day, a big announcement was made in the town. A famous fashion company was holding a competition for tailors. The winner would get a big cash prize and a job in the city. Ravi's friends told him to participate but he was unsure. "I am just a simple tailor. How can I win such a big contest?" he said.

His wife, Meena, smiled and said, "You must try. You are talented and this is your chance." Encouraged by her words, Ravi decided to take part. He worked day and night on a special dress. He carefully stitched every piece of fabric, adding beautiful patterns by hand. When he finished, he felt proud of his work. His children also admired the dress and told him he would surely win.

On the day of the competition, Ravi saw many talented tailors with fancy designs. He felt nervous but stayed hopeful. When the judges saw his dress, they were amazed. "This is wonderful! Such fine stitching and unique design," one of them said. After much discussion, Ravi was declared the winner!

Tears filled Ravi's eyes as he accepted the award. The prize money helped him expand his shop, and soon, he got many new customers. A few months later, the fashion company offered him a big job in the city. His life changed forever.

Ravi had once doubted himself but now he knew-hard work, belief and the courage to try could make dreams come true.

Q.2 Write an original short story in which a woman, her strange neighbour and a police officer form the main characters. **(ICSE Specimen 2025)**

Ans. **The Mysterious Neighbour**

It was a quiet evening in the residential neighbourhood when Meera noticed something unusual. A new tenant had moved into the house next door–a house that had been vacant for months. She hadn't seen anyone come or go but she could hear strange noises at night, like muffled footsteps and odd sounds coming from the house. Curiosity gnawed at her but she dismissed it as nothing more than overactive imagination.

One evening, as Meera was returning from her walk, she saw the new neighbour standing by his gate. He looked out of place, with a hurried and anxious demeanor. His eyes darted nervously around and Meera felt a strange chill.

"Good evening," she said, trying to break the silence.

The man quickly glanced at her and gave a stiff nod but didn't speak. His odd behavior made Meera uneasy. Over the next few days, she noticed stranger occurrences -unexplained lights at odd hours and the man often seen leaving and returning at strange times. Meera couldn't shake the feeling that something was wrong.

One afternoon, she noticed a police officer standing outside her house. She walked over and learned that there had been a report of suspicious activity at the house next door. The officer had come to investigate. Meera, feeling uneasy, mentioned the strange behaviour of her new neighbour.

The officer's face grew serious. "Ma'am, you're not mistaken. We've been watching that house for some time. The man living there is suspected of involvement in a series of robberies in the area."

Meera's heart raced. Her curiosity had led her into an unexpected and dangerous situation. The officer assured her that the investigation was ongoing but for now, she was safe.

The following week, the house was empty again. The mysterious neighbor had vanished, leaving behind only questions and the quiet echoes of a dangerous secret.

Q.3 Write an original short story entitled. 'A Strange Visitor'. **(ICSE 2024)**

Ans. **A Strange Visitor**

It was one of those days when everything seemed to go wrong. I was buried in debt and had no idea how to pay it off. To make matters worse, I had unwittingly invested all my savings into a fraudulent scheme.

For months, I had been receiving large returns and I thought everything was fine. But the truth hit me hard when I discovered that the people behind the scheme had vanished, leaving me with enormous debts in my name. I was left to face the consequences alone while the scammers disappeared without a trace.

On that bleak day, my mind was clouded with worry and regret. I decided to step outside to clear my head. The crisp winter air nipped at my skin and the fields around my home were covered in a blanket of frost, creating a quiet, almost magical scene. I lived in rural Ireland, a place where silence often reigns, making everything seem even more overwhelming.

As I walked by my house, I noticed a man sitting on a large stone. His appearance was unusual-his old-fashioned clothes looked out of place and he seemed distant yet oddly comforting. Concerned, I approached him and asked if he was okay but he didn't reply. I offered him food and warmth, inviting him into my house to escape the cold. Without a word, he followed me inside.

Once settled by the fire, I made him tea and offered him bread and biscuits. He silently drank the tea, lost in thought. When I went to collect his cup, a sudden knock on the door startled me. I opened it but there was no one there. When I turned back, the man had vanished, leaving no trace.

To my surprise, I found a small pouch on the stool where he had sat. Inside, there were 20 gold coins.

I couldn't believe my eyes. I kept the coins, hoping he might return but he never did.

Since that strange encounter, my situation has improved, though I still don't understand what happened. Was it just a coincidence or did the mysterious visitor help me in my time of need? I'll never know but I remain deeply grateful for the unexpected kindness that brought hope back into my life.

Q.4 Write an original short story entitled. 'A Narrow Escape'. **(ICSE Specimen 2024)**

Ans. **A Narrow Escape**

It was a bright Sunday morning when my friends, Arjun and Maya and I decided to take a hike through the forest near our village. We had often heard stories of hidden waterfalls and beautiful trails and we were excited to explore the wilderness. The air was fresh and the scent of pine trees filled our senses as we ventured deeper into the woods.

As we walked along a narrow path, the sounds of birds chirping and leaves rustling made the journey feel peaceful. After about an hour, we reached a steep hill covered in dense bushes. Arjun, even the adventurous one, suggested we climb to the top to get a better view. Maya and I hesitated but eventually agreed. The climb was difficult, with sharp rocks and tangled roots making it tricky to ascend.

Halfway up, I lost my footing and slipped. My heart raced as I slid down the hill, grasping at branches and rocks but everything was too loose. I was falling fast when, out of nowhere, a strong hand grabbed my wrist. It was Arjun. He had climbed down after hearing me scream and caught me just in time.

Shaken but unharmed, I caught my breath. Arjun helped me back up to the path, his face pale with fear. Maya, who had watched the whole scene unfold, was visibly relieved. We all sat down for a while, grateful to be safe.

We decided to head back home, not wanting to push our luck any further. As we walked back through the forest, I couldn't stop thinking about how close I had come to serious danger. That narrow escape taught me the importance of caution and the value of looking out for each other in times of need.

Q.5 Write an original short story that begins, with the words. 'He was the strangest boy I had ever met ......' **(Competency Based Que.)**

Ans. **He was the Strangest Boy I had Ever Met**

He was the strangest boy I had ever met. It was the first day of school after the summer holidays and Everyone was buzzing with excitement. There was one boy in our class who immediately caught my attention. His name was Aditya and he was unlike anyone I had ever seen before.

He had messy, untidy hair that he did not comb and brush. His uniform was worn out. But what struck me the most were his eyes. They were a bright shade of green, almost glowing and had a faraway look, as if he was always lost in a world of his own.

The moment he sat down beside me, he didn't say anything. He just opened his notebook, scribbled something and stared out of the window. I tried to start a conversation but he barely responded. Instead, he pulled out a small sketchbook from his bag and began drawing.

His sketches were amazingly-detailed, intricate and full of life. There was something almost magical about his drawings, as if they captured the essence of the world around him in ways no one else could.

Over the next few days, I tried to get to know him better. However, Aditya was always elusive. He spoke in soft, almost inaudible tones, never making eye contact for long. Yet, there was an undeniable aura of mystery around him. He would often disappear during lunch breaks, wandering in the schoolyard as though searching for something.

One afternoon, I followed him secretly. He led me to the edge of the school grounds, where he stood silently, staring at a small patch of wildflowers. Without a word, he knelt down and sketched the flowers, their petals delicately drawn in his book.

I realised then that Aditya wasn't strange at all.

He simply saw the world differently-a world full of beauty and wonder that most of us missed in our rush to grow up. And in his quiet way, he taught me to see it too.

This image and story inspire testament to the fact that children, with their prejudiced mind and boundless heart, can teach adults the fundamental value of friendship, diversity and unity.

Q.6 **Write an original short story in which two children and their school teacher are the main character. (ICSE 2023)**

Ans. **The Best Friends**

Ramu and Suresh were really good friends. They had been classmates since they started school and loved to create mischief. They always pranked teachers but their pranks never hurt anyone. Though they were pranksters of the school, they were loved by all. One could find them playing sports in the field, working on projects together and even participating in debates taking opposite stands.

Once their English Teacher Mr. Sullivan had read the poem 'The Tale of Custard the Dragon' in the class and started a discussion on bravery. The discussion was healthy till a classmate stated that Suresh was not as brave as he showed and told the class that Suresh was scared of lightning. Suresh who was sitting quietly got upset when Ramu did not defend him.

He asked Ramu to do the same but Ramu did not say a word. Thus, it led to a fight between the best friends.

Mr. Sullivan got worried for he did not want the best friends to fight over something as trivial as this. So, he called the boys and explained the situation to them but in vain. The boys did not even want to talk to each other. So, Mr. Sullivan decided to play a small prank on the boys to prove his statement. He called the boys to the restricted part of their Convent School which was claimed to be haunted.

When the boys reached the area, the door of the room closed by itself and strange sounds came from the room. The boys were scared and started beating the door so someone could hear them. But no one came to help them. They even looked out to find a way to escape the haunted room and saw a window with a broken pane.

Together, they rushed towards it and helped each other escape the room. When they were finally out of the room, they hugged each other for both of them were safe. Outside, they saw Mr. Sullivan who was standing with a smile.

He told the boys about his plan to reunite them and explained that Ramu had requested him for the discussion so that Suresh learns to defend himself and be bold. Ramu told Suresh how he had heard someone call Suresh a wimp and wanted Suresh to prove them wrong. Suresh easily understood Ramu's explanation and apologised for starting the fight.

Q.7 **Write an original short story entitled. 'Lost and Found'. (ICSE Specimen 2023, 19)**

Ans. **Lost and Found**

This happened around the time when I was in the fifth grade. My 13th birthday had arrived and I was ecstatic. My father gave me a new bicycle as a gift. I was very happy to see it. I spent the entire day on it, going to different places. I flaunted it to all of my friends. They also wanted to ride my bicycle. Once, I drove it to a park nearby. I had a great deal of fun there. In my overjoyed state, I forgot to bring my bicycle home.

When I arrived at my house, I went for a walk with my friends. It is then that I realised that I'd forgotten my bicycle in the park. It had been a long night. I was taken aback. I wondered whether or not to inform my father. I came to the conclusion that if I told him, he would scold me. I also knew that we won't find it that late in the evening.

When I came home, I discovered that my father already knew about my lost bicycle. I couldn't figure out how he knew that it wasn't in the garage. He became enraged and demanded to know where my bicycle was. There was nothing I could do. I told him what had happened and how I had mistakenly left it at the park. His anger only grew after hearing that. He continued to scold me. Late after that, I went to sleep and as soon as it was morning, I went to find my bicycle.

I went to my friends' house and asked for their help. They agreed to help me and said that we should start looking in the park first. They accompanied me but my bicycle was nowhere to be found. I was afraid that it had been stolen. But, I reasoned to try harder.

I inquired of the park's guard if he had seen any green bicycle. He stated that he had found a bicycle there the day before and had kept it in a secure location.

I was overjoyed and went to get it. Soon I returned home after thanking the guard for his kindness and honesty.

I showed the bicycle to my father. We were both overjoyed. Now, I think a thousand times before leaving my bicycle anywhere. That day, I realised the true worth of my bicycle.

Q.8 **Imagine a situation where a child runs away from home but later returns. Why did he or she run away? What made him/her come back? Write an original short story entitled. 'Finding My Way Home'. (ICSE Specimen 2022 Sem II)**

Ans. **Finding My Way Home**

Freedom and space are two important parts of any teenager's life. We crave it but when we get it, we retaliate. That is exactly what Ramya did about a year ago when she decided to flee from her home at the age of 14. Ramya's decision was not sudden. It had a reason- her parents' constant nagging.

Her mother had always interfered in her life. She had to know where Ramya had been all day, who she was with, what she did and so on. The nagging nature was so overwhelming that Ramya should needed her approval for everything. Her father didn't fare any better. He was often nodding his head in agreement with whatever she said and Ramya hated it.

She needed space but her mother refused to give it to her. One day, fed up of her mother's nagging, she thought that she should flee. She had about two thousand rupees. So hurriedly she put her things in a bag. She left for school the next day but arrived at the bus station unsure of where she was heading. She decided to visit her ancestral village, which was a 100 kilometres away from Delhi.

She had never ridden a local bus alone before but she got a ticket and ascended the vehicle slowly. After three hours of journey, the bus reached its destination but Ramya could not recognise it. She had visited the village 2 months ago and depended on her memory to go her grandparents' home.

She decided to look out for a friendly face to get some help. However, she found none. So, she sat down and started crying. Suddenly, an old gentleman came and sat next to her. After some time, he asked Ramya if she was okay and what the matter was. Ramya told him everything and the man advised her to return to her parents. He suggested that Ramya should tell her parents how she feels and that they would listen to her. Parents are their children's sole well-wishers. Ramya realised how reckless she had been in running away and decided to go back.

Soon, with the help of the gentleman, she returned home. When she reached her home, she found her parents were crying. They were surrounded by the police and the neighbours. When Ramya made her presence known, her mother ran to her and hugged her. Ramya also started crying and told everyone the matter. She, then, apologised and promised to never do it again.

Q.9 **Write a short story in which the main characters are an old woman, a small child and a little puppy.**

(ICSE 2021 Sem II)

Ans. **The Lost Puppy**

A little girl named Sophie found a puppy near a tree when she was going back to home from school. The puppy looked weak and was afraid of people passing by. She went close to him but he stepped back.

He tried to hide behind the tree. Seeing this, Sophie took out a water bottle and a packet of biscuits from her bag and offered them to the puppy. Hesitantly, the puppy came out and sniffed the biscuits, sensing no danger, he hungrily ate the biscuits and drank the water.

Meanwhile, Sophie was gently petting the puppy who seemed to like it as he started wagging his tail. When Sophie realised that the puppy was not scared, she inspected him for injuries. She found that his leg had a huge cut and so she took him to the nearby veterinary clinic and got him medicines and band aids.

While inspecting the puppy, Sophie had also noticed that he wore a collar indicating that he was someone's pet. However, she could not find the name of the owner on it. So, she decided to look for the puppy's owner herself.

She went to nearby homes but to no avail. Since no one was there to look after the puppy, she decided to take him home. On reaching home, she gave him a bath, cleaned him thoroughly and put medicine on his injury. Meanwhile, she also put up an advertisement in the locality so that Tabby, the name she had given to the puppy, could be found by real owner. After a few days of advertisement, an old lady came up to Sophie and told her that she was the owner of Tabby.

The lady told her that she went out for a couple of days and left her puppy with the neighbours. But he ran from their house and ended up meeting Sophie. Tabby also started licking the lady's face and wagged his tails in excitement. Seeing this, Sophie was sure that Tabby belonged to the lady. He happily went away with her. Sophie would visit the old lady's house whenever she missed him.

Q.10 **Write an original short story entitled 'The Secret'.**

(ICSE 2020)

Ans. **The Secret**

Rohan was a fun-loving teenager. He was fourteen years old and a student of eighth standard in a reputed school. His happy family included his parents and his seven-year-old sister, Rhea. His father was a doctor and mother was a homemaker. One day, Rohan found a diary in their storeroom while playing with his sister. The diary had an attractive leather cover with golden border. He took it and kept it with his books.

The next day, Rohan opened the diary and found that it was an secret old diary that belonged to his mother. He started reading it. It contained beautiful descriptions of his mother's childhood, her village, ancestral home, etc. Next, he found the description of the marriage ceremony of his parents and their new life. But the real surprise still waited for him.

After few pages, it was written that he was the adopted child of his parents. They adopted him from an orphanage five years into their marriage. This secret left him absolutely shattered. He felt betrayed and ran away from home immediately.

Rohan roamed for many hours. Being exhausted, he sat on a bench in a park. There, he saw an old lady coming with a large tiffin-box. She distributed puri-aloo to all poor children. All the children called her 'Amma' (mother). After finishing their meal, they started reading.

Looking at those children, Rohan got into thinking about his parents, how they treated him and fulfilled all his demand's. He realised that his parents loved him unconditionally. They never differentiated between him and his sister, who was their biological child. He realised his mistake and returned home.

His anxious mother asked him where he had gone for such a longtime. He replied that he was very busy with his cricket match and forgot the timing. She served his favourite meal Rajma-chawal. Rohan realised it was his real home and decided that he would never think about the 'secret' anymore.

Q.11 Write an original short story in which two children and their grandfather are the main characters. (ICSE 2019)

Ans. What Sarita Did with Grandfather's Coins

Every month, Sarita and her younger cousins would go for Sunday lunch at their grandparents' house. The children would always wait excitedly for the moment their grandfather would give them a few coins, so that they could buy something for themselves. Then, all the children would run off to buy chewing gum, ice cream or potato chips.

The adults in the family felt that the children would never learn to manage their money. So, they told the children that they would have to show, over a period of one year, just what they could manage to get with those few coins.

The two smallest children paid no attention to this and continued spending the coins on sweets. However, Ajit, a ten year old boy, had a will of iron.

He saved all the coins he was given. At the end of the year he had collected more money than anyone. He won the competition hands down. His cousins learnt from him the advantages of knowing how to save and be patient.

The eldest cousin was Sarita. She was 12 years old. Poor Sarita didn't enjoy the end of the competition because even though she had a wonderful secret plan, she had spent her money without giving her plan enough time to work. But that didn't stop her from continuing with her plan.

When she was about to complete the second year of her plan, Sarita surprised everyone by turning up at her grandparents' house with a guitar and a lot of money.

Her playing was even more impressive. She played the guitar really well.

Then, Sarita told everyone how she did it. She had got to know a poor guitarist who played in the park. She offered him all the coins her grandfather had given her, if he would teach her how to play

On seeing Sarita's excitement, the guitarist agreed and taught her happily for months.

Then, the guitarist loaned her a guitar so they could play together in the park, as a duo. They were so successful that gradually she managed to buy her own guitar.

Sarita would always tell people how it was possible, with just a few coins well spent, to make your wildest dreams a reality.

Q.12 Write an original short story entitled. 'The Gift'. (ICSE 2018)

Ans. The Gift

Ayesha woke up on her fifteenth birthday, expecting a day filled with surprises and celebrations. But something felt... off. The house was unusually quiet. There were no colourful balloons, no streamers and, worst of all, no sign of her mother's cheerful singing that always woke her up on special days.

Feeling a little let down, she headed to the kitchen. Her younger brother, Rohan, was sitting at the table, completely absorbed in his comic book. Without looking up, he muttered, "Oh, uh, happy birthday." Her father was there too but he seemed busy with his newspaper and coffee.

Ayesha tried to brush it off but the disappointment lingered. Was everyone too busy to care? By the afternoon, she couldn't take it anymore. She marched to her mother's room and knocked. "Mum, did you... forget my birthday?" she asked, trying to keep her voice steady.

Her mother opened the door, a warm smile on her face.

"How could I forget, my love? Come with me," she said, taking Ayesha's hand. In the living room, a small box sat on the coffee table. It wasn't wrapped in shiny paper or topped with a bow-just a simple box with her name scrawled across it. "Go on, open it," her mother urged.

Inside, Ayesha found an old scarf, a bundle of faded photographs and a letter. She looked up, puzzled.

"That scarf belonged to your grandmother," her mother said gently. "She wore it every day, even when she was working hard to build this home for us. The photos are from simpler times when life wasn't easy but we had each other. And the letter... that's from me."

Ayesha unfolded the letter, her eyes scanning the words. 'My darling Ayesha, this isn't just a birthday gift. It's a reminder of the love, strength and sacrifices that make us who we are. These memories are your roots. Hold onto them-they'll guide you wherever life takes you.'

Tears filled Ayesha's eyes. She realised this wasn't just any gift-it was a piece of her family's story, something far more precious than anything money could buy.

That evening, they sat together, sharing stories and laughter. For the first time, Ayesha understood that the best gifts weren't things you could hold-they were the ones that stayed in your heart forever.

Q.13 Write an original short story that begins with the words. "It was raining hard that night. In my hurry to get into the house, I didn't notice the black car parked across the road. I realised something was wrong when.........." (ICSE 2017)

Ans. A Pleasant Surprise

It was raining hard that night. In a hurry to get into the house, I didn't notice the black car parked across the road. I realised something was wrong when I heard strange muffled voices coming from inside the car. Was I being followed? Were there some robbers sitting inside that car ready to rob any one of the houses or what was it? Who exactly was sitting in the car and why were they parked here?

I was really terrified when suddenly I saw a man all dressed in black getting out of that car. While I was trying to observe him, he started walking towards me. "He must've noticed me", I thought while I was shivering from the chill in the rain and most probably because I was wet. As soon as I tried to ring the bell of the house, that man called out, 'Excuse me.'

I was terrified at that man's call and wanted to run away but could not. The man asked me if I knew a mechanic nearby as he was a stranger to this city and was heading towards Delhi, where his mother was admitted in a hospital. I was still not sure whether I should trust that man but, at the same time, my father opened the door as I had rung the bell.

I just decided to go inside the house when my father happened to have a glance at that stranger. Suddenly, my father screamed with excitement, "Oh Shreekant! How come you are here? You had disappeared suddenly." That man looked at my father and came running towards him and screamed "Oh Pulkit, is this your house? Are you settled in this city?" My father replied him in affirmation and further asked him to come inside as the weather was really bad.

I was totally confused as I didn't know the stranger and my father was asking him to come inside. My father introduced me to that man, who was his class fellow some 22 years back. After finishing college, they had not been in touch with each other. My father was really excited meeting his old class fellow. He called a mechanic to get his car repaired and invited him to stay and rest till the rain got over.

So, initially what was scary for me, turned out to be a pleasant surprise for my father.

Q.14 **Write an original short story which illustrates the truth of the statement. 'One lie leads to another'.** **(ICSE Specimen 2017)**

Ans. **One Lie Leads to Another**

Saira was a sixteen-year-old girl belonging to a middle class family. She went to a really expensive private school as she was smart in academics. She was friends with many wealthy students but her best friend was Anna. She was very good at studies and was also interested in extra-curricular activities. Besides studies, she talked to Saira about fashion, jewellery, concerts and parties, etc.

Although Saira was not really interested in these things before, hearing about them made her want to do all the things that Anna did. One day, Anna told her that she was going to 'The Towers' with some friends and asked her to join them. Saira knew that her parents would never allow her to go with Anna but she really wanted to have fun so she decided to go with them.

Next day, Saira told her mother that she would be late from school as there was an extra class and took some money from the college savings. She felt uneasy about lying to her parents but forgot all about it soon. When her parents asked her about the extra class, she again lied that she had been working on a project with her science teacher.

After some days, Anna again asked her to join them somewhere and Saira agreed. And a series of excuses continued. As a result, her studies were affected while her college savings were getting reduced.

One day when Saira's mother was cleaning her cupboard, she noticed that the money Saira had saved for college had reduced significantly. When she asked Saira about it, the latter got afraid. She did not want her mother to find out that she goes out with Anna. So, she lied and said she did not know about it.

Her mother started scolding their maid thinking that she was the culprit. The maid was terrified and started crying which made Saira feel guilty. She was frightened but she also wanted to save the innocent maid so she decided to lie yet again. She told her mother that she had taken the money to buy some books. Her mother was surprised and doubtful. So, she asked Saira to show her the books but Saira couldn't. Finally realising that she cannot escape the situation, Saira told her mother everything. Her mother got angry and scolded Saira.

She decided to take the rest of the saved money so that Saira could not spend it recklessly. She also told Saira that she wasn't allowed to stay back in school until her teacher informs her of the same. Saira realised that her one lie led to several others that she had lost the trust that her mother reposed in her. She promised that she would never lie again and apologised to her mother.

Q.15 **Write an original short story that begins with the words. "The day started off well enough, whoever thought it would ...."** **(ICSE 2016)**

Ans. **Presence of Mind**

The day started off well enough, whoever thought it would end otherwise. We were going to Mumbai to spend one week with my elder sister who is settled there. We had booked the plane tickets in advance.

My younger sister and myself were very happy and excited to meet her for not only were we meeting her after three years but also she was expecting her first child. Finally, the flight time approached and the formalities were completed.

We were just about to board the plane when a loud announcement terrified us. "All passengers about to board Indigo flight 753 should immediately deboard and gather in the waiting hall. The flight is cancelled".

The announcement was repeated many times. We were all very shocked, disappointed and somewhat enraged.

I, along with my sister, came down in the hall and sat in a corner chair. It was 11p.m. and I could see the dark airport road outside. I was thinking of my mother's premonition that it would be an unlucky hour for a journey. As I was so excited about the Mumbai trip, I never paid any attention to my mother's words.

Suddenly, an old lady came rushing and said that a time bomb had been found and some terrorists were suspected to be inside the airport.

We all were very scared and prayed for our safety. Suddenly, there was a commotion as security personnel were seen running after someone. As the person was running with great speed, they were not able to apprehend the suspect terrorist.

He was holding a gun in his hand and as he passed the hall he started shooting randomly. An old lady who could not move or act very fast became his first victim.

I was very terrified but kept my cool. As the terrorist was shooting and running, it became very difficult to catch him. Suddenly, I had an idea. I bent down and slowly started crawling towards the terrorist. As his back was turned towards me, I gestured to the security personnel to come closer.

Still bent down, I pushed him hard in the legs, his gun fell down and immediately he was overpowered by two security personnel.

He was very angry and tried to catch hold of me but before he could do anything he was captured and taken to a secret place where they would interrogate him.

I was surrounded by people in the hall who congratulated me for my presence of mind and courage. As our flight was cancelled and we were too terrified to travel the next day, we decided to return home.

I had been so excited that morning but never knew the breathtaking adventure I would go through by the end of the day.

Q.16 Write an original story that begins with the words. "He was the funniest boy I had ever met. He would make everyone laugh .... " **(ICSE 2015)**

Ans. **Varun and his Humour**

He was the funniest boy I had ever met. He would make everyone laugh even in the most trying times. Blessed with great humour, Varun was one of the most wanted person in our parties for he could make everyone forget their worries. No amount of sadness could dampen his spirit.

I remember once when the three of us friends including Varun had failed the chemistry exam badly. Our parents had been called and we were told that most certainly we would have to repeat the year. That was a very hard time but even then no look of worry could be spotted on Varun's face or in his behaviour.

His cheer was undiminished even when his father suffered a major financial loss in business.

Even during that time, Varun was known to spread cheer around. He always pushed his worries to the backseat and dedicated himself towards making others happy.

However, the loss of his pet dog Veeto, some months ago, immersed him in grief. That was the only time that robbed him of his smiling face. For days, he did not speak to anyone and shut himself up in his room. We could not see him like that so all of us friends decided to do something to dispel his gloom.

One day, we all went to his place and rang the doorbell of his house. There we kept a little box, slightly open from one side and hid ourselves so that he could not see us. When he opened the door, he was surprised to find no one. He picked up the box with a look of amazement on his face. He took the lid off and there came out a puppy, quite like Veeto.

He held him in his hands and started to play with it. It brought the smile back on his face. Then, we all came into his sight and uttered with excitement, 'Surprise!' Indeed, that little effort from our end, helped Varun come out of his sorrow.

Q.17 **Write an original short story that begins with the words "This story pertains to ...."**

Ans. **Real Kindness**

This story pertains to a chance encounter that taught thirteen-year-old Aarav the true meaning of kindness and courage. It was a rainy evening and Aarav was walking home from the library, clutching his umbrella tightly.

The roads were muddy and most people were rushing to find shelter. As he crossed the bus stop, he noticed an elderly man sitting on a bench, drenched and shivering. Beside him was an old leather bag, water seeping into its worn edges.

Something about the man seemed off. He looked lost, glancing around nervously. Aarav hesitated for a moment but then walked up to him. 'Excuse me, sir, are you okay?' he asked.

The man nodded weakly. "I missed my bus... and I don't know how to get home." His voice was trembling and Aarav could see that he was struggling.

Aarav wasn't sure what to do. It was getting late and his parents would worry if he didn't return soon. But leaving the man alone in this state didn't feel right.

'Where do you live?' Aarav asked.

The man fumbled in his bag and pulled out a crumpled piece of paper. It had an address scribbled on it. Aarav recognised the area-it was across town and the last bus had probably already left. 'Come with me,' Aarav said, making up his mind. 'I'll help you.'

He hailed a passing auto-rickshaw and used the pocket money he had saved to pay the fare. On the way, the man opened up. He had come to the city to visit his grandson but had gotten confused in the unfamiliar streets. The bag he carried was filled with gifts for his family.

When they finally reached the address, the man's face lit up. His family rushed out, hugging him tightly and thanking Aarav profusely. As Aarav walked back home in the rain, he felt a warmth in his heart that no sunshine could match. That day, he realised that sometimes, courage isn't about grand acts-it's about stopping to help someone when no one else does.

Q.18 Write a short story to illustrate the proverb. 'Knowledge is power'.

Ans. Knowledge is Power

'Vijay Bhaiya Zindabad, Jeet Mubarak', shouted the motley crowd of people assembled at the stadium to welcome their new leader as he walked in to address them. A tall, lean, strikingly handsome man, dressed in spotless white chooridar pajama kurta, walked up to the podium, raising his hands to acknowledge the greetings of the people. He was profusely garlanded by the elite of the town who had come to honour their elected representative to the State Assembly.

Vijay's trek to glory was not all that easy. After completing his schooling in the village, Vijay went to Varanasi for higher education. He eventually completed his masters degree in agriculture from Banaras Hindu University. Unlike other youth, Vijay returned to his native village to put his knowledge to practical use for the benefit of the villagers. His scientific methods of farming soon caught the attention of the villagers.

His willingness to help others and compassion for the well-being of the villages won their hearts. Having gained their confidence, he formed self-help groups comprising village youth and with the help of an NGO developed a proper drainage system for the village. To reduce the problem of potable drinking water, he drew the attention of the district authorities to install hand pumps in the densely populated parts of the village.

His knowledge of science came in handy to produce gobar gas from cow dung. This became an alternate fuel for the oppressed housewives of the village. Thus, in a span of five years, he transformed the village into a small town having all the basic amenities.

Vijay's good work soon caught the attention of the opposition party. Seeing a sure winner in him, they gave him a ticket to contest the election as their party candidate. The rest was indeed history, with Vijay emerging victorious in the elections. This very well illustrates the aptness of the proverb 'knowledge is power'.

Q.19 Write a story that concludes with the sentence. 'Every cloud has a silver lining'.

Ans. Every Cloud has a Silver Lining

'You are under arrest'. I looked back and saw the police officer accompanied by his juniors. I was whisked into a car and taken like a high profile criminal. The car stopped in front of the Crime Branch Headquarters where the SSP and other senior officers were waiting for me. As I stepped out of the car, newsmen flashed their cameras. It was chaos as I was taken inside a room for interrogation. I was frightened and had no idea about what was happenings and was totally disordered.

At last, someone dressed in civil uniform came and started questioning me, "How do you know Dawood? What are your plans?" The questions pouring in caused a more puzzling environment. The police was already issuing statement mentioning the details of how they had trapped Chetan, Dawood's man in Pune. All kinds of stories were circulated within hours. The evening newspaper had splashed my photograph on the front page and every channel worth its name had a footage of me as breaking news.

I told him that I was innocent but no one paid any heed to it. I also heard some of the police officials talking about using third degree on me so that I would reveal the truth. I was terrified at the thought of it. But the truth was that I was innocent and no one wanted to believe that.

After great difficulty, I understood the entire situation. The much talked about criminal, Dawood was sending orders to his counterparts in India. These orders were given on a mobile number which was similar to mine. The police intercepted some messages and played them for me. I said the voice was not mine.

They recorded my voice and sent the record for the audio and voice forensic analysis. Finally, it was proved that the voice was not mine. Then, they went into the details of the number again and enquired whether it was 98919XXXXX. I told them that my number was 989981XXXX. Only then, they realised their folly.

Eventually, I was allowed to go and all the charges levelled against me were dropped. I was also interviewed by many news channels. I became a star overnight. After it was all over, I realised that 'Every cloud has a silver lining'.

Q.20 Write an original short story that begins with the words. "I was returning to India after having completed my studies from abroad. The yearning to meet my parents and friends grew ...."

Ans. **The Hijacking**

I was returning to India after having completed my studies from abroad. The yearning to meet my parents and friends grew with every passing minute as

I boarded the plane. Seated next to me was a boy who was about five years old. He was going to visit his grandma in India and was travelling alone.

Next to him were two old ladies in their late fifties, who despite their gray hair were bubbling with excitement and chattering excitedly causing some distraction.

No sooner had the plane taken off from Heathrow Airport, than the boy jumped out of his seat removing his seat belt and started roaming about in the plane.

He was very candid and spoke to every one in the plane. The old ladies called the boy and gave him two chocolates. The air-hostess brought some snacks and tea, which was indeed very tempting. After having my refreshment, I settled down to complete a novel that

I had brought with me. I had almost completed my novel when I heard the captain requesting passengers to fasten the safety belts, as we were about to land at the Palam airport. Just then, a young man seated behind me got up and caught hold of the boy, placing a knife on his neck. He warned us to stick to our chairs.

Entering the cockpit, he ordered the pilot not to land the plane. Suddenly, one of the old ladies collapsed on the floor. Seeing this, the other lady shouted at the hijacker for having caused a heart attack.

The hijacker's attention was momentarily diverted. Sensing this, a well built young man sitting in the front passage just near the hijacker, knocked the knife out of his hand. Wild and noisy disorder prevailed for a while, as the others pounced on the unarmed hijacker, freeing the boy in the process. He was overpowered and everybody heaved a sigh of relief. The plane finally landed at the airport and the hijacker was promptly arrested.

We were all accorded a warm welcome from the waiting crowd which had gathered at the airport as news of the hijacking had spread. The child leaped into the open arms of his grandma who hugged him lovingly. It was indeed a very eventful homecoming for all of us.

Q.21 Write a story that ends with the words. '......... would not have to go through all this.

Ans. **Advice not Taken**

The ability to make effective decisions is a fundamental requirement for both professional success and personal happiness. A teenager is restless, keen to learn, willing to try new flavours of life and finally aggressive in behaviour. As a teenager, we feel that our decisions are right and perfect and so we do not prefer to listen to advice of our elders.

Teenagers are friendly and so am I. I would prefer to be in a park with all my friends than in Mauritius with my family. Once, my friends and I decided to go out and watch a movie at PVR. On the other hand, there was a family function that day. I asked my mother if

I could go out with my friends that day and the clear and obvious answer was, No! "How can you be out when there is a family event?" she said. I stood hard on my decision and compelled her to stand with it.

The difficult part was over as I had convinced my mother and did not have any pressure of missing the event. Like all mothers, my mother advised me not to go out to crowded places and insisted on carrying a cell phone. We all left before the scheduled time as we decided to roam around and spend some time in the gaming centre.

After that, we went to book tickets for the movie. Luckily, we got the tickets of the show and all our seats were in the same row. But, little did we know that our luck would stay with us just for a short while. Hardly had the movie begun, than a group of men barged into the theatre hall and started creating a chaos.

They asked all of us to leave the screening hall. Then, they began damaging the chairs, lights and were creating a rampage. All of us were suddenly taken aback. Some panicked, some rushed out, some stayed in their places and some were confused like us. The exit doors got jammed as all the audience started rushing out. It was almost like a panic scene.

Soon, the police arrived and the situation was under control. They took us aside and made sure that we were safe. They asked us why we had come without our parents and advised us not to go to alone to such places. Disappointed, I came home and also felt guilty for not taking my mother's advice. If I had taken my mother's advice, I would not have to go through all this.

PICTURE COMPOSITION

Picture composition refers to a creative writing task where students write a story description or interpretation based on a visual image provided. The image could depict a scene, an object, an event or even an abstract idea. This exercise assesses the student's ability to observe, interpret and express thoughts clearly and imaginatively.

Do's and Don'ts for Picture Composition

Do's	Don'ts
Analyse all elements in the image (people, objects, setting) before writing.	Don't describe unnecessary elements that don't contribute to the theme.
Start by describing the scene and setting the context.	Avoid leaving out important details that can help the reader visualise the scene.
Add details to make the composition engaging and interesting.	Don't overcomplicate the story.
End with a meaningful conclusion that ties back to the main idea or theme.	Stick to the visual cues and don't add unrelated content.

Sample of Picture Composition

Study the picture given below. Write a story or a description or an account of what it suggests to you. Your composition may be about the subject of the picture or you may take suggestions from it; however, there must be a clear connection between the picture and your composition.

Life is nothing but a series of dramatically charged situations that choose to change when least expected. Often great courage is demanded to adapt oneself to these situations which are more than often cruel and rarely generous. It is to one of these cruel situations that Aarti found herself subjected to. Aarti was a 10-year-old girl born to a poor family of nomads that wandered from city to city performing various acrobatics to earn their daily bread. Unfortunately, her father was paralysed when he was hit by a speeding car and lost the use of his legs.

Being the only child of her parents, she was left with no other option but to help her mother to earn their daily bread. Aarti was an excellent tight rope walker and people would marvel at her performance. Ever since she was 8 years old, she had earned a name for herself in this field. Aarti had always aspired to perform in the city. Her mother was very apprehensive about this, being a common village people and having never visited the city. When Aarti did get an opportunity, her mother refused to go but sent Aarti along with her uncle.

In the city, Aarti performed at many places and earned a name for herself. On the way back to her village, she was dumbstruck to see the destruction caused by the flood. A few survivours informed distraught Aarti that her family had been swept away in the devastation. She felt her whole world crashing in, had it not been for the reassuring presence of her beloved uncle and aunt, she felt she could have died.

Aarti, however, got on with life with great fortitude. She continued with her tight rope walking. Soon, she was chosen to be one of the many performers at the centenary celebrations of one of the most prestigious colleges of Delhi. Her performance was very much appreciated and applauded and she was awarded a special prize of ₹ 1 lakh.

Being in the limelight, she was immediately noticed by the owner of a prestigious circus who offered her a very lucrative job which she accepted. Today, Aarti is a famous performer. Her dedication towards her perseverance was the ultimate winner.

Teacher's Remarks

- Written in a story format.
- Opens with the idea that life is full of unexpected and challenging situations.
- Introduces a character in accordance with the picture which makes it interesting.
- Highlights a tragic indicident which makes the reader sympathise with the story in the composition.
- Concludes on a positive note, attributing the character's success to her dedication and perseverance.

EXAM ORIENTED QUESTIONS

Q.1 Study the picture given below. Write a story or a description or an account of what it suggests to you. Your composition may be about the subject of the picture, or you may take suggestions from it; however, there must be a clear connection between the picture and your composition. **(ICSE 2025, 20 M)**

Ans. In a small village, a mother and her children worked in their vegetable garden. Every morning, they stepped into their green fields, caring for their plants with love. Their hard work made the crops grow fresh and healthy. It was not just about growing food; it was about connecting with nature and learning patience.

One bright morning, the family was harvesting brinjals. The mother, dressed in a pink saree, smiled as she handed the vegetables to her children. The boy, wearing a vest, held a basket filled with colourful brinjals. His younger sister, in a blue dress, stood nearby, watching happily. Their faces glowed with joy and satisfaction. They knew that their efforts had borne fruit and their happiness was pure.

For them, farming was not just work-it was a way of life. They enjoyed growing their own food and felt proud of their efforts. The mother had taught her children that nature rewards those who care for it. With patience and dedication, their small garden provided enough vegetables for their daily meals. Sometimes, they even shared extra produce with neighbours. This created a strong bond among the villagers.

The village believed in working together. People helped each other during planting and harvesting seasons. They knew that unity made life easier and happier. Unlike cities, where people bought everything from markets, villagers valued the food they grew with their own hands. It was fresh, healthy and free from chemicals. Their connection with the land was deep and meaningful.

As they gathered the last batch of brinjals, the children laughed and played. The mother looked at them with love, knowing she was teaching them valuable lessons-hard work, teamwork and gratitude for nature.

The picture of this happy family in their green fields shows the beauty of simple living. It reminds us that joy comes not from wealth but from the satisfaction of honest effort, the love of family and the strength of a close-knit community.

Q.2 Study the picture given below. Write a story or description or an account of what is suggested to you. Your composition may be about the subject of the picture or you make suggestions from it; however there must be a clear connection between the picture and your composition. **(ICSE Specimen 2025)**

Ans. The picture of three Children, each from seemingly different cultural backgrounds, standing hand in hand in a lush green park evokes profound narrative about friendship, diversity and unity. This image not only captures a moment of innocent friendship but also serves as a poignant reminder of how friendship transcends all boundaries- cultural, racial or social.

In the heart of Maplewood Park, three children- Ayesha, Sophie and Juan are playing together. Ayesha is a gentle soul with a passion for nature. Juan is the thinker among the trio always curious, always questioning. Sophie is the notorious one- playing pranks on everyone around.

One sunny afternoon, as they played in their favourite part of the park, the three friends decided to embark on a 'treasure hunt', a game they invented where they would look at unique leaves, stones and anything interesting or unusual that the park had to offer. This particular day, however, they decided the greatest treasure would be to find the 'Heart of the Park', a mythical tree said to be the oldest and wisest in the park, according to local legend.

Their quest was not just a journey across the park but a journey into each other's lives. As they wandered, they shared stories from their diverse backgrounds. Ayesha spoke of her family's tradition from India. Sophie described her favourite German fairy tales and Juan recounted his grandmother's tales from Mexico. No language, religion or culture stood between them. They were united by the simple joy of playing together.

This picture is a beautiful reminder of the importance of inclusivity and unity in our communities. It shows how friendships, forged in the innocence of childhood, break down barriers. The children's laughter and carefree spirits are a testament to the idea that at the core of all humanity, we are more alike than we are different.

As they continue their game, one can only imagine how their bond will grow stronger, not because of their shared similarities but because of their acceptance and respect for each other's differences. This image teaches us that unity in friendship isn't just possible, it's something we can all work towards, one simple gesture at a time.

Q.3 **Study the picture given below. Write a story or a description or an account of what it suggests to you. Your composition may be about the subject of the picture, or you may take suggestions from it; however, there must be a clear connection between the picture and your composition.** **(ICSE 2024)**

Ans. A few weeks ago, I had the pleasure of visiting my Grandma's village, which is situated on the outskirts of the city. I was immediately captivated by the sight of straw and clay houses, which gave the village a rustic charm.

The children were playing on swings tied to the trees, their laughter filling the air. Everything around me felt lively yet peaceful and I couldn't help but feel a sense of calm as I took in the natural surroundings.

It was such a refreshing break from the noisy city life.

After a delicious lunch, lovingly prepared by my Grandma, I decided to take a walk around the village. The cool breeze, flowing gently through the trees, was incredibly soothing and made the walk even more enjoyable.

As I strolled, I came across a group of young children sitting in a circle under a massive banyan tree. In the center of the circle was a carrom board placed on the ground. The children looked up at me with bright, welcoming smiles and invited me to join their game. I politely declined but asked about the carrom board.

Their faces lit up as they told me that they had bought the carrom board from the village fair using money that my Grandma had given them.

It was their first time playing with it and their excitement was infectious. I felt a deep sense of happiness knowing that my kind Grandma had helped these children buy the game, allowing them to enjoy their time together.

The children began setting up the game, arranging the pucks in a circle and even played rock, paper, scissors to decide who would take the first shot. Their enthusiasm and simple joy made me appreciate the little things in life. It reminded me to savour each moment and cherish the small acts of kindness that can make a big difference in someone's day.

Q.4 **Study the picture given below. Write a story or a description or an account of what it suggests to you. Your composition may be about the subject of the picture or you may take suggestions from it; however, there must be a clear connection between the picture and your composition.** **(ICSE Specimen 2024)**

Ans. The old fort stood in silence, its weathered stones telling tales of past rulers and their opulent lives. Once a mighty symbol of power and grandeur, the passage of time had stripped it of its former glory.

Now, it lay abandoned, its vast halls echoing with emptiness. Neglected and forgotten, the fort seemed to mourn the loss of its past, its beauty hidden beneath layers of dust and decay. Yet, within its crumbling walls, something remarkable was about to unfold.

Amidst the desolation, a passionate teacher arrived with a vision that would transform the fort into a beacon of hope. Seeing the dilapidated state of the building, she saw potential where others saw ruin. Her unwavering determination sparked a light in the hearts of the children from the nearby village, who had long been trapped in the cycle of poverty.

The teacher set to work immediately. One by one, she repaired the broken windows, cleared away the debris, and cleaned the rooms, each step bringing the fort closer to its new purpose.

With limited resources, she reached out to the community, gathering donations for books, desks and stationery. Slowly but surely, the fort began to take on a new life, not as a symbol of past battles, but as a place of learning.

The teacher believed that education was the key to breaking the chains of poverty. She understood that her students, each with their unique challenges, needed personalised attention. With patience and dedication, she tailored her lessons to their needs, encouraging them to dream big and strive for excellence.

The fort, once a place of neglect, became a symbol of resilience. Its crumbling walls no longer represented despair, they stood as a testament to the strength and determination of the children who studied there.

As the classrooms began to buzz with energy, the once-forgotten students discovered their innate potential. Education gave them the hope and opportunity to break free from the chains that had bound them for so long.

The fort, transformed into a haven of learning, became a powerful reminder that with determination, education can turn even the most abandoned places into beacons of hope and possibility.

Q.5 **Study the picture given below. Write a story or a description or an account of what it suggests to you. Your composition may be about the subject of the picture or you may take suggestions from it; however, there must be a clear connection between the picture and your composition.** **(ICSE 2023)**

Ans. Dog was the first animal that humans tamed when they settled down and started practicing agriculture. They have been rightfully called a 'man's best friend'.

Dogs have always been very helpful and have always shared a special relationship with us. These fluffy creatures protect us from dangers, are the most loyal creatures and stand by our side in thick and thin.

Regardless of their role in helping humans over the generations, a lot of dogs are stray and lonely in the streets. They often don't have anyone to help them. People even behave rudely to them at times. Since they can't voice their emotions, it is important for humans to try to understand them and help them by providing any sort of assistance they may need, as is shown in the given picture.

It is important to be compassionate towards them and all other animals because they are living beings and need help, just like humans.

Just by treating the dogs well, we can make sure that those animals who wander on the streets are able to survive and lead a good life. Even a little act of kindness such as protecting them from the rain or the cold can act wonders.

Dogs are amongst the most loyal creatures and they would go to any length to protect the people they care about. They don't need money or any material possessions, only to be treated with kindness, care and compassion and they would be some of the best companions.

Their symbiotic relationship with humans is the reason why we have co-existed together for many years and the dogs on the streets have survived for many years even without proper resources. It is our duty, to help them, to do our part and preserve the bond that exists between our species, the foundations of which were laid thousands of years ago when the first dog became a part of the human community.

Q.6 **Study picture given below. Write a story or a description or an account of what it suggests to you. Your composition may be the subject of the picture or you may take suggestions from it; however, there must be a clear connection between the picture and your composition.** **(ICSE Specimen 2023)**

Ans. Hunger is a long existing and draining problem in India. People, mostly children, from poorer backgrounds might go days without eating. This has burdened India with the huge problem of child malnutrition.

Children who do not get food end up suffering from a lack of nutrients, which weakens them, causes diseases and can even stunt their growth. India, in fact, has the world's highest burden of child malnutrition. Low income has become the primary cause of the issue of malnutrition. Although investments are made and money is directed towards child welfare, there is only a marginal growth. However, it has rightly not stopped anyone from trying. Several initiatives have also been taken by the Indian Government, including Narendra Modi's vision of 'Kuposhan Mukt Bharat' and various NGOs to put an end to this problem. One such NGO is the No Hungry Child Organisation.

It works for underprivileged background children providing them the Nutritious meal and Education support. They feed hungry children in a clean and open environment, providing food in adequate quantities and simultaneously ensuring that no food goes to waste.

India has the maximum number of children in the world suffering from malnutrition and the claimed aim is to increase awareness on the issue. The first 1000 days of a child are critical for cognitive development, physical growth and immunity.

In an attempt to achieve this, Horlicks launched the 'Horlicks Mission Poshan' with actor Amitabh Bachchan as the campaign ambassador. The focus is that during the first 1000 days of a child, they will be addressing the issue of malnutrition, stunting and infant mortality.

In addition to these organisations, we can also play our part in ensuring an end to hunger and child malnutrition. We need to connect and reach far and wide as it is critical for mass awareness to bring in these positives change in the society.

In addition to raising awareness, we must raise funds and actively engage on-ground to make child hunger a subject of mass movement. It is only through everyone's contribution that we can eradicate this social evil.

Q.7 **Study the picture given below. Write a short story, description or an account of what it suggests to you. Your composition may be about the subject of the picture or you may take suggestions from it.**

(ICSE 2022 Sem II)

Ans. I was passing by a motor garage when I saw him working. I was stunned to see a 12-year-old boy, covered in dirt and car oil trying to repair a car. I went to him and asked him his name.

He told his name was 'Chhotu' as his employer used to call him that. I asked him why he was not at school at that time and was instead working there. Chhotu got emotional and told me his story. He told me that a few months ago he also went to a nearby government school.

But one day, his father died in a road accident and his mother had no money left to send him to school. He had to become the bread earner of the family to support his mother and 3 younger siblings. As a result, he dropped out of the school and started doing menial works and then joined this garage a few months ago.

I was so touched by his story that I wanted to do something for him.

I held his hands and told him that he would be going to school from the next day and that he could work in the garage part-time. I also told his employer the same and he agreed. Next day, I went to Chhotu's house and talked to his mother and got him ready along with his siblings to get them admitted in the nearby school.

They felt so happy knowing that they would be going to school. Their mother thanked me a million times. I tried to help their mother by getting her associated with a famous NGO who helps women in distress. They impart them vocational trainings free of cost to make them self-reliant. Chhotu also promised me that he would work hard to become a respectable and learned man in future. I felt so content after helping the child. My soul was filled with happiness.

Q.8 **Study the picture given below. Write a short story or description or an account of what the picture suggests to you. Your composition may be about the subject of the picture or you may take suggestions from it.**

(ICSE Specimen 2022 Sem II)

Ans. I have often seen the little children in the nearby slum going to the nearby bangle factory to earn a meagre living. The small, frail-looking children always seem to be distressed going into the dingy region and while coming out, their faces tell nothing but a story of misery and helplessness.

Many-a-time, I had wanted to help the children but never came up with an idea of how I would do it and honestly I forgot about it until a few days before my birthday. I had wanted to do something different this year for my birthday and was looking for ideas. I did not want to throw a party this year and did not know exactly what I wanted.

One day, while returning from school, I saw those children playing in the dirt and was immediately struck with an idea. I wanted a day of fun and frolic for these children and so went to my parents with the idea.

At first, they were surprised but soon they rejoiced that I wanted to bring joy to those underprivileged. The next day, my father went to the slum and talked to their parents for it.

It took him a while but with a promise that the money of the day will be paid by him, the parents agreed. Next, he went to the factory owner who apparently was my father's friend. He also agreed and finally the day arrived. I along with the children went to the nearby park where we played a lot of games.

Then, we came to my house and played some more. We also clicked a lot of pictures and watched a movie. After that, we ate McD meals which was loved by all of them.

It was noon and we decided to go to the nearby zoo. All of the children were very happy and I felt elated for not only was I satisfied on seeing the little children happy just like me but I was also very pleased with the fact that I got to bring that joy on their faces.

Q.9 Study the picture given below. Write a story, a description or an account of what it suggests to you. Your composition may be about the subject of the picture or you may take suggestions from it; however, there must be a clear connection between the picture and your composition. **(ICSE 2020)**

Ans. The given picture shows five children, seemingly from a humble background trying to click a selfie. The only difference is that they don't have a mobile phone. But there is one thing that they have that strikes out invariably irrespective of the fact that they are just pretending to take a selfie. That thing is the genuine smile on their face. They may not have the perfect tool for clicking a selfie but they have smile that indicates their joy.

In this century, no one can refuse that money has become a deciding factor for the quality of life we are leading.

But the problem is that nowadays people have started linking money with happiness. We will have to understand that money helps us in acquiring the comforts and luxuries of life but it does not guarantee happiness.

Money doesn't make you laugh when you are lonely. Indeed, money can help you buy a mansion, a fancy car or branded clothes that might make you happy but these things don't last for long. Soon, you will start seeing that your neighbours have a better house, more cars and many other things that you don't have. At that moment, money will no longer be a source of happiness.

Happiness isn't a quality like height, weight or income that can be measured easily. It is a complex, indistinct state that is developed by momentary simple pleasures. It is the tendency to feel positive emotions and holding a sense of purpose.

Happiness is not having a lot of privilege or money. It's much more than that. It is our ability to connect with others, to have meaningful relationships and to have a better community. People who say they are happy have strong connections and communications with other people. That is a sort of recipe for happiness.

This picture of these children smiling with pure innocence reflects their happy souls and gives us the clear message that we should stop searching for happiness in materialistic things. All we need is a big smile from within the heart and the world will be a happy place.

Q.10 Study the picture given below. Write a story, a description or an account of what it suggests to you. Your composition may be about the subject of the picture or you may take suggestions from it; however, there must be a clear connection between the picture and your composition. **(ICSE 2019)**

Ans. When I went to the local market outside my coaching centre during the lunch break to eat something,

I observed a very common sight at the nearby small shop which sold all kinds of packaged food items such as chips, sweets, etc.

The nearby primary school had just got over and there was a crowd of students around this shop, jostling each other to buy food items. I realised that the children were simply wasting their pocket money on such snacks which are tasty but have very little nutritional value.

In fact, such snacks are injurious to the health of children. They are generally deep fried and heavily spiced, being high in calories, fat, sugar and salt.

Children and teenagers these days are more prone to eating such foods daily while they neglect homemade food. They are leading themselves towards danger through their unhealthy lifestyle.

These foods affect their health adversely, whatever may be their age group, weight and health condition. The foods is considered as high in calories; however, one who eats them ends up getting easily exhausted and needs more food frequently. These items do not provide an appropriate level of energy which is required by children of this age.

Thus, the child develops the tendency of craving for food more frequently. What the children acquire from these foods is not healthy nutrition but unhealthy fats. They feel a lack of oxygen, which causes poor functioning of the brain. They absorb cholesterol from such types of foods. The cholesterol forms plaque in the arteries and creates problems for the heart.

A high level of bad cholesterol damages the liver and also increases weight. According to research, such children are overweight or obese and are highly prone to heart and liver disorders. They are more prone to become diabetic and lethargic because of the high amount of sugar collecting in their body. They also get high blood pressure because of the high amount of sodium in the salt. Thus, such children should be trained by their parents to follow healthy eating habits and not waste their pocket money on such items.

Q.11 **Study the picture given below. Write a short story, description or an account of what the picture suggests to you. Your composition may be about the subject of the picture or you may take suggestions from it; however, your composition must have a clear connection with the picture.** **(ICSE Specimen 2019)**

Ans. Lakshmi was the third child in the family of five children. Her mother was a poor labourer who worked at the nearby construction site along with her father. Lakshmi was 7 years old and used to accompany her parents to the construction site. One day, the manager at the construction site offered to employ Lakshmi at a meagre pay. Her parents accepted, considering it an additional income for their family.

The small girl was forced to do hazardous work without proper compensation. She was risking her life just to keep her family's body and soul together. So tragic was her condition that she had turned into a physical and mental wreck. Her weak and fragile body seemed to suffer from disease.

Lakshmi would keep breaking stones in a corner, crying and regretting her fate. Such was her misery that in the days when she should be going to school and playing, she had to work hard for sustaining herself. Instead of smiles and carefreeness, her face was writ large with a worry for earning her bread.

This picture can be labelled, 'The Plight of Child Labour'. It is a serious blot in the efforts to project our nation as a dynamic country. The root cause of child labour is poverty and to some extent ignorance. This girl Lakshmi has become symbolic of all child labourers who are exposed to the difficulties of the world at such a tender age. It is a pity to see her shouldering the responsibilities of her family.

The government should realise the grimness of the situation and take strict actions to ban child labour. Additionally, adopting a multi-prolonged problem- solving approach is required. Furthermore, this should be incentivised by the provision of education and vocational based skills training for each child in the poor families. The combination of the right information complemented by the right rewards will combat child labour and in the longer run, poverty.

Q.12 **Study the picture given below. Write a story, a description or an account of what it suggests to you. Your composition may be about the subject of the picture or you may take suggestions from it; however, there must be a clear connection between the picture and your composition.** **(ICSE 2018)**

Ans. While I agree that girls from all corners of the nation are coming out of shells and taking positions that were denied to them, I had never expected to see a women's cricket match cheered by all. But I did see the image. Last week, a cricket match was held in Muzaffarnagar, my friend's village. I was in his village because both of us were going on a road trip together and I had to pick him up.

He told me about the match and I went to watch the game thinking it to be an all-boys cricket match. But I was in for a surprise when I saw three girls playing with the bat and ball as if warming up. I thought maybe they were just kidding. But no, the girls were actually part of the team that was playing the match that day.

My shock was just wearing off, when I found another the entirety of the villages coming forward to support the girls. My friend, looking at my face told me that this was how it was in their village. Girls were not discriminated. In fact, girls were told to go to school, get educated, work and participate in all extracurricular activities including sports.

Soon, the teams were ready to play the game and what a game it was. The girls performed astoundingly.

The first team totaled at 215 runs in 15 overs while the second team took the lead by 218 runs in just 12 overs. While the girls were playing, the village elders were cheering and complementing the girls for their improvement and performance. I was stoked.

The image of Indian villages being orthodox, limiting and traditional was completely shattered by the village. Contrary to my opinion, my friend's village was more open and accepting of its female population than many communities residing in cities.

Q.13 **Study the picture given here. Write a story, a description or an account of what it suggests to you. Your composition may be about the subject of the picture or you may take suggestions from it; however, there must be a clear connection between the picture and your composition.** **(ICSE 2017)**

Ans. In the modern world, where the talks of animal rights had taken the world by storm, we talk about cruelty to animals. Human beings taking advantage of their intelligence treat animals in violent and immoral ways. But here what we see is a close bonding between a baby elephant and daughter of Mahendra, the caretaker of the elephant.

Mahendra lives in a small house on the outskirts of a jungle near Bengaluru. Herds of elephant are seen in jungles and Mahendra is employed at a plantation where elephants root out stumps with their heavy feet. So, many times Mahendra has taken the baby elephant to his house and his daughter Kavya has developed a great affinity with it. Both have seemingly become really good friends.

Kavya roams around in nearby areas surrounding, plantation and spends her time enjoying the company of the baby elephant. Who says man is an enemy of animals. Kavya and the baby elephant are a living example of close bonding between man and animals. What animals need is love and sincerity and they will prove more faithful and helpful than other human beings. This bonding proves that 'Haathi Mera Sathi' or the elephant is my friend.

Q.14 **Study the picture given below. Write a story or a description or an account of what it suggests to you. Your composition may be about the subject of the picture or you may take suggestions from it; however, there must be a clear connection between the picture and your composition.** **(ICSE Specimen 2017)**

Ans. It is plight of the India that even after 76 years of independence, the country can still find a large number of children employed to earn money. Child labour is a curse that the nation is facing since long. The curse is most rampant in the agricultural sector wherein the illiterate parents find in children an extra pair of hands to work in farms. Once can find many children carrying large haystacks on their heads when they visit any farm.

It is sad that even with many governmental efforts that ban child labour, it is still rampant in many places. The reason for child labour essentially springs from one root cause-Poverty. The lack of proper livelihood is directly connected to a limited access to quality education, inadequate agricultural technology and traditional attitudes towards children's participation in agricultural activities.

Child labour in the agriculture industry can easily be divided into hazardous and non-hazardous. Hazardous child labour is majorly health and opportunity destroying. The constant exposure to pesticides, long working hours, the vulnerability to cuts from sharp knives and other health issues along with the inability to get proper education destroy the future of the child.

None-hazardous child labour highlights that participation in some agricultural activities is not always child labour. Age-appropriate tasks that are of lower risk and do not interfere with a child's schooling and leisure time can be a normal part of growing up in a rural environment.

Especially in the context of family farming, small-scale fisheries and livestock husbandry, some participation of children in non-hazardous activities can be positive as it contributes to the inter-generational transfer of technical and social skills and children's food security. Improved self-confidence, self-esteem and work skills are attributes often detected in young people engaged in some aspects of farm work.

Therefore, it is important to distinguish between light duties that do not harm to the child and child labour, which is work that interferes with compulsory schooling and damages health and personal development, based on hours and conditions of work, child's age, activities performed and hazards involved.

Q.15 **Study the picture given below. Write a story, a description or an account of what it suggests to you. Your composition may be about the subject of the picture or you may take suggestions from it, however there must be clear connection between the picture and your composition.** **(ICSE 2016)**

Ans. Everybody is waiting for the rains to arrive. The city has already had a long dry spell. The weather has been very hot, the power cuts and water shortage have added to the misery. A lot of people have fallen ill due to the intense heat and few have died also.

Not only the humans, but the animals also are having a hard time in this burning heat. The monsoons were scheduled to arrive in the city but the wait is still on for the season's first rain. A few people are organising *havans* so as to please the rain god. Some have left the city and gone to the mountains to get respite from the heat.

Finally, the rain came when we least expected it. It seemed that people had lost hope after waiting for too long. It was afternoon time and suddenly it started raining. The downpour was very heavy and lasted for 2 hours.

I was studying for my class test when it rained. I saw a girl and a boy playing in the rain from my window. Although they had umbrellas, they threw it away and were enjoying getting wet. Everyone was joyous and enjoyed the rain. Children were dancing and playing in the rain. They also made paper boats and floated them in the water.

This reminded me of my childhood days. I also used to come out in the rain and play with my friends. The weather had become cooler after the rain. When I finished studying, I had a cup of tea with *pakoras*. Everyone in my home was very happy as finally, it had rained after a long wait. It was such a great relief for everyone!

Q.16 Study the picture given below. Write a short story, description or an account of what the picture suggests to you. Your composition may be about the subject of the picture or you may take suggestions from it; however, your composition must have a clear connection with the picture. **(ICSE 2015)**

Ans. The world's population of tigers requires some basic necessities in order to survive. These are water, food which comprises of only preys as tigers are carnivores and forests where these animals can conceal themselves. When any of the above-mentioned requirements are not available, their chances of survival diminish naturally. Today, world over, tigers face this situation.

As human population and exploitation continues to grow, the forest cover tends to shrink. As more and more space is needed by the human population and the infrastructure they require–towns, roads, buildings, etc., more and more forests and other natural habitats are being destroyed to make room for it.

Human beings are rapidly encroaching into wild areas which were once ruled exclusively by the tigers. Loss of habitat is only driving this animal to the verge of extinction. Without tall trees or grass, tigers and other animal can be easily hunted down by anyone. Moreover, without the forests, even the tiger's prey cannot survive, so the former will ultimately die of starvation.

However, the government has taken a view of the grim situation and has reserved some essential forest covers as wildlife sanctuaries and national parks.

This particular percentage of the reserved area is not to be touched by man and his activities.

Thus, we as humans, must realise our social responsibility and make an effort to let the tigers and other wild animals have their natural habitat intact. For if they are robbed off their home, ecological balance gets disturbed.

Q.17 Study the picture given below and write a story or a description or an account of what it suggests to you. Your composition may be about the subject of the picture or you may take suggestions from it; however, there must be a clear connection between the picture and your composition.

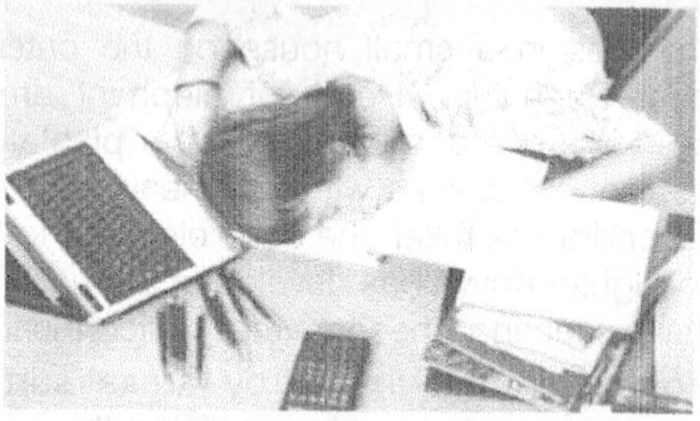

Ans. Today, the world has become so competitive that it has caused a sharp rise in the expectations of parents. Expectations always create pressure on children. This pressure sometimes acts as a catalyst but very often it proves fatal, resulting in a child trying to eliminate himself or developing an inferiority complex. This in turn causes them to withdraw into a shell. The picture depicts an overburdened student.

Very often, children fall off to sleep while studying due to sheer exhaustion. The parents expect their child to wake up at 4 am and get down with their studies, get ready and then attend school, again get down with their books at night and prepare themselves for the next day.

During exams, it gets worse. The child is expected to perform miracles and is goaded to despair in a quest for obtaining a high rank and percentage. The child, on their part, tries hard to live up to the high expectations of their parents and in doing so, mentally and physically wears themselves out. Some succeed while others are not so fortunate.

Parents are only concerned with their expectation but have no time to understand the psyche of their child. They don't take out time to understand their child's mentality, their weaknesses or strengths and their interests. They don't even know if their child would be able to cope up. At times, they try to fulfill their unfulfilled ambitions through their child and here lies the problem.

Every child is a gift of God and is born to achieve greatness in their own way. Children should be nourished properly in order to prepare them for the burden of studies.

It is, therefore, strongly recommended that the parents should understand the fact that a child must be allowed to grow up according to their natural instincts. Parental discretion and direction is definitely a must but to mould a child according to your own ambitions is wrong.

Q.18 **Study the picture given below and write a story or a description or an account of what it suggests to you. Your composition may be about the subject of the picture or may take suggestions from it; however, there must be a clear connection between the picture and your composition.**

Ans. The picture shows a heartwarming moment between a grandfather and his grandson in their backyard. The grandfather, an older man with silver hair and a gentle smile, is on all fours, pretending to be a horse.

His little grandson, dressed in a t-shirt and shorts, is laughing with pure joy as he rides on his grandfather's back, holding onto his shoulders.

The warm, peaceful atmosphere of the garden, with the grass beneath them and flowers in full bloom, makes everything feel like a moment out of a fairytale. Though the grandfather is clearly older and a bit tired, his face is lit up with happiness as he plays with his grandson.

The little boy, filled with excitement, grips his grandfather with all his strength, his innocent laughter ringing out. He feels safe, loved and completely at ease in his grandfather's care. For the child, this is not just a game-it's an experience filled with trust and joy.

The grandfather, though he may not have the energy of youth, is happy to take on this playful role. He knows that these moments matter. He's not just being the 'horse' for his grandson; he's creating memories that will last a lifetime. It's the kind of love and care that only family can provide.

This simple yet beautiful scene is a reminder of the importance of family. The bond between a grandfather and his grandson is built on love, laughter and shared moments, teaching us that these small gestures are what truly matter in life.

Q.19 **Study the picture given below and write a story or a description or an account of what it suggests to you. Your composition may be about the subject of the picture or may take suggestions from it; however, there must be a clear connection between the picture and your composition.**

Ans. The light of the dying Sun was shimmering on the sand. The beaches of Lakshadweep Islands were illuminated by the showers of beautiful and peaceful light. My grandpa lived at Kadmat island in Lakshadweep and we visited him.

This season like always, the Lakshadweep Adventure Sports Championship was going to be organised. I like wind surfing a lot and so I got my name registered immediately. At last, the day arrived. I had practised for it day and night and was quite confident of winning it. Vaasu also instilled a lot of confidence in me.

The day dawned bright and clear as I took my grandpa's blessings and set out for the starting point with Vaasu on my tail. The spectators crowded the beach, moving their handkerchiefs and throwing flowers.

At last, the trumpet sounded and the whistle blew up. I trapped the wind in my sail and the board lurched forward. I could hear Vaasu, 'Di, you can do it!' Hearing this, I zipped through all the contestants. Everybody was dumbstruck but cheered madly. The track was not an easy one. After 2 km, I saw a boy approaching me very fast. It appeared as if he was determined enough to overtake me.

The last 3 km route was the toughest part of the race. Sometimes, he left me behind and sometimes I left him behind. Then, there came a steep turn and unfortunately for him, a lot of turtles clogged his way.

He was a bit confused and tried to scrap past them. However, he could not control the speed and crashed down. Before he could recover from the blow, I crossed the finishing line. My grandpa and Vaasu came walking through the water and hugged me. The first prize was a real big trophy and along with that I got a beautiful new surfboard and some surfing gear.

Q.20 Study the picture given below and write a story or description or an account of what the picture suggests to you. Your composition must have a clear connection with the picture.

Ans. The picture shows a group of smiling students posing for a photograph in front of a historic monument. The foreign students, with their backpacks and wide grins, stand alongside their local hosts, who seem equally excited. A sense of joy and camaraderie fills the air as they stand shoulder-to-shoulder, their arms around one another, capturing the final moments of an unforgettable exchange programme.

This week-long programme brought together students from different countries and cultures, giving them an opportunity to bond and learn.

Over the past few days, they had participated in a variety of activities as a group. They attended workshops, cooked traditional dishes and exchanged stories about their homes. The bonds of friendship grew stronger with every shared laugh, every new discovery and every group effort.

The photograph is taken on the last day of the programme. By now, the foreign students have travelled extensively across the host country, exploring local markets, museums and natural wonders. Each place they visited became a treasure trove of memories and the hosts played the perfect guides, sharing the stories and history of their land with pride.

As they smile for the camera, you can sense the bittersweet emotions behind their happy faces. The local students will miss their new friends, who had become a part of their lives in such a short span of time.

The foreign students, on the other hand, will take back more than just souvenirs-they will carry home an understanding of a new culture, lifelong friendships and a heart full of cherished memories.

This exchange programme proves that despite differences in language, traditions and lifestyles, the joy of human connection can bring people closer. It's a reminder that the world is much smaller than we think and that true friendships can transcend borders.

Q.21 Study the picture given below and write a story or description or an account of what the picture suggests to you. Your composition must have a clear connection with the picture.

Ans. Statue of Liberty is one of the seven wonders of the world. It is the pride of America and represents it in the world. The story behind the Statue is that it was a gift from the French to the United States in honour of the first hundredth anniversary of American Independence in 1886. It was designated as an American National Monument.

This masterpiece was created by Frederic Auguste Bartholdi, who got the idea about the design of Liberty when he was on a visit to the US. He got a creative thought about designing a statue which will represent freedom all over the world.

It is located in the New York Harbour on Liberty Island. The Statue of Liberty is 46 m (151 ft) tall and the surface of the statue is composed of hammered copper sheets that were riveted to an iron framework. The statue is made up of concrete; therefore, its base and pedestal increase the height of the monument to 93m (305 ft) high. 'Liberty Enlightening the World' is the second name of the Statue of Liberty.

The statue depicts a woman escaping from the chains. Her right hand holds a burning torch in order to represent liberty. The Liberty has seven rays on the top of her head which symbolise the seven seas and continents.

Even in the fluctuating climate of The United States, Liberty's body remains unaffected from any unexpected change in nature because its green patina (a green or brown film on the surface of bronze or any other metals) gives the Liberty an excellent copper exterior which lasts for a long time and does not get affected by weather.

Lady Liberty is built and placed in order to give immigrants arriving from abroad a welcoming signal. In conclusion, the Statue of Liberty is really famous around the world as it represents the basic principle of freedom.

06

LETTER WRITING

Letter is a written message sent to people who are far away from us. We usually write letters to our friends and relatives. Although with the advent of telephones, mobile SMSs and chat–the importance of personal letter writing has become less popular, this art is still required in most forms of formal communication. The art of letter writing is no more an ornamental accomplishment but something that every educated person must acquire for practical purposes.

Types of Letters

Letters can be broadly classified into two main categories– Formal letters and Informal letters

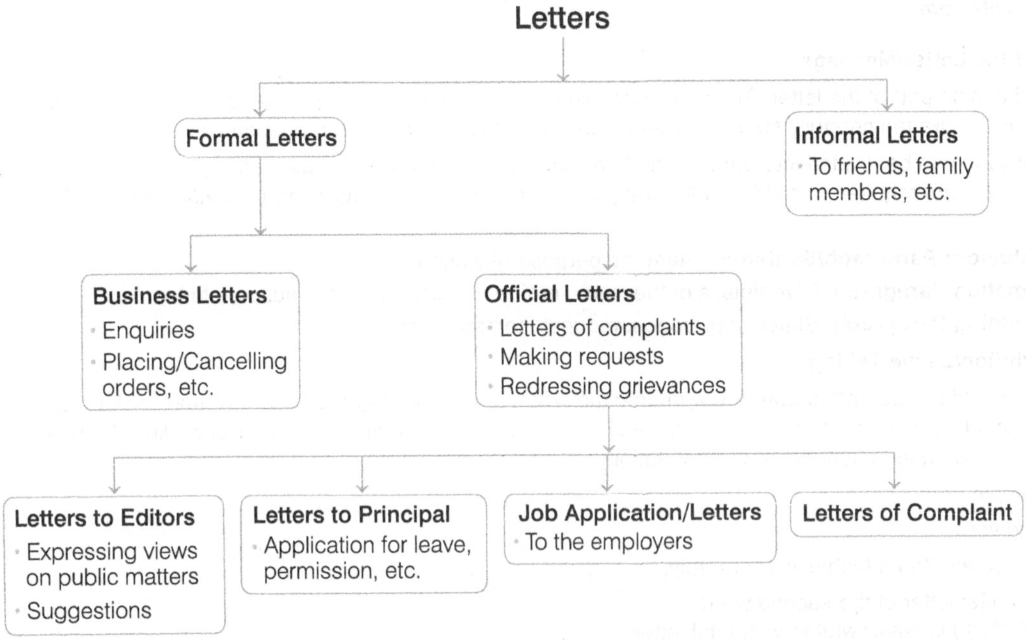

Formal Letters

Formal letters are meant to be addressed to the heads or managers of civil, public or private companies, such as the Police Commissioner, Director, Branch Manager, Chairman, Mayor, etc. The tone of such letters must be positive, polite and formal. Also, the message must be to-the-point and short. Informal language and jargons should be avoided in these type of letters. Formal letters are written to serve the following purposes

Do's and Don'ts for Formal Letters

Do's	Don'ts
Use formal language and courteous tone.	Use any jargons, informal language and casual tone.
Use proper format	Use abbreviations
Write clearly and directly.	Write unnecessary information.

Element of a Formal Letter

1. **Sender's Address**

   This portion includes the sender's full address. It is written at the top of the page. Specify the house number first, followed by the street, town/state and pincode.

   Example 2334/31, Mangal Pandey Nagar
   Ekta Park
   Meerut-250002

2. **Date and Receiver's Address**

   While writing date, always remember the day is written in figures, month in words and year in full figures. The receiver's address comprises of the receiver's name/designation and the complete address.

   Example 12th December, 20XX
   The Editor
   The Times of India
   Daryaganj
   New Delhi–110002

3. **Salutation**

   The salutation, used in formal letters, is a greeting to whom the letter is addressed. The salutation is written below the subject line and is never followed by any other word.

   - Dear Sir/Ma'am,

4. **Body of the Letter/Message**

   This is the main part of the letter. The writer's message or purpose of writing the letter comes in this part. So, it must be drafted carefully so as to create a convincing and appealing impact on its readers.

   The message can be divided into paragraphs to distinguish or mark the subject matter properly. If the matter is too short, it is not required to divide it into paragraphs. The body of the letter can be divided into the following parts

   - **Introductory Paragraph/Sentence** State the purpose of writing.
   - **Information Paragraph** Give details of the issue, problem (cause, effect, solution, etc.)
   - **Concluding Paragraph** States your hopes, request, comment, etc.

5. **Subscription/Leave Taking**

   A letter should not be ended abruptly with only the writer's name or signature for that may look rude. There should be proper leave- taking followed by your name. It is a courteous way of ending the letter. The expression used must match the salutation.

   For example,
   Thanking you,
   Yours sincerely/Yours faithfully/Yours truly,

   Note The first letter of the second word (here 's', 'f', 't') is never written in capital letter.

6. **Name and Signature**

   It is written just below the subscription and includes the sender's name and his/her signature. If applicable, the sender's designation may be added in brackets.

Suggested Specimen of Formal Letter *(Issued by Council)*

Format

Write a letter to the Police Commissioner of your city drawing his/her attention to the menace of hawkers outside your school. Tell him/her what dangers they pose and offer solutions for their rehabilitation.

Letter	Part
Flat 236, Black C, Hill Crest View Apartments, Salem Street, Coonoor-26.	Sender's Address
23rd February, 20XX	Date
The Police Commissioner, Police Commissioner's Office, 6, Cavalry Road, Coonoor-3	Receiver's Address
Dear Sir,	Salutation
I write to draw your attention to the menace of hawkers outside St. Paul's School in Nehru Nagar of our town. I am the Secretary, Swach Bharat Club, St. Paul's School.	Introduction In describes the purpose of writing.
The hawkers sell open food and cheap toys. A number of our school students cluster around them and the lane in front of our school is blocked, dirty and congested. I would request you to look into this problem and have the hawkers move into the field behind our school. This would ensure that they are not deprived of their livelihood and the area in front of our school is kept clean and congestion fee. The hawkers must also be warned about the importance of necessary hygiene and the sale of clean food. This will ensure that students do not fall sick after eating food sold by the hawkers.	Informative Paragraph Always change the paragraph while making a new point.
I hope that you will consider my suggestion and take the necessary steps as outlined in my letter to you to deal with the menace of hawkers outside the school.	Conclusion Having hope/comment /request.
Thanking you, Yours faithfully, / Yours truly, Santosh Haldar	Salutation and Complimentary Closure.

EXAM ORIENTED QUESTIONS

Formal Letters

Q.1 There is no bus stop in your locality. Write a letter to the Municipal commissioner of your town/city complaining about the problem. Offer possible solutions. **(ICSE 2025, 10 M)**

Ans. H.No. 45, Greenwood Colony,
Rajgarh Road, Guwahati – 781003

4th March, 20XX

The Municipal Commissioner,
Guwahati Municipal Corporation,
Guwahati – 781001

Dear Sir/Ma'am,

I am writing to bring to your attention the lack of a bus stop in our locality. Many people, including students, office workers and senior citizens, face great difficulty because of this. We have to walk a long distance to catch a bus, which is very inconvenient, especially during bad weather.

I request you to kindly arrange a bus stop in our area. A suitable place for it would be near Lachit Nagar Point on Rajgarh Road. This will help many people and make travel easier for everyone.

I hope you will consider our request and take action soon. Thank you for your time and support.

Yours sincerely,
Reshmi Saikia

Q.2 The garbage bins in your locality have not been cleared regularly resulting in the overflow of garbage in the area. Write a letter to the municipal commissioner in town/city, complaining about the problem. Offer some suggestions for the removal of garbage and maintenance of cleanliness. **(ICSE Specimen 2025)**

Ans. C3, 103
Arihant Arden,
Greater Noida West

24th January, 20XX

The Municipal Commissioner,
Noida Municipal Corporation,
Noida

Dear Sir/Ma'am,

I am writing to bring to your attention the persistent issue of garbage bins not being cleared regularly in our locality, Arihant Arden. This negligence has led to an overflow of waste, creating unhygienic and unpleasant living conditions for the residents.

The garbage bins in our area have not been cleared for several days, resulting in piles of waste spilling onto the streets. The foul odour emanating from the garbage is unbearable and it has attracted stray animals and pests, posing a severe health risk to the community.

We understand the challenges faced in waste management but regular and timely clearance of garbage is essential to maintain cleanliness and public health. To address this issue, the frequency of garbage collection vehicles in our locality can be increased. Assign dedicated staff to monitor and maintain the cleanliness of garbage bins should be employed.

I sincerely request your immediate attention to this matter. The residents of our society are willing to cooperate with any initiatives taken by the municipal authorities to resolve this problem.

Thank you for your time and consideration. I look forward to a prompt resolution to this issue.

Yours faithfully,
Himanshi Mehra
Secretary, RWA

Q.3 You wish to stage a play to create awareness about the importance of saving electricity. Write a letter to the Manager of a nearby shopping mall/supermarket requesting permission to use the space in front of the shopping mall/supermarket to stage the play.
Give him/her details about your requirements and state why the play will be beneficial to the shoppers. **(ICSE 2024)**

Ans. 16, ABC Apartments,
Nashik

1st June, 20XX

The Manager,
XYZ Shopping Mall,
Nashik

Dear Sir/Ma'am,

I am writing on behalf of the Live Happy Youth Club to inform you that we are planning to organise a small play aimed at raising awareness about the importance of saving electricity. We would be grateful if you could kindly grant us permission to use the area in front of your shopping mall for this event.

Though the play focuses on a social cause, it is designed to attract a larger crowd, which will increase foot traffic to your mall. Along with the awareness message, the play will offer an element of entertainment, encouraging more people to visit and in turn, boosting your overall sales.

We sincerely hope you will consider our request and allow us to stage this event at your premises. We are looking forward to a positive response. Thank you for your time and consideration.

Yours faithfully,
PQR
Secretary, Live Happy Youth Club

Q.4 As someone who enjoys gardening, you would like other students in your school to experience its benefits. Write a letter to the principal of your school seeking permission to start a club for students to learn about gardening. Give specific reasons for your request and explain why the club would meet after school hours. **(ICSE Specimen 2024)**

Ans. The Principal,
DAV School,
New Delhi

9th May, 20XX

Dear Sir/Ma'am,

I hope this letter finds you well. I am writing to seek your permission to start a Gardening Club in our school. As someone who enjoys gardening, I have come to realise the many benefits it offers, not just in terms of cultivating plants but also in promoting mental well-being, environmental awareness and teamwork.

The Gardening Club would provide a platform for students to learn about various aspects of gardening, from planting and caring for flowers and vegetables to understanding sustainability and eco-friendly practices.

I propose that the club meet after school hours, as this would not interfere with regular academic schedules and would give students the flexibility to engage in hands-on activities without the pressure of school work.

I believe this initiative will not only enrich the students lives but also contribute to making our school environment greener and more beautiful. I would be grateful for your approval and support.

Thanking you,

Yours sincerely,
XYZ
Class IX, Section B

Q.5 A certain book/chapter has been included in your syllabus. You have heard that a film version is now available. Write a letter to the Manager of a film theatre near your school requesting that the film be shown. Tell him/her why it will be beneficial to the students. **(ICSE 2023)**

Ans. XYZ School,
PQR City,
New Delhi-02

21st September, 20XX

The Manager,
Cinepolis,
PQR City
New Delhi-02

Dear Sir/Ma'am,

It is to inform you that I am a student of the ABC School, PQR City. Recently, our syllabus has been altered and the book 'Pride and Prejudice' by Jane Austen has been added to it. Since it is a new addition to the syllabus, most of the students have very little idea about the novel.

It has recently come to my knowledge that the film version of this book has also become available. The movie is considered to be a good adaptation of the book and has received positive reviews. I feel that the movie would be helpful to most of the students in understanding the culture, customs and norms of those times.

By watching the movie, they would also be able to learn the pronunciation of the words that they find in the book. They confess that watching a movie makes them concentrate much more and it would be helpful to them in understanding the novel and doing well in the exams.

Therefore, I request you to premiere this movie for the students of our school in your film theatre. Looking forward to a positive response.

Thanking you,

Yours sincerely,
ABC

Q.6 Break time at your school is only for a duration of fifteen minutes. Write a letter to your Principal requesting for an extension in the break-time from fifteen minutes to half an hour. Given reasons for your request and explain in what way an extended break would make a difference to you as a student. **(ICSE Specimen 2023, ICSE 2015)**

Ans. The Principal,
St. John's School,
Dwarka,
New Delhi

21st September, 20XX

Dear Sir/Ma'am,

Respectfully, I would like to inform you that I, Anant Sharma, am a student of Class X in your school. This letter is intended to make a request to extend the fifteen minutes break to half an hour. The purpose of a break time is to provide students with some time to relax and recharge their minds and fifteen minutes is not enough for that. We barely finish our lunch in that time. If we get a half an hour lunch break, we will able to take a walk and even play few games.

These physical activities will benefit each student as they spend the entire day in a stationary position. Some physical activity will be good both for their body and their brain.

Kindly grant us an extension in our break time.

Thanking you,

Yours sincerely,

PQR

Class X

Q.7 You are being considered for a Head Boy/Head Girl position in the school. Write a letter to the Principal explaining why you think you would make a good Head Boy/Head Girl. Why does the role interest you? Describe ways in which you would carry out your responsibilities. **(ICSE 2022 Sem II)**

Ans. The Principal,

XYZ School,

New Delhi

22nd July, 20XX

Dear Sir/Ma'am,

This is to share with you that I, Neha Sharma, of Class XI have been nominated for the position of the Head Girl of the school.

A Head Girl is a mature, hard-working and talented individual. She is seen as someone with a friendly and positive approach to work. It is a role that requires patience, respect, care, the ability to work well in a team and to support the reputation of the school. Being open-minded and being able to communicate with the younger students are also important qualities required.

I firmly believe I have the necessary skills and qualities to represent the school as the Head Girl. It can be seen by my contribution in the last term, I was able to continue all of my extra-curricular activities both during and after school, in addition to completing my academic work in time and performing well in the Mock examinations. Moreover, it would give me an opportunity to develop my public speaking and leadership skills, which shall be useful later on in life.

Therefore, I am confident that I will be able to balance additional school activities with school work.

Thank you for the time and consideration,

Yours obediently,

XYZ

Class XI-A

Q.8 You have planned to organise a health camp at school. Write a letter to the Manager of a supermarket requesting sponsorship for the event. Name the event and explain how it will benefit both the community as well as the supermarket. **(ICSE Specimen 2022 Sem II)**

Ans. ABC School,

PQR City

14th March, 20XX

The Manager,

ABC Supermarket,

PQR City

Dear Sir/Ma'am,

Every year, we at ABC Public School put in a lot of effort to help individuals and improve their lives. We are currently striving to generate funds in order to host our upcoming health camp school at our school for the people in our neighbourhood. That is why, we are currently seeking sponsors to assist us in achieving our objective.

Therefore, I would like to request you to be one of our sponsors by contributing a small fraction of the overall project cost. If you agree, your name will appear on printed materials and signage for our event. This will get your name across many people residing in our neighbourhood. Your generosity means the world to us.

Hoping for a positive reply.

Thanking you,

Yours sincerely,

PQR

Q.9 Some taps in your locality are left open all day resulting in a tremendous waste of water. Write a letter to the Municipal Commissioner of your town/city, complaining about the problem. Suggest ways in which this waste of water can be prevented. **(ICSE 2020)**

Ans. House No. 222,

Shakti Nagar,

Amritsar, Punjab

15th September, 20XX

The Municipal Commissioner,

Punjab

Dear Sir/Ma'am,

This is to bring to your notice the tremendous wastage of water occurring in our area. The Municipality has installed various public taps to facilitate the water supply. It is especially helpful for those households which do not have submersibles at their homes.

This has caused two problems: first, there is a lot of wastage of water and second, this water gets collected along the roads leading to waterlogging. This has caused a lot of inconvenience for the residents.

I, therefore, request you to look into the matter and get the taps repaired. Also, to prevent the excessive wastage of water, these public taps could be replaced by underground water pipelines with connection to every household.

I hope you will take the matter into consideration and act accordingly as soon as possible.

Thanking you,

Yours faithfully,
XYZ

Q.10 **You want to start a new club in your school. Write a letter to your Principal requesting permission to start the club, explain your role in it and give reasons to prove that the club will be beneficial for the school.** **(ICSE 2019)**

Ans. The Principal,
Sunlight Public School,
Ghaziabad

8th July, 20XX

Respected Sir/Ma'am,

This is to inform you that we, the students of Class IX, have written this letter to request you to allow us to start a nature club in our school. The objective of the club will be to inform as many students as possible about our environment and to study animals, birds, flowers and plants and how to conserve them. We plan to hold weekly excursions and meetings on Saturday afternoons when school gets over. I myself have experience of running such a club in my previous school last year. It has helped to increase our general knowledge and I am sure that it will benefit the school.

We hope you will permit us to start the nature club for the students whose activities can be monitored by a teacher whom you nominate.

Thanking you,

Yours obediently,
ABC
Class IX, Section A
Roll No. 20

Q.11 **You have accidentally left your suitcase behind when you got off the train. You only realised it after the train left the platform. Write a letter to the Station Master reporting your loss and request that the suitcase be located and kept till you claim it.** **(ICSE Specimen 2019)**

Ans. XYZ Apartments,
PQR City

21st May, 20XX

The Station Master,
PQR City

Dear Sir/Ma'am,

This is to inform you that I, Shivam Shah resident of Mumbai, came to Kolkata by the ABX express PNR No. 12345 seat 23C. I have forgotten my suitcase on my reserved seat. The suitcase is dark blue in colour and had some Marvel stickers on it.

Therefore, I request you to find my suitcase and keep it with you safely till I can claim it. I am hoping to come and collect the suitcase in a day or two.

Kindly understand and oblidge.

Thanking you,

Yours faithfully,
XYZ

Q.12 **The traffic outside your school is very heavy and chaotic. Write a letter to the Deputy Commissioner of Police (Traffic) pointing out the danger of such heavy and chaotic traffic in a school zone. Suggest possible solutions for the problem.** **(ICSE 2018)**

Ans. Brahma Public School,
Hindu Colony, Dadar,
Mumbai - 400014

17th October, 20XX

The Deputy Commissioner,
Mumbai Police (Traffic),
Mumbai – 400009

Dear Sir/Ma'am,

This letter brings to your kind attention the regular harassment our school students face on Bhadkamkar Marg due to regular traffic jams at the time when school opens in the morning and when it closes in the afternoon.

We all are aware that the number of vehicles and commuters on the roads is continuously increasing and that there is no proportional increase in the width of the roads to accommodate this increased traffic.

We observe that jams occur because of all kinds of vehicles being parked irresponsibly for long periods of time on the road near our school.

If your department arranges two traffic constables on duty at the time of the school's opening and closing, they can create awareness among the drivers about traffic rules and regulations. Further, they can regulate the traffic at that time to improve the situation.

I believe that the department will fulfill its duties to combat this problem of traffic jams in our school zone.

Thanking you,

Yours sincerely,
ABC
(Head Boy)

Q.13 A number of loose electric wires are hanging from a lamp post near the main gate of your school. Write a letter to the Municipal Commissioner explaining the problem, the danger it poses and suggest a quick solution. **(ICSE 2017)**

Ans. Apeejay School,
New Delhi

20th April, 20XX

The Municipal Commissioner,
New Delhi

Respected Sir/Ma'am,

This is to inform you that I, a student of Class X, Apeejay school, Saket, New Delhi, have written this letter to bring to your notice the precarious situation all school students and staff members face everyday when they enter the school. Near the main gate of our school, a lamp post had been erected a few years prior. But it was not maintained. But recently, some loose electrical wires are seen hanging out of it. They are extending to the main gate of our school.

We have requested the local authorities to repair these wires as they pose a literal threat to the lives of students and staff members. There is always a fear of getting electrocuted if any one unintentionally or intentionally touches them.

Despite repeated requests, nothing has been done so far. Therefore, it is requested to treat the matter urgently and get the wires set at their proper place to avoid any calamity or loss of life.

Thanking you in anticipation.

Yours faithfully,
XYZ
(Head Boy)

Q.14 Write a letter to the Editor of a local newspaper telling him/her what you think about global warming, its effects and what people should do to prevent it from getting worse. **(ICSE Specimen 2017)**

Ans. XYZ Apartments,
PQR City

30th April, 20XX

The Editor,
The Times of India,
PQR City

Dear Sir/Ma'am,

Through the columns of your esteemed newspaper, I would like to make everyone aware of global warming, its effects and what we people should do to prevent it from getting worse.

One of the most common news in the present world is the sinking of many cities due to rapidly rising sea water levels. We all know the cause- global warming or the long-term heating of Earth's surface observed. Sometimes, we experience extreme heat or we encounter rains in the most unexpected season while monsoon has become just a dry spell.

It is because of our carelessness towards the environment that has caused this increasing global warming and its dire effects. We can try to use less electricity, try to travel from public transport and follow the Reduce, Reuse and Recycle policy.

I request you to highlight this issue on your esteemed daily to spread awareness among citizens and stop the unjust abolition of greenery in localities.

Thanking you,

Yours sincerely,
ABC

Q.15 A company has been marketing spurious medicines behind claims that its product could be effective in preventing the avian flu or other forms of influenza. Write a letter to the Drug Controller General of the Directorate of Health Services, examining the claim of the company and explaining the harm these kind of claims could cause.

Ans. 24/7, Charkhop Pharmacy Stores,
Andheri West,
Mumbai

2nd December, 20XX

The Drug Controller General,
Directorate of Health Services,
Mumbai

Dear Sir/Ma'am,

This is to draw your attention towards the marketing of a spurious medicine, 'Oxeprazole capsules and injections', by XYZ India Ltd. It claims that these medicines are effective in preventing the avian flue and other forms of influenza. Such huge claims have attracted the doctors who are readily prescribing these medicines to their patients.

Many patients of the avian flu have used these medicines and their condition has further deteriorated. Some of them have developed severe side effects. Many have even been on the brink of losing their lives.

I, therefore, request you to examine the claims of this company thoroughly and prevent any more such medicines from flooding the markets so that innocent lives may be spared. Moreover, a ban should be issued on the production of such medicines.

Your immediate action in this regard would be highly appreciated.

Thanking You,

Yours faithfully,
ABC

Q.16 **Recently, the paper leaking of the esteemed NEET and NET exam have created an uproar regarding the efficiency of our education system. In order to increase the reliability of such competitive exams, the Government of India has introduced the Public Examinations (Prevention of Unfair Means) Act, 2024. You recently researched upon the act while preparing for an inter-state debate competition. Write a letter to the editor of your local daily, expressing your views on this act.**

Ans. A4, 205
Ecovillage 1,
Noida

8th November, 20XX

The Editor,
Jagran Daily,
Sector 52,
Noida

Dear Sir/Ma'am,

Through the columns of your esteemed daily, I would like to draw the attention of all towards the new act passed by the government of India regarding 'unfair means' used in public examinations.

Time and again, we have heard about the news of leaking of question papers and bypassing security measures in public examinations by the students.

The act recently passed will allow the government to keep a check on any unfair means being used in the examinations by students or any other person responsible. The act sets up a severe punishment structure for the offenders which involves imprisonment and financial liability.

Successful implementation of the act will require collaboration between authorities and exam conducting bodies. Public awareness and continuous improvement will be required to maintain the standards. I hope that the act is properly implemented considering the favourable welfare of the students.

Yours sincerely,
Sanjam Singh

Informal Letters/Personal Letters

Informal letters include the letters written to family members, relatives, friends and acquaintances. There are no formal rules as such on how to write these types of letters. Since they are intended to express feelings and share some life events, they are written in a friendly manner. The style of writing may depend upon an individual's nature and mood. If you are writing to an elderly person, you should use the language which is respectful and courteous. While writing to friends, one can use casual, friendly language.

Do's and Don'ts for Informal

Do's	Don'ts
Use a friendly tone.	Use overly formal phrases.
Share your thoughts, feelings or experiences openly.	Engage in overdramatisation.
Maintain a logical flow of thoughts.	Skip important details of any events.

Element of an Informal Letter

Informal letters consist of following parts

1. **Sender's Address and Date**

   Sender's address and date of writing the letter (sender's name is never written in the heading part)

2. **Greeting/Salutation**

   This consists of greeting and name of the recipient or the sender's relation with the recipient, e.g. Dear Ashi.

   (a) For Parents
   Dear/My dear father/mother, etc.

   (b) For Relatives
   Dear uncle/aunty, etc.

   (c) For Brother/Sister/Cousin, etc.
   Dear/My dear (name), etc.

   (d) For Acquintances
   Dear Mr (last name)/Ms (name)

3. **Body of the Letter/Message**

   (a) Introduction/Opening

   - This may begin with enquiring howabouts, e.g., 'How are you?', 'How are you (Akshay/Rahul)?' or 'I hope you are hale and hearty', 'I hope you are doing well', or 'It's been a long time since I have heard from you.'
   - The letter may also being with acknowledging/thanking for the previous letter/gift received, e.g. 'Thank you for such a precious gift of yours' or by apologising if you are writing/replying after too long.
     e.g., "Hi Preeti.
     I received your letter, but I was so busy with my new project that I could not reply earlier."

   (b) Main Body of the Letter

   - Here, you write about the actual purpose of your letter, sharing the current events happening in your life, school, college, etc.
   - Try to write your message according to the theme of the question asked.
   - While you share your experiences, your feelings, ask questions in between to arouse interest of the reader. This will give your letter a touch of live conversation.
   - Also, give replies to the questions of the recipient if he/she has written to you earlier.

4. **Closure/Concluding Sentence**

   Even if you are writing an informal, friendly letter, you cannot end it abruptly. So, give your letter a proper closure with the consent of the reader. e.g. 'Hope to see/hear from you soon'.

   Also, you may convey love to family members and good wishes to friends and acquaintances. e.g. 'Convey my regards to aunty and uncle', 'Love to little Chinu', etc.

5. **Subscription or Leave-Taking**

   As in formal letters, informal letters too need to be courteous and respectful to the person you are writing to. Below the subscription, comes the signature or name of the writer as e.g.

   - **Family Members and Relatives** Your affectionate/loving son/daughter/brother/sister/nephew, etc.
   - **Close Friends** Yours lovingly/loving friend

Suggested Specimen of Informal Letter *(Issued by Council)*

Format

Imagine that you are in a boarding school and have performed poorly in your terminal examination. Write a letter to your mother, explaining the reasons for your poor performance and tell her how you plan to do better in the forthcoming examinations.

Jingle Bells Residential School
Igatpuri - 422 402 ← Sender' address

10th October, 2018 ← Date

My dear Mummy / Mother, ← Salutation/Customary greeting

I know that you are very disappointed with my half yearly report that you must have received last week. I am truly sorry for a poor performance and I am feeling very depressed at having let you down so badly. I do not want to make excuses but this last term I have been in and out of the infirmary several times. I had a bad attack of malaria and was unable to attend classes for about a week.

Barely had I got over this when I broke out in a rash because of the medication and I had to go back into the infirmary. As result of this, I missed many classes and I scored very poorly in three subjects.

I have now picked up health and have requested my teachers to give me some extra assignments. I also plan to do group study with some of the other boarders of my class.

I am sure that this will help me to catch up with my studies and I promise you I will score much better marks in the next unit tests.

Please do not be worried about my health, I am much better. I look forward to meeting you during the mid-term break.

← Body of the letter

Yours lovingly,/Yours affectionately,/Your loving son,
Sanjiv ← Subscription and Signature

EXAM ORIENTED QUESTIONS

Informal Letters

Q.1 Your grandmother has taught you a special skill. Write a letter thanking her. Explain how you will use that skill and why it is important to you. **(ICSE 2025, 10 M)**

Ans. Sector 66,
Noida 201301

4th March, 20XX

Dear Grandma,

I hope you are doing well. I am writing this letter to thank you for teaching me gardening. I really enjoyed learning how to plant seeds, water them and take care of the plants.

This skill is very special to me because it connects me to nature and reminds me of you. I will use it to grow my own flowers and vegetables. It will help me keep the environment green and beautiful. Gardening also teaches me patience and hard work.

I will always remember the time we spent together in the garden. Thank you for your love and guidance. I feel luck to have you as my grandmother.

Take care and stay healthy.

Yours lovingly,
Nilima

Q.2 Your uncle was unable to attend your birthday party but has sent you one thousand rupees as a gift. Write a letter thanking him, telling him how would you spend that money, explaining the reason for this particular choice. **(ICSE Specimen 2025)**

Ans. 194A, Second Floor
Old Gupta Colony,
Delhi

25th January, 20XX

Dear Uncle,

I hope you are doing well. I missed you dearly at my birthday party but I completely understand that you were unable to attend due to your commitments. Your thoughtful gift of one thousand rupees truly brightened my day and I am writing to thank you for your kindness.

After careful thought, I have decided to spend the money on buying a set of books. These include some novels by my favourite authors and a few reference books that will help me in my studies. Reading is my passion and I feel this is the best way to use your generous gift.

The reason for this choice is that books are not only a source of knowledge but also a means to relax and explore new ideas. I believe they will not only help me academically but also inspire my creativity and broaden my imagination. Each time I read these books, I will be reminded of your encouragement and support.

Thank you once again for your thoughtful gesture.

It means a lot to me and I truly appreciate your love and generosity. I hope to meet you soon and tell you more about the books I've chosen. Please take care of yourself and I look forward to seeing you soon.

With love and regards,
Satakshi

Q.3 You recently read an interesting book that impacted you deeply. Write a letter to your friend highlighting the parts that impressed you. Explain two ways in which you would like to make changes in your behaviour or actions based on what you have read. **(ICSE Specimen 2024)**

Ans. 110, Model Town,
Delhi

17th March, 20XX

Dear Anjali,

I hope you're doing well! I recently read 'The Alchemist' by Paulo Coelho and I wanted to share my thoughts with you. The book left a huge impression on me, especially the idea of pursuing one's "Personal Legend"-our true purpose in life. The protagonist, Santiago, goes on a journey to find treasure but along the way, he discovers that the real treasure is not material wealth but the lessons and wisdom gained from following your dreams.

Another part that stood out was the concept of listening to your heart and trusting the signs the universe sends you.

Inspired by the book, I plan to make two changes in my life. First, I want to stop procrastinating and start working more seriously towards my goals. Second,
I will learn to trust my gut feelings and be more confident in my decisions, instead of letting fear or doubt hold me back. I truly think you'd enjoy this book, and I'd love to hear your thoughts if you read it!

Yours lovingly,
ABC

Q.4 Your school had taken you on an outing to an amusement park which your friend could not join due to ill-health. Write a letter to him/her describing the various activities you did throughout the day. Also, tell him/her how much you missed him/her. **(Competency Based Que.)**

Ans. 56, Patel Nagar,
Delhi

25th April, 20XX

Dear Riya,

I hope this letter finds you in better health. I really missed you on our school trip to the amusement park today. It wasn't the same without you and I kept thinking how much fun we would have had together.

The day started with a ride on the Ferris wheel, which offered a breathtaking view of the entire park. From the top, everything looked so small! After that, we headed straight to the roller coaster. You know how much I love it and I'm sure you would have screamed with me all the way down! Later, we played some games at the arcade and I even won a stuffed toy-a cute little bear, which I kept as a souvenir for you.

We had lunch at the food court, where I tried a giant pizza. It was delicious but I wished you were there to share it with me! Afterward, we went on the bumper cars and laughed so much, especially when Arjun bumped into a pole!

I missed you so much today. Everything was fun but without you, it felt incomplete.

I hope you get well soon so we can plan another trip together. Take care and I'm looking forward to seeing you back at school!

Yours affectionately,
Ripan

Q.5 You have had to shift to a new house recently. Write a letter to your grandmother telling her what you miss about your old house. Tell her also what you like about your new house and what you plan to do to make it comfortable for yourself. **(ICSE 2023)**

Ans. XYZ Apartments,
PQR City

17th November, 20XX

Dear Grandmother,

I hope you are in the best of health and taking your medication on time. I miss you and the rest of the family more than I can describe in words. Ever since I left our house, I have felt alone. When I was there with all of you, I was always having fun. It was good to always have some company.

In my new house, there is no television, roof or balcony. The house is tiny and that makes it easier to take care of. I can clean it pretty easily too. Also, I have a personal bedroom and study, as well as an entire wall that I can use for posters without having to share it with my siblings.

However, the house still needs a lot of work to make it more comfortable. I also have to buy new covers, cushions and blankets for my bed to have a comfortable sleep. I hope you would visit me once I have made the house more comfortable.

Yours lovingly,
Priyanka

Q.6 Your friend has been unwell and unable to attend school for two weeks. An interschool drama competition took place during the period. Write a letter to your friend telling him/her about the event and your role in it. **(ICSE Specimen 2023, 19)**

Ans. 3-397/B, Kavita Vihar,
New Delhi

17th November, 20XX

Dear Anamika,

I hope you are doing better now. It's been a long time since you got sick and you have missed a lot in the school during this time. For one, you scored the highest marks in the Internal Assessments. I heartily congratulate you. Second, there was an Interschool Drama Competition organised on Children's Day by the school. The play chosen by our school was Shakespeare's Macbeth and I got selected for the role of Malcolm.

Had you been there, I am sure you would've nabbed the role of Lady Macbeth. I missed you on the day of the audition but I also knew you would've wanted me to give my best so I worked diligently. Finally, on the day of the competition, everyone performed elegantly and tried their best.

Our school won the first prize. My happiness knew no bounds. The drama team went for a party after school and everyone talked about how much we missed you.

I pray for you to get well soon. Hoping to see you soon.

Yours lovingly,
XYZ

Q.7 Your favourite aunt/uncle has asked you what you would like as a gift for your birthday. What gift would you choose (specify) and why would you choose this? Write a letter to your aunt/uncle thanking her/him for the kind thought and telling her/him about the gift of your choice. **(ICSE 2022 Sem II)**

Ans. 25/89-B, Ground Floor,
Laxmi Nagar,
Delhi

1st June, 20XX

Dear Uncle/Aunt,

I hope this letter finds you in best of your spirits and health. I am good here and want to tell you that I was overjoyed to receive your present. A big thank you for sending such a beautiful camera.

I know you couldn't attend my birthday party due to your busy schedule but I missed you. I was overjoyed at receiving your blessings and the DSLR Camera on my birthday. It is the best present I have ever received. All my friends have also liked it very much. The camera works so well. I took a lot of pictures on my birthday which I will show you on your next visit. I have a keen interest in photography and would like to pursue it as my professional career. I am even planning to join a professional course in the same during summer vacations for which I have already taken permission from mummy and papa. I'm so excited that I'll be able to learn to use the camera professionally.

Once again, thank you very much for the gift. It is really a lovely present.

I am looking forward to your visit.

Yours lovingly,
ABC

Q.8 You have been given a small sum of money to buy a gift for a friend. What gift would you choose (specify) and why would you choose this? Write a letter to your friend telling him/her about the gift and how it will benefit him/her. **(ICSE Specimen 2022 Sem II)**

Ans. XYZ Apartments,
PQR City

14th March, 20XX

Dear ABC,

I hope this letter finds you in the best of health and spirits. I am really excited for your birthday party and guess what I have finally bought your gift. From the time I heard that you are about to head to London for your higher studies, I had an idea of what I wanted to gift you. I wanted to give you something which will allow you to remember us all. I decided to buy a Fujifilm Instax camera for you. It comes with film sheets so that you can get polaroid pictures instantly. It also has a selfie mode and is easy to carry and use. With this, you can click artsy and beautiful snaps of beautiful locations, yourself and your near and dear ones. You can prepare cute diaries and boards with the pictures and look them up as and when you wish.

Do let me know if you love my idea and I will place the order for the same so that I can meet you up with your gift! Meet you soon.

Your loving friend,
XYZ

Q.9 You have changed your school recently. Write a letter to your friend in your old school telling him/her what you like about your new school but also what you miss about your old school. **(ICSE 2020)**

Ans. House No. 125,
Sector 1, IMT,
Manesar, Gurugram,
Haryana

24th March, 20XX

Dear Yug,

Hope this letter finds you in good health. I am writing this letter to tell you about my new school. It has been a month since I joined this school after my father was transferred here. The name of my new school is Modern Public School and it is a lot bigger than our school. There is also a spacious cafeteria that serves good quality food. The teachers are extremely knowledgeable and teach very well.

But I still remember the fun I used to have in my old school. I especially miss those hobby classes that were conducted every Thursday. What fun we used to have during the dance class! Although I have made new friends, nobody can replace you.

I hope I will be able to see you soon. Eagerly waiting for you!

Yours affectionately,
PQR

Q.10 Your friend has not fared well in the recent examinations. Write a letter to him/her expressing your concern. Give him/her some advice on how to score better marks and offer to help him/here to improve his/her performance. **(ICSE 2019)**

Ans. B-103, Sajeevani Society,
MG Road,
New Delhi–110019

27th March, 20XX

Dear Mohit,

How are you? I came to know from your brother, whom I met yesterday, that you had not fared well in your Class IX final exams. I am very concerned about this because you were always serious about your studies and I did not expect this.

I miss you so much now that you are away at boarding school. When you come here to spend the summer holidays, we will have lots to talk over.

I am sure you can do much better in the Boards next year if you learn to study without help from coaching. I feel you had adjusted yourself to coaching till you studied here upto Class VIII. I don't attend any coaching either. I study by myself every day in the evening and revise each lesson taught in class that particular day. This keeps the lessons fresh in my mind. At the time of exams, I just need to go through my notes to refresh my memory. You can use this method when you come here and obtain as good results as I get.

More news when we will meet. Take care of yourself.

I look forward to meeting you in the second week of May.

Your loving friend,
ABC

Q.11 Your uncle has offered to get you a pet for your birthday. Write a letter to him telling him what you like, give reasons for your choice and tell him how you take care of your pet. **(ICSE 2018)**

Ans. House 365 - E,
Malviya Nagar,
Patna - 800003

15th February, 20XX

Dear Uncle,

Namaste. How are you? I am sure you are healthy and fine. Even I am doing well here.

As you know very well, next week is my birthday. You know your gifts are always valuable to me and delightful. I remember you were telling me, when you visited our home last month, that you were planning to give me a puppy as my birthday gift.

Uncle, I am eagerly waiting for this gift from your side. I am quite excited about it. Since a long time, I have been interested in looking after a puppy and you are fulfilling my wish. As you very well know, dogs are very faithful pets and can also guard a home against intruders. I can train up the puppy to be a good guard dog.

I understand that keeping pets in the house is not easy. We have to take good care of them. I assure you that I will take good care of it. I will keep writing to you regularly about its training and progress.

I am eagerly awaiting its arrival. I am making preparations for its stay in my room.

Thanks once again.

Please convey my respects to Aunty and regards to Sunny.

Yours affectionately,
XYZ

Q.12 You were a part of an organising committee for an inter-school event which was very successful. You and the other committee members were congratulated and praised at the school assembly by the Principal. Write a letter to your grandmother telling her about the event and your feelings at being recognised and praised in front of the school. **(ICSE 2017)**

Ans. St. Thomas Boys Hostel,
Roorkee,

20th April, 20XX

Dear Grandmother,

How are you? I miss you everyday. I am very excited and happy right now. Last week, my school had organised an Inter-School Quiz Competition in which six schools had participated. An organising committee was formed by our school principal. The committee's function was to chalk out the programme and to look after the participants and accompanying teachers coming from other schools. I was selected as a member of that organising committee. The event went off smoothly and the guests were looked after properly. Timely distribution of snacks, water and serving of lunch were all responsibilities of the members of the organising committee which were taken care of with minute details.

Next day, during morning assembly, the principal congratulated all the members of this organising committee. The principal praised our efforts in front of the whole staff and students. It was a proud moment for all of us. As I was also a part of it, I was very happy as everyone appreciated our work. It was a great feeling to be recognised and praised in front of the whole school and staff members.

I wanted to share this proud moment with you. I know you would also feel very proud of me and bless me for the future.

With regards,
PQR

Q.13 Your school recently held a Silver Jubilee celebration. Write a letter to your friend who was unable to attend, giving details of the function and your role in it. **(ICSE 2016)**

Or **A friend of yours has been out of station for a month and there was an important event function held in the school while he/she was away. Write him/her a letter describing the event/function and your role in it and why your friend was missed.** **(ICSE Specimen 2017)**

Ans. WZ-1263, Nangal Raya,
New Delhi–46

5th March, 20XX

Dear Rashi,

How are you? I hope that you are enjoying your trip. While you were on leave, we celebrated the Silver Jubilee of our school. A special function was organised to celebrate the Silver Jubilee. We gathered in the auditorium for the function. The Principal gave a small speech before the function started. He told us about the history and the foundation of our school.

The function started with a cultural programme. It was organised by the students of Class XII and depicted the diverse culture of our country. The next programme was a fashion show. I also participated in that show and represented our class. Everyone cheered for me when I came on the stage. I was adjudged the best dressed female by the judges.

The party was followed by a snacks. We also got a chance to meet the honourable Chief Minister of Delhi, who was the Chief Guest on this occasion.

We enjoyed the celebrations a lot. It would have been a more fun if you also had been present on that day.

I wish that you come back soon and join school.

Your best friend,

XYZ

Q.14 You were taken by your school to visit a place of historical interest. Write a letter to your classmate who was unable to go on the trip telling him/her about the trip, why it was important and what you gained from the experience.

Ans. 18/5, New Rajender Nagar,

New Delhi

18th December, 20XX

Dear Parth,

I hope this letter finds you in the best of your spirit and health. I am good too. You might be curious to know about our trip and I am also very excited to tell you all about it. I must say that it was really fun and full of excitement which you unfortunately missed.

We left early morning at around 7 am from the school and reached the railway station to board the train to Amritsar. We reached Amritsar in the afternoon.

After settling in the hotel, we had our lunch and went to Wagah Border. It was immensely beautiful sight and the parade enthralled us to no extent. After paying our respect and honour to the martyrs of Indian Army, we left for the hotel.

The next morning, we went to the Jallianwalla Bagh and were told about its history.

After spending an hour there, we left for the Golden Temple. First and foremost, the temple was marvelous in the shining Sun. There was peace and serenity. It was a soothing experience. We sat there till lunch and then left for shopping in the nearby market. I bought Punjabi Pappads, Jutti's and a beautiful suit for my mother. While in the market, we were mesmerised by the beauty of the monuments. Some of the students also entered into gol-gappa competition and gulped as many as 60-70 of them. The scene left all of us in peels of laughter.

All in all, it was a fun trip.

If you would have been with us, you also would have enjoyed it. Hoping to catch up with you in school.

Yours lovingly,

ABC

Q.15 You have just acquired an unusual pet. Write a letter to your friend telling him/her about it. Give details about the care you have to take in looking after and feeding the pet.

Ans. 22, Bhawara Vihar,

M.G. Road,

Agra

3rd April, 20XX

Dear Parul,

It's after ages that I'm writing to you again. I am quite eager to tell you about my newly acquired pet. You can't even think what it is. It's neither a dog nor a bird in a cage. It's a baby monkey which I got from my uncle. He rescued it from the jungles of Assam.

He was just a month old when I got it. He was too young then to have his normal diet of fruits and breads. He, thus, survived on milk. We had to feed him through a feeding bottle. Sometimes, we also gave him cerelac. My sister found him quite funny and named him 'Bunny'. After a few days with us, Bunny took a special liking towards me and we soon became best of pals.

Bunny is more like a family member now. But he is only 6 months old. We don't allow him to eat anything from outside. My mother cooks for him. He eats boiled rice and vegetables mashed into a paste. Everyday after his meals, he needs a banana. He is more pleased if it's provided by me. I have also cut a portion of a discarded mattress and made a soft bed for him too

Come soon to my place and visit Bunny. You will find him very lovable and he is quite friendly too

Yours lovingly,

PQR

07

NOTICE

Notice is an important form of written communication used by individuals and organisations to convey information about functions, events and occasions or to announce something that has happened or is about to happen. It is direct and formal in language. Its style is straightforward.

Do's and Don'ts for Notice Writing

Do's	Don'ts
Use lucid language and third person pronouns.	Use any jargons, informal language and casual tone.
Use present tense or future tense.	Use first person pronouns.
Adhere to the word limit.	Write incomplete information.
Include value points like date, time and venue.	Exaggerate the content.

Points to be Kept in Mind While Write a Notice

- Do not use the word NOTICE.
- Give a clear Title based on the Event.
- The body should include what, when, where and who is involved, keeping it formal and concise.
- Do not make a box around the Notice.

Suggested Specimen of Notice *(Issued by Council)*

Format

Your school is hosting an interschool debate competition. Write a notice for your school informing them of the event.

Ans. **War of Words**

Inter-School Debate Competition
on 8th December, 20XX
from 9:00 a.m. to 12 noon
at Centenary Hall, St. Hilda's School

All pupils from Classes IX and X who wish to participate are to give their names to Mrs. T. Baker on or before 1st December, 2017.

TYPE 1 **Notice for Meeting**

This type of notice requires the following details

- Purpose of the meeting or agenda
- Date and time/duration of the meeting
- Details of persons to attend/departments to attend
- Venue, specific instructions for the persons called for the meeting

Sample Notice

You are Abhishek/Avantika of Class X, Translam Academy, Kanpur. Being an Activity Coordinator, draft a notice to all the other Activity Council Members to discuss and plan the activities for Christmas Day celebration.

Ans.

IT'S CHRISTMAS TIME!

Meeting regarding activities for Christmas Celebration

on 23rd December, 20XX

at 10:30 a.m.

in Biology Lab, Translam Academy, Kanpur

All the Activity Council Members are hereby informed to attend the meeting with the purpose of discussing activities for Christmas Day celebration.

TYPE 2 **Notice for Events**

These notices include invitation for competition, tour, celebration, annual sports, cultural event, etc. This type of notice requires the following details

- Who can participate in it
- Occasion should be mentioned
- Number of days (in case of tours/visit)
- Expenditure estimate
- Last date for depositing the advance (tour/visit)
- Any specific instructions

Sample Notice

You are the Secretary of the Environment Club of Dharmik Sandhya Public School. Write a notice to invite students to the tree plantation drive organised by the Club on the World Environment Day.

Ans.

Plant it up

Tree Plantation Drive

5th June, 20XX, Monday

9:00 a.m. to 4:00 p.m.

School Playground

All are invited to participate.

TYPE 3 **Notice for Seminar/Workshop/Debate or any other Literary Event**

These notices should include the following details

- Speakers/Chief Guest/Honourable Persons should be mentioned
- Who can attend it
- Date/Time should be mentioned
- Specific instructions should be mentioned
- Duration of the programme should be mentioned

Sample Notice

You are the Captain of Meerut Public School, Shastri Market, Meerut. Write a notice informing the students about a guest lecture by Mr. Rajiv, an environmentalist, on the topic 'Conservation of Water'.

Ans.

SAVE WATER!

Guest Lecture on Conservation of Water

on 3rd November, 20XX

from 10:30 a.m. to 11:30 a.m.

in the Auditorium, Meerut Public School, Meerut

Chief Guest–Mr. Rajiv, a renowned environmentalist

Attendance of Class X students is compulsory. For more information, contact the school captain.

TYPE 4 Notice for Appeal/Warning

These notices include the following details

- Whom to appeal/warn
- Issuing authority (if different from the person signing the notice) should be mentioned
- A slogan or message
- Important instructions
- Courteous way to appeal
- Name and designation of the issuing person
- Any punishment (if required, in case of warning type only)

Sample Notice

Recently, it was in the news that a hurricane hit Odisha and around 13 districts were affected. Being the Head of Environment Society of your school, draft a notice to the students and staff appealing for donations of relief products like clothes, money, books and other articles.

Ans.

GIVE TILL IT HURTS!

Appeal for Donations

5th December, 20XX

10:00 a.m. to 1:00 p.m.

Auditorium, Deewan Public School, Mysore

Students can donate money, clothes, books, articles like blazers, etc. for the victims of the hurricane.

Certificates will be given to the highest contributors.

EXAM ORIENTED QUESTIONS

Q.1 Your school is hosting an Inter-School Story Writing Competition. Write a notice informing the students about the event. **(ICSE 2025, 10M)**

Ans.

Inter-School Story Writing Competition

Our school is hosting an Inter-School Story Writing Competition. Students from all classes can participate. The event will be held on 6th March, 20XX, in the school auditorium. Interested students must register by 5th March, 20XX. For details, contact your class teacher.

Q.2 Your School is hosting an Art and Craft Exhibition. Write a notice informing pupils at your school about the event. **(ICSE Specimen 2025)**

Ans.

SHOW YOUR SKILL!

Art and Craft Exhibition

25th December, 20XX

9 a.m. to 12 p.m.

School Auditorium

All the students from Class IX to XII are requested to register their names with the Head Girl by 20th December, 20XX.

Q.3 Your school is organising a student conference on the theme 'Youth for Digital India'. Write a notice for your school notice board inviting students from Classes IX to XII to submit essays for this conference. **(Competency Based Que.)**

Ans.

YOUTH FOR DIGITAL INDIA

An Enlightening Student Conference

30th August, 20XX

8 a.m. to 11 a.m.

School Auditorium

All pupils from Class IX to XII are requested to register your names with your class teacher by 22nd August, 20XX.

Q.4 Your school is hosting an Inter-School Debate Competition. Write a notice informing the students at your school about the event. **(ICSE Specimen 2024)**

Ans.

War or Words

Inter-School Debate Competition

On 9th December, 20XX

9:00 a.m. to 12 noon

at Auditorium, DAV Public School

All pupils of Classes IX and X who wish to participate are to give names to your respective class teacher on or before 1st December, 20XX.

Q.5 Write a notice to be put up in your school informing the pupils of Classes IX and X about the Remedial Classes to be held after the school hours and asking them to register their names for it. **(ICSE 2023)**

Ans.

Remedial Classes

For Classes IX and X

Monday to Friday

2:30 to 4:00 p.m.

in Respective Classes

Register your names with your class teacher.

Q.6 Your school is hosting an Inter-School Music Competition. Write a notice informing your school the event.
(ICSE Specimen 2023)

Ans.

FLAUNT YOUR MUSICAL TALENT!

Inter-School Music Competition

20th September, 20XX
11:00 a.m. to 2:00 p.m.
in Respective Classes

Participate and win exciting prizes!

Q.7 22nd March is celebrated as World Water Day. The school Dramatics Club is planning to stage a one act play to mark the occasion and create awareness. Write a notice to be put up on the school notice board giving details of the event.
(ICSE 2022 Sem II)

Ans.

Save Blue. Live Green.

World Water Day Celebration

On 22nd March, 20XX (World Water Day)
from 1:30 p.m. to 3:00 p.m.
in Auditorium, Delhi Public School

All the students are hereby invited to the one-act play, to mark the occasion and create awareness. The play will be followed by an interactive session.

Q.8 You are the President of the school Science Club. You and your team are planning to organise a creative mask-making event using renewable materials. Write a notice to be put up on the school notice board giving details of the event.
(ICSE Specimen 2022 Sem II)

Ans.

Creative Mask Making Event

22nd March, 20XX
9:00 a.m. to 1:00 p.m.
Science Room

Event Details

- Use only renewable material
- Come dressed traditionally

All of you are hereby requested to attend the event and honour the contribution made by children in our formation.

Q.9 Your school is organising a fete/carnival to raise funds for victims of the recent floods in your State. Write a notice to be put up on the school notice board giving details of the event.
(ICSE 2020)

Ans.

For the Ones in Need

Fund Raising Carnival

on 8th April, 20XX
from 11:00 a.m. onwards
in Vidyasagar Public School, Bihar

Students are requested to be a part of the fest and bring their parents and friends. There will be various food stalls, games and rides. A lucky draw will also be organised. The coupons for the lucky draw can be obtained from the reception.

All are invited to participate and help the victims of the recent floods in the state.

Q.10 Your school is hosting an Inter-School Quiz Competition. Write out a notice to be displayed in your school giving all details for the event. **(ICSE 2019)**

Ans.

Puzzlers

Inter-School Quiz Competition

on 5th September, 20XX

4 p.m. onwards

in Auditorium, Sunlight Public School, Ghaziabad

The events of the function are as follows

- Welcoming the Chief Guest, Ms. R Shastri, MLA
- Announcement of the rules, introduction of the teams and the Quiz Master
- Actual conduct of the quiz
- Presentation of prizes to the winners and runners-up
- Address by Chief Guest
- Vote of Thanks by the Principal
- Refreshments

All faculty, staff and students are requested and welcome to attend.

Q.11 **You are the President of a children's club in your locality. You and your team are planning to organise a programme to celebrate Teachers' day. Write a notice to be put up in the local supermarket giving details of the programme to create an awareness of the event.** **(ICSE Specimen 2019)**

Ans.

Thank you Teacher!

A cultural programme to celebrate Teachers' Day

on 5th September

from 5:00 p.m. to 7:00 p.m.

at Community Centre, South City Mall

All teachers who are residents of the South City Complex are cordially invited.

Q.12 **You are the Secretary of Tours and Trips Society of Translam Academy International, Meerut. The school is organising a 20 days historical tour to some important places in South India. You have been asked by the Activity Coordinator to put up a notice inviting students interested in visiting those places. Write this notice to be put up on the school notice board.**

Ans.

20 Days Historical Tour

(A visit to Chennai, Mysore, Rameshwaram, Kanyakumari and Bengaluru)

1st April to 20th April

₹ 2500 Fare

Interested students need to submit

- Parents' approval letter
- Fees by 24th March

For further details, contact Ms. Saini, Senior Co-ordinator

Q.13 **You are Secretary of AVM Housing Society. You are going to organise a Blood Donation Camp. Write a notice urging the members of your society to come in large numbers for this noble cause. Invent all the necessary details.**

Ans.

DONATE BLOOD! GIVE LIFE!

Blood Donation Camp

on 15th March, 20XX from 11 a.m. onwards in

Community Hall AVM Housing Society, Ghaziabad

Residents above the age of 18 and below 50 years

with good medical health are urged to volunteer in large number for this noble cause.

Qualified doctors will be available to carry out the procedure.

Q.14 You are School Pupil Leader of Rani Laxmi Bai Senior Secondary School, Gwalior. Draft a notice for your school notice board inviting the names of the students who want to participate in the cultural programme organised in aid of the victims of the recent Assam floods.

Ans.

Cultural Test

(A charity event to aid the victims of Assam floods)

25th December, 20XX
11:00 a.m. onwards
School Auditorium

All students are requested to give your names to volunteers.

Q.15 You are the Principal of St. Thomas School. Write a notice informing students and parents about the 'Obesity Camp' to be organised by Jessa Ram Hospital.

Ans.

SHED THE FAT!

Obesity Camp

30th March, 20XX
9:00 a.m. to 5:00 a.m.
MI Room, St. Thomas School, Hyderabad

Renowned Dr. Ajay Gupta will be the Chief Guest of the camp and will share knowledge on obesity and its ill effects. All students should inform their parents about this event.

Q.16 Young astronauts have to be selected for 'Mission NASA'. The preliminary round will be conducted in Modern School. Write a notice inviting students who wish to become astronauts to take the preliminary round for final selection. You are the Director of Science Research Centre.

Ans.

CHASE YOUR DREAM!

Preliminary Round for Mission NASA

19th July, 20XX

Time Phase I Timings 8:30 a.m. to 9:30 a.m.
Phase II Timings 10:00 a.m. to 11:00 a.m.

Modern School, Barakhamba Road

Interested students of Class XI and XII should enrol themselves with the Science Club Manager at Modern School.

Q.17 You are the President of the Literary Club of your school. You have organised an Inter-School Debate Competition on the occasion of the Silver Jubilee celebrations of your school. Write a notice informing the students of your school about the competition.

Ans.

SPEAK YOUR MIND!

Debate Competition

18th December, 20XX
11: 00 a.m. onwards
Saraswati Auditorium, Sophia International, Kanpur

Topic : 'Nuclear Armament is India's Best Defence against Cross-border Terrorism'
Last date for submission of names is 10th December upto 4:30 p.m. in the Activities Room.

E-MAIL WRITING

E-mail or electronic mail is a message distributed by electronic means from one computer user to one or more recipients *via*, a network. With the advent of the digital age, e-mail plays an important part in everybody's life. It is one of the most popular and fastest way of sending messages anywhere in the world and can be used in formal as well as informal contexts.

Parts of an E-mail

- **Recipient's Address** The first thing you need to enter when composing an e-mail is the recipient's address. An example of e-mail address is: sakshiwrites@gmail.com. When sending a message to multiple recipients, be sure to separate all addresses with a comma.
- **Subject Line** The subject line is the second part of your e-mail that the recipient will see. It essentially tells what the e-mail is about.
- **Cc and Bcc** Another option when sending a message to multiple recipient's is to use the Cc or Carbon copy and Bcc or Blind carbon copy fields.
- **Body** The body is where you actually write the message that you want to send.
- **Attachments** Attachments are similar to enclosures in a traditional mail. If you have files that you want to share with your recipient(s), you can include them as attachments to the e-mail.
- **Signature** Some e-mail systems allow you to enter a signature that will appear automatically at the bottom of every message you send. This feature is optional and can be turned off and on as needed.

Steps for Writing an E-mail

1. Type the e-mail id of the recipient(s) in the 'To', 'Cc' and 'Bcc' fields.
2. Compose the subject of the e-mail in the subject line.
3. Attach any files that you want to send with the e-mail using the 'Attach' or 'Insert' option.
4. Write the proper salutation (like Dear Father, Hi Bhawna, Sir/Ma'am, etc.)
5. Write the body of the e-mail.
6. End the mail with a proper close.

E-mail Etiquettes

It refers to the do's and dont's of the things to be kept in mind while writing e-mails.

1. **Do not Leave the Subject Line Blank**
2. **Include Proper Salutation as per the E-mail Type** One must include proper salutation before starting to write an e-mail. The salutation used should depend on the recepient of the e-mail.

   Example- Sir/Ma'am
3. **Avoid using Abbreviations and Acronyms**
4. **Grammar and Language** The message should be conveyed using correct grammar and simple language. The traditional rules for punctuation is to be maintained in the e-mail.
5. **Add Appropriate Closing** One should use proper closing of the e-mail before hitting the send button. The closing of the e-mail should be appropriate.

   Examples
   - Yours obediently
   - Yours sincerely
   - Yours faithfully

Suggested Specimen of E-mail *(Issued by Council)*

Format

Write an e-mail to the Principal of a neighbouring school requesting him/her to send a team of teachers to judge the event.

Ans. principal@stflorence.org

Request to appoint judges for a talent search event.

Dear Ma'am,

It is our pleasure to share with you that we are conducting a talent search contest for the students of Classes 8th, 9th and 10th.

This is to be held on the 24th July, 2018 from 9 a.m. to 4 p.m. in Music, Art, Dance, Magic, Acrobatics and Stand-up Comedy.

We request you to send a team of three teachers from your school to judge the talent search, Everybody's Got Talent.

Anticipating a positive response,

Yours faithfully,
Maya Gilani
Cultural Secretary, Student Council
St. Agnes' School

EXAM ORIENTED QUESTIONS

Q.1 Write an e-mail to a famous person inviting him/her to be the Judge on the occasion. **(ICSE 2025, 10 M)**

Ans. abc@gmail.com

Invitation to Judge Our Public Speaking Competition

Dear Dr. Tharoor,

I hope you are doing well. We are organising an Inter-School Public Speaking Competition on 28th March, 20XX at St. Xaviers College, Gurgaon. We would be honoured if you could be the judge for the event. Your presence and guidance would inspire our students.

Please let us know your availability.

Thanking You

Yours faithfully
Ravi Shashank
St. Xaviers College

Q.2 Write an e-mail to a local artist inviting his/her to inaugurate the exhibition and be the chief guest on the occasion. **(ICSE Specimen 2025)**

Ans. rishabh07@gmail.com

Invitation to inaugurate Art and Craft Exhibition

Dear sir,

I hope this e-mail finds you well and thriving in your creative endeavours. I extend an invitation to you to be the Chief Guest at our upcoming Art and Craft Exhibition, which will be held on 30th July, 20XX at 10 a.m. in our school auditorium.

We believe that your presence and your inaugural address will greatly inspire and motivate our young artists.

Looking forward to the possibility of your positive response.

Yours faithfully,
Tanish Goyal
Principal

Q.3 Write an e-mail to an entrepreneur involved in the field of Information Technology to deliver the keynote address at the Student Conference to be organised by your School **(Competency Based Que.)**

Ans. xyz@gmail.com

Invitation to deliver a keynote address

Dear Sir/Ma'am,

It is with extreme pleasure that we, ABC School, is hosting the eagerly awaited Student Conference on Careers in Information Technology for all students.

In this regard, it would be our utmost pleasure if you could join us and give a keynote address to our students.

The details of the event are as follows

Date : Friday, 3rd August, 20XX
Time : 8 a.m. to 11 a.m.
Venue : The Assembly Area, ABC School

Your work as an entrepreneur and your words will act as key motivation for our students. Hoping for a positive response.

Thanking you,

Yours faithfully,
Ashvik Bhardwaj
(Principal, ABC School)

Q.4 **Write an e-mail to a famous artist in your city requesting him to judge and select the best painting in the competition.** **(Competency Based Que.)**

Ans. soniya@painter.org

Invitation to judge the Inter-School Painting Competition.

Dear Sir/Ma'am,

This is to share with you that the Arts Club of the school is organising an inter-school painting competition on the occasion of Independence Day. For the same, we shall be honoured if you could grace us with your presence on the occasion and judge the competition. Your presence will boost the morale of the students and inspire them to take up arts as a profession.

Hoping for a positive reply.

Yours sincerely
Praveen
(Secretary, Arts Club)

Q.5 **Write an e-mail to the Principal of a neighbouring school to request him/her to send their dance teacher to act as a judge for the competition.** **(ICSE 2024)**

Ans. principalanju@gmail.com

Invitation to judge the Inter-School
Dance Competition

Dear Sir/Ma'am,

With great pleasure, I would like to share with you that Delhi Public School, Delhi is going to organise an Inter-School Dance Competition on 31st January, 20XX from 11:00 a.m. onwards in the school auditorium. For the same, we would love to have the dance teacher of your school over as a judge of the competition.

Kindly accept our invitation and increase the glory of the competition. Hoping for a positive response.

Thanking You,

Yours obediently,
Neelam Tyagi
Principal
Delhi Public School

Q.6 **Write an e-mail to the principal of a neighbouring school informing him/her of the inter-school debate competition being held at your school and requesting him/her to send a team of students to participate.** **(ICSE Specimen 2024)**

Ans. anuradha09@gmail.com

Invitation for Inter-School Debate Competition

Dear Sir/Ma'am,

I hope you are doing well. I am writing to inform you that our school, is organising an Inter–School Debate Competition on 17th March, 20XX. We would be delighted if your school could send a team of students to participate in this event. The competition promises to be an excellent platform for students to showcase their debating skills and engage in intellectual discussions with their peers.

Please confirm your participation by 1st March, 20XX. Looking forward to the possibility of your positive response.

Yours faithfully,
Anita Gupta
Principal

Q.7 **Write an e-mail to the Principal of a neighbouring school inviting their pupils to attend the classes if they so wish. Give all details of the classes to be held.** **(ICSE 2023)**

Ans. principal.dps.2013@yahoo.co.in

Invitation for students to attend foreign language classes

Dear Sir/Ma'am,

The school is going to organise Spanish, German and French classes for the students of Classes IX-XII from the 20th September, 20XX. The school has invited teachers and language experts from embassies to help the students in spoken as well as written languages.

The classes would last three months and would take place after school hours (2:30 p.m.-4 p.m.) from Monday to Friday. This is a great opportunity for the students to get acquainted with foreign languages.

The students of your school are welcome to attend these classes if they wish. Each student can pick one language to learn from the three given languages. Kindly send the interested students to our school for the same.

Thanking you,

Yours faithfully,
Anita Kumar
(Head Girl)
Vidya Public School

Q.8 **Write an e-mail to the Principal of the neighbouring school informing him/her of the event and requesting him/her to send a team to participate.** **(ICSE Specimen 2023)**

Ans. principal.dps.2013@yahoo.co.in

Request to send a team for participation in the Inter-School Music Competition

Dear Sir/Ma'am,

The school is going to organise an Inter-School Music Competition on the 20th of September, 20XX. Five schools from the city will be participating in the competition. The winning team will be honoured with Gold Medals and prize money.

Kindly send a team from your school to participate in the event.

Thanking you,

Yours faithfully,
Anita Kumar (Head Girl)
Vidya Public School

Q.9 **Write an e-mail to the Principal of a neighbouring school requesting him/her to send a team of children to participate in the interactive session which will follow the play on 'World Water Day' celebration.** **(ICSE 2022 Sem II)**

Ans. principal.abc@xyzschool.com

Interactive Session on World Water Day

Dear Sir/Ma'am,

This is to inform you that Delhi Public School, Delhi is going to organise a one-act play on World Water Day, i.e., 22nd March, 20XX in the School Auditorium to mark the occasion and create awareness. The play will be followed by an interactive session on the same. You are requested to send a team of children to participate in the interactive session.

It will be a great opportunity for students of both the schools to interact with one another and improve their knowledge.

Kindly send the names of the participants by
4th March, 20XX.

Thanking you,

Regards,
PQR
(Principal)
Delhi Public School

Q.10 **Write an e-mail to the General Manager of a local hospital requesting him/her to send a senior doctor to talk to the participants at the event about the quality of mask which would give them the best protection.** **(ICSE Specimen 2022 Sem II)**

Ans. GMHospital@sthospital.com

Request to send a team of doctors

Dear Sir/Ma'am,

This is to request you to kindly send a team of doctors to our area for health meeting against Covid-19 protection including mask quality. People here are living below the poverty line and are unable to afford a health checkup.

This health checkup would be very beneficial for them because then they may approach their concerned doctors and get their treatment done. This initiative of yours would be appreciable.

Anticipating a positive response,

Yours faithfully,
ABC
Principal
(ABC School)

Q.11 **Write an e-mail to the Principal of a neighbouring school inviting him/her to send their students to attend the fete/carnival.** **(ICSE 2020/19)**

Ans. principalgloriaschool@gmail.com

Invitation for attending the carinval

Dear Ma'am,

With extreme pride and pleasure, we would like to invite your students to attend and participate in the carnival being organised by our school on 8th April, 20XX. The carnival will begin at 11 o'clock in the morning. The purpose of this carnival is to raise funds to help the victims of the recent floods in our state. There will be a lot of interesting games and rides. Attractive food stalls have also been arranged.

We request you to kindly grace the occasion with your presence.

Thanking You,

Yours obediently,
Sarita
(Head Girl)
Vidyasagar Public School

Q.12 **Write an e-mail to the Principal of a neighbouring school requesting him/her to send a team of three members to participate in the Quiz Competition.** **(ICSE 2019)**

Ans. principal@ bhairavschool.com

Invitation for Inter-School Quiz Competition

Dear Sir/Ma'am,

This is to share with you that our school has been honoured to host the Inter-School Quiz Competition of the district this year. Ms. R Shastri, MLA, has kindly consented to be the Chief Guest.

A notice giving details of the event is attached to the mail. You are requested to arrange to send a team of three students to participate on behalf of your school.

You are requested to provide the names as well as the contact details of the students as well as staff members by 28th March, 20XX. For further details, kindly contact the undersigned.

Thanking you,

With Regards

Ravi Saroha

(Head Boy)

Q.13 Write an e-mail to the General Manager of XYZ publishing asking for quotations for publishing your school magazine 'The Buds' on a monthly basis. **(ICSE Specimen 2019)**

Ans. inquiry@xyzpublishing.com

Request for Quotations for School Magazine Publication

Dear Sir/Ma'am,

I am writing on behalf of Angel Public School, Indirapuram, as we are exploring publishing options for our school magazine, 'The Buds'. The magazine showcases the creative talents of our students, including articles, poetry, artwork and photography.

We plan to publish the magazine on a monthly basis, starting from February 20XX.

Please provide us with a detailed quotation, including costs for printing, design assistance and any additional services you offer.

We look forward to your response by 31st January, 20XX.

Yours sincerely,

Akshat Negi

Editor-in-Chief/Secretary,

School Magazine Committee

Q.14 As a member of your residential society, write an e-mail to Inspector of Local Police Station, Mr. Sharma, informing him about miscreants who ride their bikes rashly every evening outside your society.

Ans. inspectorsharma10@yahoo.com

Miscreants in the area

Dear Sir,

This is to inform you that we, the residents of Siddhartha Nagar, have written this mail to bring to your notice that a few guys are riding their bikes very rashly in the evening hours in the main road of the colony. As you know that this is the time when children play on the road and elderly go for an evening walk these rash drivers can lead to accidents and mishaps. In fact, many of these people are seen bullying and harrassing women, children and even the elderly.

Therefore, we request you to look into the matter and help us make our locality safe for all.

Thanking you,

Yours sincerely,

Vaibhav Kumar

Q.15 You are the President of the Nature Club of your school. You wish to subscribe to the 'Nature for All' magazine for the school library. Write an e-mail to the Subscription Department of the magazine requesting them to send the details of the subscription plans.

Ans. theweek@subscriptionenquiring.com

Subscription enquiring for 'Nature for All'

Dear Sir/Ma'am,

This is to inform you that I, the President of the Nature Club of Springdales School, Dhaula Kuan, New Delhi, happened to go through a copy of your magazine at your stall in the recently concluded Book Fair at Pragati Maidan. I found your magazine very interesting and wanted to subscribe to it for our school library so that students can benefit from it. Kindly send me the details of the cost of its subscription and the various plans available for the same. I would appreciate if you could give us some discount over and above the regular subscription rates as we would be using it for educational purposes.

Looking forward to your correspondence.

Yours faithfully,

Naveen Kaul

(President, Nature Club)

Q.16 Write an e-mail to the Manager of Smart Automotive Company, Mr. Ahmed, regarding the poor quality of service facility available in the city.

Ans. ahmedsac@gmail.com

Poor service quality in the city

Dear Mr. Ahmed,

This is to inform you that I recently bought Fiat Palio from your store in Nagole with Receipt no. 1100XX. Recently, I faced small problem with car AC and brought the car for maintenance. But to my utter surprise, the showroom staff told me that service is not available in their showroom and they asked me to take the car to the nearby service center.

After much struggle, when I reached the service centre no one was there. I decided to wait when one very rude staff told me that they are busy and are not going to take my car for service. Dejected I had to drive the car to another service centre where they took my car for service. However, even here I was left unsatisfied. The AC which was faulty had been removed and the car was very dirty. Further, I was charged a hefty amount for refusal.

Such a poor behaviour and service was not expected. Hence, I request you to look into the matter, improve it and get my car serviced again.
I hope for a early redressal.

Yours faithfully,
Pramit Chopra

Q.17 Write an e-mail to your School Counsellor requesting him/her to take a session on the topic "How to choose the right stream in Class XI". Invent necessary details.

Ans. Pqr@gmail.com

Session on choosing the right stream in Class XI

Dear Sir,

I am a student of Class X-D of your school. After a few months, we would be promoted to Class XI and face the dilemma of choosing the right stream that is suitable to our aptitude. Making a wise decision at that stage is very important for a student and their future career prospects.

Therefore, I request you to conduct a session on 'How to choose the right stream in Class XI' for us in our free period. This would help us in getting prepared in advance for the process and thus, avoid making a last minute blunder in the crucial decision-making process.

Thanking you,

Yours obediently,
ABC
Class X-D

Q.18 You are Saurabh/Saumya of Class X of Happy School, Daryaganj, New Delhi. You wish to participate in a Robotics Contest being organised by a Infocom Private Company. Write an e-mail to your Principal requesting him to nominate your name for the Class IX-X level, giving him the detail of the Robot that you want to display in the contest.

Ans. principalhappyschool@gmail.com

Nomination for entry in Robotics Contest

Dear Sir,

I am a student of Class X-B of your school. I most humbly request you to nominate my name in the Class IX-X category of the upcoming Robotics Contest being organised by Infocom Pvt. Ltd.

The Robot that I have made for the contest can mimic a human's voice. It is also capable of reciting a few nursery rhymes. I am quite confident that my entry would bag the first prize in the contest.

Kindly nominate my name on the behalf of our school.

Thanking you,

Yours obediently,
Saurabh Jain

Q.19 Write an e-mail in the form of a congratulatory e-mail addressed to the three students individually. Mentioning the names of 'First Three Positions' won by students of your institute at the National Games. You are the Head of the Sports Department of your institute.

Ans. rohitbiswas@gmail.com

Heartiest Congratulations

Dear Rohit,

I am thrilled to extend my heartfelt congratulations on behalf of our school on securing the First Place at the National Games 2025! Your exceptional performance and unwavering dedication have brought immense pride to our institute, and your success serves as a shining example for all your peers.

Your achievement in 800m Sprint is a testament to your hard work, discipline and talent. Representing our institute on such a prestigious platform and excelling among the finest athletes is no small feat, and you have truly made us proud.

We are confident that this milestone is just the beginning of many more successes to come. Your determination and perseverance inspire us all to aim higher and work harder.

On behalf of the entire Sports Department and the institute, I once again congratulate you on this remarkable accomplishment. We look forward to celebrating your victory at a special felicitation ceremony soon.

Wishing you continued success in all your future endeavours!

Yours sincerely
Aman Sharma
Head of the Sports Department

09

UNSEEN PASSAGES

Comprehension involves a thorough understanding of the given passage consisting of one or more paragraphs. It is meant to test the comprehending (understanding) skills of a student.

In the examination, there will be a passage followed by different types of questions that are to be answered on the basis of the information given in passage.

Format of Questions

This question comprises a passage of about 450 words followed by three types of questions as follows

1. **Vocabulary Based Questions** The first question is based on vocabulary. It includes choosing the correct synonym or meaning of the given word.
2. **Short Answer Type Questions** The second question contains 5 subjective or short answer type questions which are to be answered in the context of the passage.
3. **Summary Based Questions** The third question is based on summary or characterisation. The students are required to answer the question in about 50 words.

Important Steps to Follow While Attempting the Question

(i) Read the passage quickly so as to get the main theme of the passage.

(ii) At this stage, do not worry about the difficult words that you encounter.

(iii) Now, go through the questions once. This will facilitate the process of comprehending the passage.

(iv) Now, read the passage carefully and comprehensively.

- This time you should read the passage slowly so as to grasp the minute details of every point talked about in the passage.
- If you try to read the passage hurriedly, you will not be able to discover every detail and will end up wasting your time in repeated readings.
- Try to make out the meanings of the words you have underlined.
- Do not try to attempt the questions, before you have completely read the passage.

Points to be Kept in Mind While Answering the Questions

- The answers must be in complete sentences.
- The answers must be relevant and to-the-point.
- No information from outside the passage should be included in the answer even if that information is related to the topic.
- The answers must be written using
  – one's own language.
  – simple, appropriate words.
  – correct grammatical English.
- The tense of the answers must be the same as that of the questions.
- Avoid using the language of the passage.

REVISION NOTES

EXAM ORIENTED QUESTIONS

Q.1 Read the following passage carefully and answer the questions that follow. **(ICSE 2025, 20 M)**

A little later, when he went to the pump to wash, he saw the school children pouring by with their **satchels** across their shoulders. They all wore the same clothes - grey shorts or skirts and light blue shirts or blouses - faded and mended and they all had their hair oiled and combed down very flat. Some went by in laughing, racing groups, others had to be led by their mothers or grandparents to the school building. This reminded him of his sisters in the village.

The boys in the kitchen now looked at him with less hostility. Jagu seemed pleased with Hari too and sometimes handed him a glass of tea in the middle of the day. When he had a few moments to **spare**, Jagu sat down at one of the long wooden tables, drummed loudly on it and sang a song in a dialect Hari did not know. When he caught

Hari listening and smiling, he smiled back. Then Hari knew that he too had a village somewhere that he called home. It was just that he was a silent, hardworking, worried man and had no time and no gift for speech.

It was the watch mender, Mr. Panwallah, who was truly a benefactor, the kindest and most helpful of all. One afternoon, during those hot, still hours when there were no customers for a change, Hari was standing in front of the eating house, idly watching the traffic because he was too tired to do anything else, and Mr. Panwallah called to him to come and sit beside him on the bench behind the counter in his shop.

"Want to help?" he asked. "Want to learn how to make a clock tick? I'm just going to open this big grandfather clock sent to me for repair - you'll be able to see the workings plain. Don't often get a piece like this anymore – wall clocks, yes and electronic gadgets – but you don't often come upon a grandfather clock like this. It's a real piece of luck, being able to show you one of this size." Look, he said, swinging open the door at the back and revealing the machinery to a fascinated Hari who felt as if the door had opened into a new and strange house. Mr. Panwallah showed Hari what was wrong with it, what had made it stop. "Interesting, isn't it? How would you like to learn? Tell you what - I'll take you on as an apprentice. You don't have much to do between two and four, do you? Of course you will have to ask Jagu first. I can pay you a little, not much, and you can help me for two hours a day. Perhaps I can make a watch mender of you."

– *Village by the Sea, Anita Desai*

Questions

(i) For each word given below choose the correct meaning (as used in the passage) from the options provided.

1. Satchels (line 3)

(a) snatching (b) scarves
(c) school bags (d) sweaters

2. Spare (line 14)

(a) share (b) offer
(c) thin (d) extra

(ii) Which word in the passage is the opposite of 'closed'?

(a) Behind (b) Fascinated
(c) Opened (d) Revealing

(iii) Answer the following questions briefly in your own words.

(a) How were the school children dressed?
(b) In what way was Jagu kind to Hari?
(c) What did the song tell Hari about Jagu?
(d) Which sentence in the passage tells us that Jagu was not a talkative man?
(e) Why were there no customers at that time of the day?

(iv) In not more than 50 words describe how Mr. Panwallah introduced Hari to watch mending.

Answers

(i) 1. (c) school bags 2. (d) extra

(ii) (c) Opened

(iii) (a) The school children wore grey shorts or skirts and light blue shirts or blouses. Their clothes were faded and mended and their hair was oiled and combed flat.

(b) Jagu was kind to Hari by giving him a glass of tea during the day and smiling at him when he noticed Hari listening to his songs.

(c) The song made Hari realise that Jagu also had a village he called home.

(d) 'It was just that he was a silent, hard-working, worried man and had no time and no gift for speech.'

(e) There were no customers because it was a hot afternoon, a quiet time for business.

(iv)

Mr. Panwallah	called	Hari	to	sit
beside	him	and	showed	him
the	inside	of	a	big
grandfather	clock.	He	explained	what
was	wrong	with	it	and
how	to	fix	it.	He
then	offered	to	take	Hari
as	an	apprentice,	paying	him
a	little	and	patiently	training
him	for	two	hours	daily.

Q.2 Read the following passage carefully and answer the questions that follow. **(ICSE Speciment 2025)**

One day, I found the pond occupied by several buffaloes. Their keeper, a boy a little older than me, was swimming about in the middle. Instead of climbing out on the bank he would pull himself up on the back of one of his buffaloes, stretch his naked brown body out on the animal's glistening **hide** and start singing to himself.

When he saw me staring at him from across the pond, he smiled, showing gleaming white teeth in a dark face. He invited me to join him in a swim. I told him I couldn't swim and he offered to teach me.

His name was Ramu and he promised to give me swimming lessons every afternoon and so it was during the afternoons especially summer afternoons when everyone was asleep that we usually met. Before long I was able to swim across the pond to sit with Ramu astride a **contented** buffalo.

Sometimes I would slip into the water. Emerging in shades of green and khaki, I would sneak into the house through the bathroom and bathe under the tap before getting into my clothes.

One afternoon, Ramu and I found a small tortoise in the mud, sitting over a hole in which it had laid several eggs. I presented the tortoise to Grandfather. He had a weakness for tortoises and was pleased with this addition to his menagerie, giving it a large tub of water all to itself, with an island of rocks in the middle. If one of the dogs bothered it too much, it would draw its head and legs into its shell and defy all its attempts at rough play.

Ramu came from a family of bonded labourers and had received no schooling. But he was well-versed in folklore and knew a great deal about birds and animals.

"Many birds are sacred." said Ramu, as we watched a blue jay swoop down from a peepal tree and carry off a grasshopper.

Both Ramu and Grandfather were of the opinion that we should be more gentle with birds and animals and should not kill so many of them.

"It is also important that we respect them, said Grandfather. We must acknowledge their rights. Birds and animals are finding it more difficult to survive, because we are trying to destroy both them and their forests."

Ramu and I spent long summer afternoons at the pond. I still remember him with affection, though we never saw each other again after I left Dehra.

Questions

(i) For each word given below choose the correct meaning (as used in the passage) from the options provided.

1. Hide (line 6)

(a) blanket (b) fur
(c) undisclosed (d) skin

2. Contented (line 17)

(a) cheerful (b) lazy
(c) satisfied (d) container

(ii) Which word in the passage is the opposite of 'easy'?

(a) Sneak (b) Difficult
(c) Labourer (d) Survive

(iii) Answer the following questions briefly in your own words.

(a) What did Ramu like to do once he had climbed on the back of a buffalo?

(b) What offer did Ramu make to the narrator?

(c) Why do you think the narrator would bathe before entering the house?

(d) Who was the large tub of water for?

(e) How would the tortoise protect itself from the dogs?

(iv) Despite the lack of schooling what did Ramu know? How, according to Ramu and Grandfather, should we treat birds and animals? Answer in not more than 50 words.

Answers

(i) 1. (d) skin

2. (c) satisfied

(ii) (b) Difficult

(iii) (a) Ramu enjoyed stretching his naked brown body out on the animal's shiny hide/back and humming to himself.

(b) He volunteered to teach the narrator to swim and provide swimming sessions every afternoon.

(c) To escape getting chastised for swimming in the village pond or when everyone was asleep, they may have had to sneak inside the home through the bathroom and bathe under the faucet to clean themselves.

(d) The tortoise was presented by the narrator to his grandfather.

(e) It would retreat into its shell and resist rough play from other canines.

(iv)

Ramu	came	from	a	family
of	bonded	labourers	and	received
no	schooling.	However,	he	was
well-versed	in	folklore	and	knew
a	great	deal	about	birds
and	animals.	We	should	be
gentle	with	birds	and	animals
and	should	not	kill	them.
It	is	also	important	to
acknowledge	and	respect	their	rights.

Q.3 Read the following passage carefully and answer the questions that follow: **(Competency Based Que.)**

If he didn't hurry it would soon be dark. And his father would be waiting for the bait. First of all he had said to his mother that he wouldn't go to the ebb. The mood had come on him to be very **stubborn**. It was a shame that he should have to go to the ebb, with the other boys playing football.

The injustice of it had hit him strongly. His father had said nothing. But if he didn't go then his father would have had to. And by two or three in the morning his father would have to be aboard.

It must be terribly cold in the dark out on that sea; out on that sea in the small hours of a sleepy morning or on a morning of hard frost, with mist coming off the water like ghosts' breath. The loneliness of the bouldered beach suddenly caught him in an odd way.

A small shiver went over his back. The dark undulating water rose from him to a horizon so far away that it was vague and lost. What a size it was! It could heave up and drown the whole world. Its waters would go rushing and drowning. He glimpsed the rushing water as a turbulent whiteness released out of thunderous sluices.

"But you can't", he half-smiled, a little fearfully, glancing at him. A short distance away, right on the sea's edge, he saw one of the boulders move. His heart came into his throat. Yet half his mind knew that it could only be some other lonely human being in the ebb. And presently he saw the back bob up for a moment again. Yes, it was a man. Seeking among the boulders there like some **queer** animal!

He looked at him carefully. There was no one else. There were just the two of them in the ebb. Here they were on this dark beach, with nobody else. A strange air of remoteness touched him. It was as though they shared this gloomy shore, beyond the world's rim, between them.

There was a secret importance in it. He stooped and began filling his bag with mussels picking big ones in a manly way. The water was now merely cool to his burning hands.

Adapted from 'Morning Tide' by Neil M. Gunn

Questions

(i) For each word given below, choose the correct meaning (as used in the passage) from the options provided.

1. Stubborn (line 4)

(a) hard to move (b) obstinate
(c) gentle (d) wise

2. Queer (line 30)

(a) weird (b) unusual (c) normal (d) strange

(ii) Which word in the passage is the opposite of 'calm'?

(a) Peaceful (b) Quiet
(c) Turbulent (d) Still

(iii) Answer the following questions briefly in your own words.

(a) What would happen if he didn't hurry?

(b) According to the passage, what would be injustice? Why would it be unjust do you think?

(c) Why did he feel he had to go to the ebb?

(d) What was the ebb, do you think? What would it be like out at sea?

(e) What made a shiver go down his back? Who were the words 'But you can't' addressed to?

(iv) Describe in about 50 words what happened after he saw one of the boulders move.

Answers

(i) 1. (b) obstinate 2. (d) strange

(ii) (c) Turbulent

(iii) (a) If he didn't hurry, it would soon be dark and his father would be waiting for the bait, implying a delay would disrupt their plans.

(b) The injustice was having to work instead of playing football, as the boy felt it was unfair to miss out on fun for a responsibility.

(c) He felt he had to go to avoid burdening his father, who would have to go alone, especially late at night.

(d) The ebb likely refers to the receding tide, with the sea being cold, isolated and dangerous, full of mist and vast, overwhelming power.

(e) The shiver came from the sea's coldness and vastness, and "But you can't" was directed to himself, trying to calm his fearful thoughts about the sea.

(iv)

The	boy	saw	one	of
the	boulders	move,	his	heart
raced,	he	was	stuck	by
fear.	He	soon	realised	it
was	just	another	person,	a
man,	seeking	among	the	boulders,
almost	like	a	strange	animal.
The	boy	felt	a	sense
of	isolation	as	they	shared
the	lonely,	dark	beach	together.

Q.4 Read the following passage carefully and answer the questions that follow. **(Competency Based Que.)**

The Belgian Consul's house was situated in the maze of narrow, smelly alleyways that made up the Jewish quarter of the town. It was a fascinating area, the cobbled streets crammed with stalls that were piled high with gaily-coloured bales of cloth, mountains of shining sweetmeats, ornaments of beaten silver, fruit and vegetables.

The streets were so narrow that you had to stand back against the wall to allow the donkeys to stagger past with their loads of merchandise.

It was a rich and colourful part of the town, full of noise and bustle, the screech of bargaining women, the cluck of hens, the barking of dogs and the wailing cry of the men carrying great trays of fresh hot loaves on their heads. Right in the very centre, in the top flat of a tall, rickety building that leant tiredly over a tiny square, lived the Belgian consul.

He was a sweet little man whose most striking attribute was a magnificent three-pointed beard and a carefully waxed moustache. He took his job rather seriously and was always dressed as though he were on the verge of rushing off to some important official function, in a black cut-away coat, striped trousers, fawn spats over brightly polished shoes, an immense cravat like a silk waterfall, held in place by a plain gold pin, and a tall and gleaming top hat that completed the **ensemble**.

One could see him at any hour of the day, clad like this, picking his way down the dirty, narrow alleys, stepping **daintily** among the puddles, drawing himself back against the wall with a magnificently courteous gesture to allow a donkey to pass and tapping it coyly on the rump with his Malacca cane. The people of the town did not find his garb at all unusual. They thought that he was an Englishman and as all Englishmen were lords it was not only right but necessary that they should wear the correct uniform.

Questions

(i) For each words given below choose the correct meaning (as used in the passage) from the options provided.

1. Ensemble (line 27)

(a) a piece of furniture (b) a group of people
(c) a collection of items (d) a type of building

2. Daintily (line 30)

(a) in a slow manner
(b) in a delicate or graceful manner
(c) in a careful manner
(d) in a carefree manner

(ii) Answer the following questions briefly in your own words.

1. Where was the Belgian Consul's house situated?
2. What made the area fascinating?
3. Why did he have to stand back against the wall to allow the donkeys to stagger past?
4. What made the streets noisy and busy?
5. Where did the Belgian Consul live?

(iii) Describe the man and his appearance in 50 words.

Answers

(i) 1. (c) a collection of items
2. (b) in a delicate or graceful manner

(ii) 1. The Belgian Consul's house was situated in the Jewish quarter of the town, in a maze of narrow, smelly alleyways.
2. The area was fascinating because the cobbled streets were filled with colourful stalls selling cloth, sweetmeats, ornaments, fruits and vegetables.
3. He had to stand back against the wall because the streets were very narrow, and donkeys, loaded with merchandise, had to pass through the alleyways.
4. The streets were noisy and busy due to the sounds of women bargaining, hens clucking, dogs barking and the cries of men carrying trays of fresh hot loaves.
5. The Belgian Consul lived in the top flat of a tall, rickety building in the centre of the Jewish quarter, which leant tiredly over a small square.

(iii)

The	man	was	sweet,	little
Belgian	consul	with	a	three-poi nted
beard	and	waxed	moustache.	He
dressed	formally	in	a	black
cut-away	coat,	stripped	trousers,	polished
shoes,	a	silk	cravat,	and
a	gleaming	top	hat.	He
carried	a	Malacca	cane	and
moved	daintily,	among	the	puddles
courteously	allowing	donkeys	to	pass.

Q.5 Read the following passage carefully and answer the questions that follow. **(ICSE 2024 Modified)**

Ashamanja Babu lived in a small flat in Bhowanipore. A Clerk in the registry department of Lajpat Rai Post office, Ashamanja Babu was fortunate as he could walk to his office in seven minutes flat without having to fight his way into the buses and trains of Calcutta.

He lived a rather carefree life as he was not the kind of person to sit and brood about what might have been had fate been kinder to him. On the whole, he was quite content with his lot. Two Hindi films and fish twice a week-these were enough to keep him happy. The only thing that week-these were enough to keep him happy. The only thing that **perturbed** him at times was his lack of companionship.

A bachelor with few friends and relatives, he often wished he had a dog to keep him company.

It need not be a huge Alsation like the one owned by the Talukdars, who lived two houses down the lane; it could be any ordinary little dog which would follow him around morning and evening, wag its tail when he came home from work and obey his orders faithfully.

Ashamanja Babu's secret desires were that he would speak to his dog in English, 'Stand up', 'Sit down', 'Shake hands' - How nice it would be if his dog obeyed such commands! That would make him really happy.

On a cloudy day marked by a steady drizzle, Ashamanja Babu went to the market in Hasimara to buy some oranges. At one end of the market, beside a **stunted** Kul tree, sat a man. As their eyes met, the man smiled. Was he a beggar? His clothes made him look like one.

Ashamanja Babu noticed at least five sewing-on patches on his trousers and jacket. But the man didn't have a begging bowl. Instead, by his side was a shoe - box with a little pup sticking its head out of it.

'Good morning!' said the man in English. Ashamanja Babu was obliged to return the greeting. 'Buy dog? Dog buy? Very good dog.' The man had taken the pup out of the box and had put it down on the ground. 'Very cheap. Very good. Happy dog?'

The pup shook the raindrops off its coat, looked at Ashamanja Babu and wagged its minuscule two inch tail. Ashamanja Babu moved closer to the pup.

Crouched on the ground and stretched out his hand. The pup gave his ring finger a lick with its pink tongue.

Nice, Friendly dog.

'How much? What price?'

'Ten rupees'

A little haggling and the price came down to seven rupees. Ashamanja Babu paid the money, put the pup back in the shoe box, closed the lid to save it for the drizzle, and turned homewards, forgetting all about the oranges.

—*Ashamanja Babu's Dog by Satyajit Ray.*

Questions

(i) For each word given below, choose the correct meaning (as used in the passage) from the options provided.

1. Perturbed (line 12)

(a) worried (b) unsettled
(c) happy (d) content

2. Stunted (line 28)

(a) prevented from growing
(b) full-grown
(c) decaying
(d) blooming

(ii) Which word in the passage means the opposite of the word 'expensive'?

(a) Costly (b) Valuable
(c) Cheap (d) Precious

(iii) Answer the following questions briefly in your own words.

(a) What kept Ashamanja Babu happy?
(b) What does this tell you about him?
(c) What is that one other thing he needed to complete his happiness?
(d) Why did Ashamanja Babu think the man was a beggar?
(e) Why did Ashamanja Babu forget about his oranges?

(iv) In not more than 50 words, narrate the series of events from the time the puppy was taken out of the box till it was paid for.

Answers

(i) 1. (b) unsettled 2. (a) prevented from growing

(ii) (c) Cheap

(iii) (a) Ashamanja Babu was happy with two Hindi films and fish twice a week. These simple pleasures were enough for him to feel content with his life.

(b) This shows that Ashamanja Babu was a simple, content person who did not require much to be happy. He found joy in small, everyday things and didn't worry much about what he lacked.

(c) The one thing Ashamanja Babu needed to complete his happiness was a dog to keep him company.

(d) Ashamanja Babu thought the man was a beggar because of his worn-out clothes with patches on them and his humble appearance. However, the man didn't have a begging bowl, which was unusual for a beggar.

(e) Ashamanja Babu forgot about his oranges because he became so engrossed in buying the puppy from the man that he completely lost track of his original intention to buy oranges.

(iv)

The	man	took	the	puppy
out	of	the	box	and
placed	it	on	the	ground.
Ashamanja	Babu	crouched	down,	stretched
out	his	hand	and	the
pup	licked	his	finger.	After
some	haggling,	the	price	reduced
to	seven	rupees.	Ashamanja	Babu
paid,	closed	the	box	and
walked	home	with	the	pup.

Q.6 Read the following passage carefully and answer the questions that follow. **(ICSE Specimen 2024)**

Tiger Talk

It was still a busy hour in the city when I entered market road. People ran for their lives at the sight of me. As I progressed through, shutters were pulled down and people hid themselves under culverts, on trees, behind pillars. The population was melting out of sight.

At the circus I had no chance to study human behaviour. Outside the circus ring they sat in their seats placidly while I cowered before Captain's whip. I got a totally wrong notion of human beings at that angle. I had thought that they were **sturdy** and fearless.

But now I found them fleeing before me like a herd of deer, although I had no intention of attacking them.

When I paused in front of a tailor's shop, he abandoned his machine and shut himself in a cupboard, wailing, 'Alas, I am undone, won't someone shoot that tiger?'

A prisoner between two constables, who had been caught for murder and was just emerging from the Court House, got his chance to escape when the constables fled, abandoning him with his handcuffs. I tore a horse from its jutka and enjoyed the sight of the passengers spilling out of it and running for their lives. A couple of street dogs invited destruction when they barked madly, instead of minding their business.

Later, I learnt from my master of the chaos that befell the city when it became known that Captain had been destroyed and that I was somewhere in the city. Sheer hopelessness seems to have seized the townspeople.

They withdrew to their homes and even there remained nervous. All doors and windows everywhere were shut, bolted and sealed Some even thought that I was some extraordinary creature who might pass through the walls and lie in wait on the roof or in the loft or **basement.**

Poor people living in huts had real cause to worry: I could have taken any of their homes apart. But why should I? One could understand their fears but why should those living in brick and cement feel nervous? It was due to their general lack of a sense of security and an irrational dread of losing their assets.

Why should a simple tiger have any interest in them either to destroy or to safeguard? I rested for a moment at the door of Anand Bhavan, on Market Road, where coffee drinkers and tiffin eaters at their tables sat transfixed, uttering low moans on seeing me.

I wanted to assure them, 'Don't fear, I am not out to trouble you. Eat your tiffin in peace, don't mind me ... you, nearest to me, hugging the cash box, you are craven with fear, afraid even to breathe. Go on, count the cash, if that's your pleasure. I just want to watch, that's all ... If my tail trails down to the street, if I am blocking your threshold, it is because, I'm told, I'm eleven feet tip to tail.

I can't help it. I'm not out to kill ... I'm too full- found a green pasture teeming with food on the way. Won't need any for several days to come, won't stir, not until I feel hungry again. Tigers attack only when they feel hungry, unlike human beings who slaughter one another without purpose or hunger ...'

— A Tiger in the School, R. K. Narayanan

Questions

(i) For each word given below choose the correct meaning (as used in the passage) from the options provided.

1. Sturdy (line 11)

(a) fragile (b) strong

(c) weak (d) unhealthy

2. Basement (line 37)

(a) attic (b) cellar

(c) a room at the bottom of the house

(d) living room

(ii) Which word in the passage means the opposite of the word 'liabilities'?

(a) Assets (b) Debts

(c) Risks (d) Obligations

(iii) Answer the following questions briefly in your own words.

(a) Which sentence in the passage tells us that the people were fast disappearing?

(b) Why was the prisoner lucky on that day?

(c) What reason does the tiger give to explain why people in brick and cement houses are nervous?

(d) The passage describes a man who is shivering with fear and clutching his cash box. What kind of a person do you think he was?

(e) How would you have reacted if a tiger walked into the street outside your school?

(iv) In not more than 50 words, describe the tiger's thoughts on how differently people behave inside and outside the circus.

Answers

(i) 1. (b) strong

2. (d) a room at the bottom of the house

(ii) (a) Assets

(iii) (a) 'The population was melting out of sight.'

(b) The prisoner was lucky because the constables, who were guarding him, fled when they saw the tiger, leaving him behind. This gave him the chance to escape.

(c) The tiger explains that people in brick and cement houses are nervous due to their general lack of a sense of security and an irrational fear of losing their possessions.

(d) The man appears to be a person who is fearful and overly concerned about his material possessions. He seems to lack courage, as he is terrified by the tiger despite it not posing any threat to him.

(e) If a tiger walked into the street outside my school, I would have been terrified and would likely have sought safety by getting inside a building.

(iv)

The	tiger	reflects	that	outside
the	circus,	people	were	fearful
and	fled	at	the	sight
of	him,	unlike	inside	the
circus,	where	they	sat	calmly
and	watched	him	perform.	He
realises	that	the	calm,	fearless
image	he	had	of	humans
was	wrong;	outside	the	circus,
they	were	quick	to	panic.

Q.7 Read the following passage carefully and answer the questions that follow. **(ICSE 2023)**

1 That huge bell never stopped ringing It got us out of bed, it **summoned** us for meals, it rang between class periods, it sent us unwillingly to bed.

2 One morning, it failed to ring or rather, there was no bell to ring. Someone had removed it and it wasn't found till late in the afternoon.

3 What a glorious day! As there was no bell to rouse us, everyone got up late and there was no morning PT. Some of us missed breakfast too. The teachers got confused and mixed up their classes. How could the school manage without it? Confusion reigned.

4 Of course, no one owned up. It could have meant expulsion. Some suspicion fell on the Sports Captain because of our **aversion** to morning PT but nothing could be proved.

5 No one was very anxious to find the bell - we were quite happy without it but it was finally discovered hanging from a branch of one of the trees.

6 'It may have been Mr. Sharma', surmised Brian. Mr. Sharma, our Maths teacher, was known to walk in his sleep. And sleepwalkers did funny things sometimes.

7 'It could be Mool Chand himself', suggested Cyrus Satralkar.

8 Mool Chand was the school chowkidar, who also had the job of banging the brass bell at appointed times. 'Why would he throw it away?'

9 'He must be as fed up with ringing it as we are of hearing it'. This was my theory. 'Perhaps, he wants a rise in salary'.

10 The identity of the culprit remained a mystery. Happily, the senior Hockey team went on a winning spree against all corners and our month-end exits were **restored**.

11 But soon there was another sensation.

12 A girl was admitted to our class!

13 The boys were scandalised. No girl had ever studied in our school before. We protested.

14 'What's the problem?' asked Mr. Knight, our class master. 'Haven't you seen a girl before?'

15 'But – but. Sir...' Tata was our spokesman. 'How will we concentrate on our studies?'

16 'When did you ever concentrate on your studies, Tata?'

17 'Are we going co-ed, sir?' Adams wanted to know.

18 'Not at all,' said Mr. Knight. 'This is a special case. She is the school accounts manager's daughter and he can't afford the Girls school fees. So, I'm sure you'll make her feel very welcome.'

19 The accountant was a popular man who also ran the school's tuck shop and allowed most of us a certain amount of credit. All our objections faded away.

20 At first, Sunita, our new entrant, was a bit of a distraction because, although she was very shy and demure, she had lovely curly hair, bright eyes, pink cheeks and a smile for everyone. All the boys were very polite and attentive to her and Brian in particular was always ready to help her.

– Collection of Stories, Ruskin Bond

Questions

(i) For each word given below, choose the correct meaning (as used in the passage) from the options provided.

1. Summoned (line 2)
(a) totalled (b) ordered
(c) requested (d) shout

2. Aversion (line 14)
(a) hatred (b) fear
(c) politeness (d) creation

3. Restored (line 33)
(a) helped (b) returned
(c) permit (d) victory

(ii) Answer the following questions briefly in your own words.

(a) Why did no one confess to having removed the missing bell?
(b) Why did suspicion fall on the Sports Captain?
(c) What made Brian think that it was Mr. Sharma?
(d) Which sentence in the passage tells you that Mr. Knight thought poorly of Tata's academic performance?
(e) Why was the accountant a popular man?

(iii) In not more than 50 words, describe the effects of the lost bell.

Answers

(i) 1. (b) ordered 2. (a) hatred
3. (b) returned

(ii) (a) No one confessed to having removed the missing bell because it would have meant expulsion from the school.
(b) Suspicion fell on the Sports Captain because of the students' aversion to morning PT.
(c) Brian thought that it was Mr. Sharma who had removed the bell because he was known to walk in his sleep and sleepwalkers did funny things.
(d) The sentence in the passage that tells us that Mr. Knight thought poorly of Tata's academic performance is: 'When did you ever concentrate on your studies, Tata?'
(e) The accountant was a popular man because he ran the school's tuck shop and allowed most of the students a certain amount of credit.

(iii)

The	lost	bell	brought	joy
to	students.	Without	it,	they
woke	up	late,	skipping	morning
PT.	The	schedule	collapsed,	children
missed	breakfast,	teachers	mixed	up
classes.	Chaos	spread	as	the
school	struggled	to	function	without
the	bell,	leading	to	widespread
confusion	and	disorder	throughout	the
day.	It	was	unforgettable	mayhem.

Q.8 Read the following passage carefully and answer the questions that follow. **(ICSE Specimen 2023, ICSE 2019)**

1 He would have gone on worrying and worrying in this way if an unexpected **distraction** had not arrived in the form of a heavily loaded car bumping over the grassy bank, dodging between the coconut trees and raising a cloud of dust in the narrow path before it came to a standstill in front of Mon Repos, the white bungalow that stood empty most of the year.

It was the de Silvas, the family that came from Bombay to spend an occasional holiday in it and bring it suddenly to life for a few days. They had bought Mon Repos a year ago from the Vakils who had been one of the first Bombay families to build holiday cottages on the Thul beach.

But they had grown too old and **frail** to come often and after the house has stood empty for several years, sold it to the de Silvas who were young and energetic and seemed heartily to enjoy life on the beach. Whenever they came, life changed for the family and the little hut, too. Immediately there was a hubbub, all kinds of excitement and expectations and of course work to be done, employment to be had and wages.

2 Hari, Bela and Kamal stood by their door under the frangipani tree, tense with excitement watching and holding Pinto back as he barked at the unfamiliar sight of a car and stranger till his voice was quite hoarse.

There was a commotion in the marshy creek that separated the hut from the house, too herons, egrets, kingfishers and moorhens all flapping into the **dense** greenery of the pandanus, the casuarina and the bhindi trees for shelter.

3 "Do you think they have come here for good?" Bela whispered.

4 "Hunh - who would live here if he had a house in Bombay?" Hari scoffed.

5 'But look how much luggage they've brought - it can't be just for a few days,' Bela said and it was true that an unbelievable number of boxes and bags and

baskets were being taken out of the car, out of the boot and off the luggage carrier so that anyone would have thought they had come to stay forever.

–Village by the Sea, Anita Desai

Questions

(i) For each word given below, choose the correct meaning (as used in the passage) from the options provided.

1. Distraction (line 2)

(a) something that stops you from thinking about something else

(b) something that helps you to think about something else

(c) something that you use for weight-training

(d) something that helps you to not be distracted

2. Frail (line 14)

(a) strong (b) funny (c) fast (d) weak

3. Dense (line 29)

(a) stupid (b) very thick

(c) a kind of tree (d) sparse

(ii) Answer the following questions briefly in your own words.

(a) Who were the Vakils?

(b) Why was the house more suited to the de Silvas?

(c) Who was Pinto?

(d) What effect did the noise have on the natural surrounding?

(e) From Hari's answer to Bela's question, what opinion does Hari have of Bombay?

(iii) In not more than 50 words, describe how the arrival of the de Silvas changed life for the family in the little hut.

Answers

(i) 1. (a) something that stops you from thinking about something else

2. (d) weak 3. (b) very thick

(ii) (a) The Vakils were one of the first Bombay families to build holiday cottages at the Thul beach.

(b) The house was more suited to the de Silvas because they were young and energetic and seemed to heartily enjoy life on the beach.

(c) Pinto was a pet dog that belonged to Hari, Bela or Kamal.

(d) The natural surrounding was disturbed by Pinto's barking. A commotion was caused in the creek that separated the hut from the house.

(e) Hari's opinion of Bombay is that the city is grand. He thinks that no person who has a house there would live anywhere else, especially the place he lived in.

(iii)

The	De Silvas'	arrival	disrupted	both
the	surroun-dings	and	the	hut's
family.	Their	visits	brought	commotion,
excitement	and	noise.	Family	members
anticipated	work,	seeing	it	as
a	chance	for	employm-ent	and
wages.	Every	visit	stirred	hope
and	activity,	making	their	presence
both	an	upheaval	and	a
promising	opportu-nity	for	their	livelihood.

Q.9 Read the following passage carefully and answer the questions that follow. **(ICSE Specimen 2022 Sem II)**

1 Father was standing in the small courtyard, wearing a dhoti and a banian, the dress which, for its very homeliness, Swaminathan **detested** to see him in; it indicated that he did not intend going out in the near future.

2 "Where are you going?"

3 "Nowhere."

4 "Where were you yesterday at this time?"

5 "Here."

6 "You are lying. You were not here yesterday. And you are not going out now."

7 "That is right," Mother added, just appearing from somewhere, "there is no limit to his loafing in the Sun. He will die of sunstroke if he keeps on like this." Father would have gone on forever without Mother's encouragement. But now her words spurred him to action. Swaminathan was asked to follow him to his 'room' in his father's dressing-room.

8 "How many days is it since you have touched your books?" Father asked as he blew off the fine layer of dust on Swaminathan's books and cleared the web that an industrious spider was weaving between a corner of the table and the pile of books.

9 Swaminathan viewed this question as a gross breach of promise.

10 "Should I read even when I have no school?"

11 "Do you think you have passed the B.A.?" Father asked.

12 "I mean, Father, when the school is closed, when there is no examination, even then should I read?"

13 "What a question! You must read."

14 "But Father, you said before the examinations that I needn't read after they were over. Even Rajam does not read." As he uttered the last sentence, he tried to believe it; he clearly remembered Rajan's

complaining bitterly of a home tutor who came and **pestered** him for two hours a day thrice a week.

15 Father was apparently deaf to Swaminathan's remarks. He stood over Swaminathan and set him to dust his books and clean his table. Swaminathan vigorously started blowing off the dust from the book covers.

He caught the spider carefully and took it to the window to throw it out. He held it outside the window and watched it for a while. It was swinging from a strand that gleamed in a hundred delicate tints.

16 "Look sharp! Do you want a whole day to throw out the spider?" Father asked. Swaminathan suddenly realised that he might have the spider as his pet and that it would be a criminal waste to throw it out.

He secretly slipped it into his pocket and, after shaking an empty hand outside the window, returned to his duty at the desk.

17 "Look at the way you have kept your English text! Are you not ashamed of yourself?" Swaminathan picked up the oily red-bound Fourth Reader, opened it, and banged together the covers in order to shake off the dust and then rubbed **violently** the oily covers with his palm.

18 "Get a piece of cloth, boy. That is not the way to clean things. Get a piece of cloth, Swami," Father said, half kindly and half impatiently.

19 Swaminathan looked about and complained, "I can't find any here, father."

20 "Run and see."

This was a welcome suggestion. Swaminathan hurried out. He first went to his grandmother.

"Granny, get me a piece of cloth, quick."

Questions

(i) For each word given below, choose the correct meaning (as used in the passage) from the options provided.

1. Detested (line 3)

(a) detention (b) detained

(c) hateful (d) hated

2. Pestered (line 37)

(a) tiny insect (b) botheration

(c) annoyed (d) annoyance

3. Violently (line 58)

(a) cruelly

(b) with great energy

(c) loudly

(d) with a lot of noise

(ii) Answer the following questions briefly in your own words.

(a) What did father's clothes show?

(b) How did mother encourage father?

(c) What did the dust on Swami's book indicate?

(d) The author says that the father spoke 'half kindly and half impatiently'. What does it indicate?

(e) What attracted Swami to the spider? What does he do with the spider?

(iii) **In not more than 50 words, describe how Swami dealt with the spider.**

Answers

(i) 1. (d) hated

2. (c) annoyed

3. (b) with great energy

(ii) (a) Father's clothes showed that he was planning to stay at home.

(b) Mother encouraged father by complaining about Swami. She said that Swami loafed in the Sun the entire day.

(c) The dust on Swami's books indicated that Swami had not touched his books in a long while.

(d) The author's statement that his father spoke 'half kindly and half impatiently' shows that his father was really angry.

(e) Swami was attracted to the spider because of the colour of its thread. He does not throw the spider away; rather, keeps it hidden in his pocket.

(iii)

After	Swami	caught	the	spider,
he	took	it	to	the
window.	As	he	held	the
spider,	he	watched	it	along
with	its	thread	which	was
shining	in	different	colours.	He
did	not	want	to	throw
it	away.	So,	he	hid
the	spider	in	his	pocket
to	make	it	his	pet.

Q.10 Read the following passage carefully and answer the questions that follow. **(ICSE 2020 Modified)**

1 Attending classes inside a railway carriage seemed unusual enough but the seating arrangements turned out to be unusual, too. At Totto-chan's previous school, each pupil was **assigned** a specific desk.

But here they could sit anywhere they liked at any time. However, the most unusual thing of all about this school were the lessons themselves.

2 Schools normally schedule one subject, for example history, during the first period, when everyone in the class just did history; then say, arithmetic in the second period, when you just did arithmetic. But here it was quite different.

At the beginning of the first period, the teacher made a list of all the problems and questions in the subjects to be studied that day.

Then, she would say, "Now, start with any of these you like."

3 So, whether you started on history or arithmetic or something else didn't matter at all. Someone who liked composition might be writing something, while behind you someone who liked chemistry might be boiling something in a flask over an alcohol burner.

This method of teaching enabled the teachers to observe as the children progressed to higher grades, what they were interested in as well as their way of thinking and their character.

It was an **ideal** way for teachers to really get to know their pupils.

4 As for the pupils, they loved being able to start with their favourite subject, the fact that they had all day to cope with the subjects they disliked meant they could usually manage them somehow.

So, study was mostly independent, with pupils free to go and consult the teacher whenever necessary. Then, pupils would be given further exercises to work at alone. It was study in the truest sense of the word, and it meant there were no pupils just sitting inattentively while the teacher talked and explained.

5 The first-grade pupils hadn't quite reached the stage of **independent** study, but even they were allowed to start with any subject they wanted. Some copied letters of the alphabet, some drew pictures, some read books and some even did physical exercises.

Just then, the boy sitting behind her got up and walked toward the blackboard with his notebook, apparently to consult the teacher.

6 Totto-chan stopped looking around the room and fixed her eyes on his back as he walked. The boy dragged his leg and his whole body swayed from side to side. Totto-chan wondered at first if he was doing it on purpose but she soon realised the boy couldn't help it.

7 The boy said brightly, "My name's Yasuaki. What's yours?" She was so glad to hear him speak that she replied loudly, "I'm Totto-chan."

–Adapted from Totto-chan

Questions

(i) For each word given below, choose the correct meaning (as used in the passage) from the options provided.

1. Assigned (line 4)

(a) allotted (b) provided
(c) given (d) attached

2. Ideal (line 27)

(a) great (b) perfect
(c) appropriate (d) general

3. Independent (line 40)

(a) available (b) free
(c) unbound (d) limited

(ii) Answer the following questions briefly in your own words.

(a) What was unusual about the seating arrangement?

(b) How did the method of teaching help the teacher?

(c) Why did the pupils enjoy their lessons at this school?

(d) What different things did the first-grade pupils do?

(e) Which sentence in the passage tells us that the boy had difficulty walking like the other children?

(iii) In not more than 50 words, describe how the children were taught.

Answers

(i) 1. (a) allotted
2. (c) appropriate
3. (b) free

(ii) (a) In contrast with the normal seating arrangement where every student is allotted a designated place to sit, the students in this school could sit wherever they liked at anytime.

(b) As the children studied their favourite subjects, the teachers had a lot of time to observe them and find out more about their interests, their way of thinking and their character. This way the teachers got to know the students well enough to help them go ahead in their studies.

(c) The pupil enjoyed their lessons at this school because they could begin their day by studying their favourite subject. In this way, they could also save the rest of the day to cope up with the subjects they found difficult.

(d) The first grade pupils were not allowed to study independently but were allowed to start with the subject of their choice. So, some of them wrote alphabet, some drew pictures, the others read books and some of them did physical exercises.

(e) "The boy dragged his leg, and his whole body swayed from side to side." This sentence tells us that the boy had difficulty walking like the other children.

(iii)

The	teacher	made	the	list
of	all	the	topics	to
be	studied	that	day.	The
children	were	then	allowed	to
begin	the	day	with	the
subject	of	their	own	choice.
They	could	discuss	their	difficulties
with	the	teachers	anytime	they
liked.	The	first	grade	pupils
also	followed	the	same	practice.

Q.11 Read the following passage carefully and answer the questions that follow. **(ICSE 2019 Modified)**

1 Billy Weaver had travelled down from London and by the time he arrived it was nine o'clock in the night and the moon was coming up.

2 "Excuse me," he asked a porter "but is there a cheap hotel nearby?"

3 "Try The Bell Hotel," the porter answered, pointing down the road.

4 Billy thanked him, picked up his suitcase and set out to walk the distance to The Bell Hotel. He had never been to Richmond before. But the man at the Office had told him it was a **splendid** city.

Billy was seventeen years old. He was wearing a new navy-blue overcoat, a new brown hat and a new brown suit and he was feeling fine. He walked briskly down the street.

5 He was trying to do everything briskly these days. The big shots up at the Head Office were fantastically brisk all the time. They were amazing.

The road was lonely and dark with a few scattered houses.

Suddenly, in a downstairs window, Billy saw a printed notice propped up against the window glass. It said Bed and Breakfast.

6 He moved a bit closer and peered through the window into the room and the first thing he saw was a bright fire burning in the hearth. On the carpet in front of the fire, a little dog was curled up asleep with its nose tucked into its belly.

The room in half-darkness was filled with pleasant furniture. There was a Piano and a big sofa and several plump armchairs; and in one corner he **spotted** a large parrot in a cage. Animals were usually
7 a good sign in a place like this, Billy told himself and it looked to him as though it would be a pretty decent house to stay in.

8 Then, a queer thing happened to him. He was in the act of stepping back and going away from the window when he felt a strange urge to ring the bell!

9 He pressed the bell. He heard it ringing and then at once the door swung open and a woman was standing there.

10 She gave him a warm welcoming smile.

11 "Please come in," she said pleasantly.

Billy found himself **automatically** moving forward into the house.

12 "I saw the notice in the window," he said, holding himself back.

13 "Yes, I know."

14 "I was wondering about a room."

15 "It's all ready for you, my dear," she said. She had a round pink face and very gentle blue eyes.

16 "How much do you charge?"

17 "Five dollars a night, including breakfast."

18 It was fantastically cheap. He could easily afford it.

Questions

(i) For each word given below, choose the correct meaning (as used in the passage) from the options provided.

1. Splendid (line 11)

(a) beautiful (b) ideal
(c) excellent (d) humongous

2. Spotted (line 32)

(a) attended (b) gazed
(c) drew (d) noticed

3. Automatically (line 44)

(a) instinctively
(b) justly
(c) usually
(d) after great thinking

(ii) Answer the following questions briefly in your own words.

(a) How did the porter assist Billy?
(b) Why did Billy want to do everything briskly?
(c) Why did Billy think animals were a good sign in a place like this?
(d) Which sentence tells you that something strange happened to Billy?
(e) How much did the room cost?

(iii) In not more than 50 words, give a brief account of what Billy saw as he looked through the window of the room.

Answers

(i) 1. (c) excellent
2. (d) noticed
3. (a) instinctively

(ii) (a) The porter assisted Billy by guiding him to 'The Bell Hotel' when Billy asked him whether there was any cheap hotel nearby.

(b) Billy wanted to do everything briskly because he admired the senior officers at the Head Office who also did everything briskly.

(c) Billy thought that animals were a good sign in a place like this because the road was lonely and dark. Further, the pet animals there made him feel that it would be a decent place to live in.

(d) The sentence which tells us that something strange happened to Billy begins in line 24 with the words, "Then, a queer .... ."

(e) The room cost five dollars a night, including breakfast.

(iii)

When	Billy	looked	through	the
window,	he	saw	a	bright
fire	burning	in	the	hearth
with	a	little	dog	asleep
on	the	carpet	in	front
of	it.	The	room's	furniture
included	a	piano,	a	big
sofa	and	several	plump	armchairs.
A	large	parrot	was	in
a	cage	in	one	corner.

Q.12 Read the following passage carefully and answer the questions that follow. **(ICSE 2018 Modified)**

1 Granny knew I'd been in the train for two nights and she had a huge breakfast ready for me.

2 Later, she told me there'd been a letter from Uncle Ken.

3 'He says he's the manager in Firpo's hotel in Simla,' she said. 'The salary is very good. It's a steady job and I hope he keeps it'.

4 Three days later, Uncle Ken was on the veranda steps with his bedding roll and **battered** suitcase.

5 'Have you given up the hotel job?' asked Granny.

'No,' said Uncle Ken. 'They have closed down.'

6 'I hope it wasn't because of you.'

7 'No, Aunt Ellen. The bigger hotels in the hill stations are closing down.'

8 'Well, never mind. Come along and have your lunch.'

9 Over lunch, Uncle Ken talked very seriously about ways and means of earning a living.

10 'There is only one taxi in the whole of Dehra', he **mused**. 'Surely, there is business for another?'

11 'I'm sure there is,' said Granny. 'But where does it get you? In the first place, you don't have a taxi. And in the second place, you can't drive.'

12 'I can soon learn. There's a driving school in town. And I can use Uncle's old car.'

'I don't think it will run now,' said Granny.

13 'Of course, it will. It just needs some oiling and greasing and a spot of paint.'

14 'All right, learn to drive.'

So, Uncle Ken joined the driving school.

15 After a month, Uncle Ken announced that he could drive and that he was taking the car out for a trial run.

16 'You haven't got your license yet,' said Granny.

17 'Oh, I won't take it far,' said Uncle Ken. 'Just down the road and back again.'

18 He spent all morning cleaning up the car. Granny gave him money for a can of petrol.

19 After tea, Uncle Ken said, 'Come along, Ruskin, hop in and I will give you a ride. Bring Mohan along too.'

20 'Mohan and I needed no urging. We got into the car beside Uncle Ken.

21 'Now don't go too fast, Ken,' said Granny anxiously. 'You are not used to the car as yet.'

22 Uncle Ken nodded and smiled and gave two sharp toots on the horn. He was feeling pleased with himself.

23 Driving through the gate, he nearly ran over a cat. Miss Kellner, coming out for her evening rickshaw ride, saw Uncle Ken at the wheel of the car and ran indoors again.

24 Uncle Ken drove straight and fast tootling the horn without a break.

25 At the end of the road there was a roundabout.

26 'We'll turn here,' said Uncle Ken 'and then drive back again.'

27 He turned the steering wheel, we began going round the roundabout but the steering wheel wouldn't turn all the way, not as much as Uncle Ken would have liked it to......

28 So, instead he went on-and straight through the Maharaja of Jetpur's garden wall.

29 It was a single-brick wall and the car knocked it down and **emerged** on the other side without any damage to the car or any of its occupants. Uncle Ken brought it to a halt in the middle of the Maharaja's lawn.

30 Running across the grass came the Maharaja himself. When he saw that it was Uncle Ken at the wheel, the Maharaja beamed with pleasure.

31 'Delighted to see you, old chap!' he exclaimed. 'Jolly decent of you to drop in again. How about a game of tennis?'

Questions

(i) For each word given below, choose the correct meaning (as used in the passage) from the options provided.

1. Battered (line 9)

(a) worn out (b) damaged
(c) thrown (d) filled

2. Mused (line 19)

(a) said funnily (b) said thoughtfully
(c) said sarcastically (d) said sadly

3. Emerged (line 62)

(a) entered (b) exited
(c) joined (d) to come out

(ii) Answer the following questions briefly in your own words.

(a) Why did Granny hope Uncle Ken would keep his job at Firpo's hotel?

(b) When Uncle Ken arrived with his luggage, Granny remarked that she hoped the hotel had not closed down because of him. What does this remark tell you about Uncle Ken?

(c) Why did Uncle Ken think that driving a taxi in Dehra would be profitable?

(d) Which sentence tells you that the narrator and his friend were waiting to be invited for a drive in a car?

(e) Why did Miss Kellner run indoors when she saw Uncle Ken at the wheel of the car?

(iii) In not more than 50 words, describe what happened after the car went through the wall.

Answers

(i) 1. (a) worn out 2. (b) said thoughtfully
3. (d) to come out

(ii) (a) Granny hoped that Uncle Ken would keep his job at Firpo's hotel as it was a steady job with a good salary.

(b) This remark tells us about Uncle Ken that he was not good at work or maybe he had created some problem due to which the hotel had closed down.

(c) Uncle Ken thought that driving a taxi in Dehra would be profitable because there was only one taxi service in the whole of Dehra; thus, there was enough business for another.

(d) The sentence which tells us this is : Mohan and I needed no urging.

(e) Miss Kellner had seen Uncle Ken nearly running over a cat, so she was afraid for her own safety. Thus, she ran indoors when she saw Uncle Ken at the wheel of the car.

(iii)

Uncle	Ken	stopped	the	car
in	the	middle	of	Maharaja's
lawn.	Seeing	this,	Maharaja	came
running	to	see	what	had
happened.	When	he	saw	it
was	Uncle	Ken,	whom	he
knew,	he	remarked	that	he
was	delighted	to	see	his
friend	and	would	like	to
play	a	game	of	tennis.

Q.13 Read the following passage carefully and answer the questions that follow. **(ICSE 2017 Modified)**

1 Every Monday, on his way back from work, Bipin Chowdhury would drop in at new market to buy books. He had to buy at least five at a time to last him through the week. He lived alone, was not a good mixer, had few friends and didn't like spending time in idle chat.

Those who called in the evening got through their business quickly and left. Those who didn't show signs of leaving would be told around eight o'clock by Bipin Babu that he was under doctor's orders to have dinner at eight-thirty.

After dinner, he would rest for half an hour and then turn in with a book. This was a routine which had **persisted** unbroken for years.

2 Today, Bipin Babu had the feeling that someone was observing him from close quarters. He turned round and found himself looking at a round-faced, meek-looking man who now broke into a smile.

3 'I don't suppose you recognise me.'

4 Bipin Babu felt ill at ease. It didn't seem that he had ever encountered this man before. The face seemed quite unfamiliar.

5 'Have we met before?' asked Bipin Babu.

6 The man looked greatly surprised. 'We met every day for a whole week. I arranged for a car to take you to the Hudroo falls. My name is Parimal Ghose.'

7 'Ranchi?'

8 Now Bipin Babu realised this man was making a mistake. Bipin Babu had never been to Ranchi. He smiled and said, 'Do you know who I am?'

9 The man raised his eyebrows and said, 'Who doesn't know Bipin Chowdhury?'

10 Bipin Babu turned towards the bookshelves and said, 'You're making a mistake. I've never been to Ranchi.'

11 The man now laughed aloud.

12 What are you saying, Mr. Chowdhury? You had a fall in Hudroo and cut your right knee. I brought you iodine. I had fixed up a car for you to go to Netarhat the next day but you couldn't because of the pain in the knee.

Can't you recall anything? Someone else you know was also in Ranchi at that time, Mr Dinesh Mukherjee. You stayed in a bungalow. You said, you didn't like hotel food. I'll tell you more: you always carried a bag with your books in it on your sightseeing trips. Am I right or not?

13 Bipin Babu spoke quietly, his eyes still on the books.

14 'Which month in Nineteen fifty-eight are you talking about?'

15 The man said, 'October.'

16 'No, sir,' said Bipin Babu. 'I spent October nineteen fifty-eight with a friend in Kanpur. You're making a mistake. Good day.'

17 But the man didn't go nor did he stop talking.

18 'Very strange. One evening I had tea with you on the veranda of your bungalow. You spoke about your family. You said, you had no children and that you had lost your wife a **decade** ago.'

19 When Bipin Babu had paid for the books and was leaving the shop, the man was still looking at him in utter disbelief.

20 Bipin Babu's car was safely parked in Bertram street. He told the driver as he got into the car, 'Just drive by the Ganga, will you, Sitaram.' Driving up the Strand Road, Bipin Babu regretted having paid so much attention to the **intruder**. He had never been to Ranchi. He had an excellent memory.

21 Unless he was losing his mind!

Questions

(i) For each word given below, choose the correct meaning (as used in the passage) from the options provided.

1. Persisted (line 14)

(a) accepted (b) forced (c) continued (d) stated

2. Decade (line 58)

(a) a period of ten years
(b) a period of fifty years
(c) a period of five years
(d) a period of indefinite time

3. Intruder (line 66)

(a) criminal (b) trespasser
(c) interferer (d) joker

(ii) Answer the following questions briefly in your own words.

(a) How did Bipin Chowdhury find time to read five books a week?

(b) How did he get rid of visitors who stayed late?

(c) Which sentence tells you that Bipin was uncomfortable?

(d) What strong argument did Bipin Babu give to prove that he was not in Ranchi at that time?

(e) What does Bipin Babu regret?

(iii) What memories of the trip does Parimal Ghose evoke to prove that Bipin Babu was indeed in Ranchi? Answer in not more than 50 words.

Answers

(i) 1. (c) continued 2. (a) a period of ten years
3. (b) trespasser

(ii) (a) Bipin Chowdhury found time to read five books a week as every day after dinner at eight thirty he would pick up a book to read and finish it before he went off to sleep.

(b) He used to get rid of visitors who stayed late by telling them that he was under doctor's order to have dinner at eight-thirty and he could no longer spend time with them.

(c) The sentence 'Bipin Babu fell ill at ease' tells us that he felt uncomfortable.

(d) The strong argument given by Bipin Babu was that in October 1958, he was with a friend in Kanpur. He said that he had never been to Ranchi.

(e) Bipin Babu regrets having paid so much attention to the stranger who was giving false claims of having met him.

(iii)

Parimal	Ghose	reminded	Bipin	Babu
of	arranging	a	car	for
him	in	Ranchi,	October	1958.
He	recalled	bringing	iodine	for
Bipin's	injured	knee	after	all
in	Hudroo.	Parimal	also	mentio ned
Bipin's	strong	dislike	for	hotel
food	and	his	habit	of
always	carrying	a	bag	filled
with	books	on	sightseeing	trips.

Q.14 Read the following passage carefully and answer the questions that follow. **(ICSE Specimen 2017)**

1 My husband Pele and I were staying in a holiday house overlooking the beautiful, lush rainforests of Indonesia. The glass walls framed a fine view across the Bagon Valley to what had been the summer palace of President Suharto.

2 The first morning we **strolled** hand-in-hand up a winding pathway, heading to the main building for

breakfast. But once we arrived at the dinning room, I realised we'd forgotten our money, so I volunteered to run back to the house.

Making my way down the path, I turned the last corner only to find a giant bird, similar to an emu, standing outside our front door.

3 "Hey baby, what are you doing?" I cooed, moving slowly so as not to frighten it.

4 Having a deep, abiding **fascination** with all creatures great and small, I wanted a closer look. This was my first mistake.

5 As I came within a few meters, he took a big breath and let out a nasty hiss, stopping me in my tracks.

6 "That's not very friendly," I said, clueless. He hissed again and I promptly made the second mistake of turning and running, instead of backing away slowly. As I rounded the corner, I heard his razor-sharp claws scrabbling on the cobblestones.

7 "Oh!"

8 His steps sounded like a drum as they hit the ground, quickly coming too close for comfort. I suddenly changed direction and headed into the trees. Dodged in and out of the **foliage**. I hoped my tactic would fool him. A crash behind me indicated no such luck.

9 Jumping over a small bush, I found myself out in the open and not far from the dining room. Picking up speed, I bolted over the plants and rockeries surrounding the perimeter and dashed through the gate. When I turned to close it, the bird was nowhere to be seen.

10 I didn't realise it at the time but I had just come face-to-face with a cassowary, a bird also found in Australia's North Queensland rainforests. Cassowarys weigh 55 kilos or more, stand about 180 centimeters tall and have saber-like toenails that can open a human from chin to groin like a zipper and kill humans.

11 "What's wrong?" Pele asked as I stumbled back into the dining room.

12 "A big bird chased me all the way from the house," I replied.

13 "What?" he asked incredulously. "You're scared of a bird?"

14 "It's as big as me and very mean," I said in a rather sulky voice.

15 "Oh, all right," he laughed. "I'll come with you."

16 Much to Pele's amusement, I stayed behind him on the path and held onto the back of his shirt as we approached the corner of the house.

17 "See! There it is. Look at the size of the thing!"

18 Pele chuckled at the hysteria in my voice. "It's all right," he soothed.

19 Calmly and confidently he walked toward the cassowary.

20 "Shoo! Go on, get out," he said.

21 He made actions with his arms as if it were a pigeon on a window ledge. The response of the cassowary was the same as before: a big hiss and a step forward.

22 "Hmm," said Pele and stopped, not so sure of himself. He tried again. "Go on."

23 The cassowary then ran a few paces at us, hissing aggressively, so we quickly retreated around a corner of the house. Pele picked up a rock the size of his hand and threw it hard, hitting the bird squarely in the chest. It didn't budge.

24 "What are we going to do?" I pleaded. This time, Pele picked up a cane chair.

25 "Stay behind and I'll keep him back. When we get to the door, open it."

26 Again, I held on to the back of his shirt and we started towards the door. This greatly displeased the already annoyed cassowary. Charging at us he ripped at the chair with those lethal claws. Pele stopped to steady the chair - and possibly his resolve.

27 Pele threw the chair at the bird and slammed the door shut.

28 Ducking the flying cane, the bird ran straight at the glass wall, only to bounce off.

29 But it didn't slow down at all. Pecking and scratching at the glass, it continued the assault with a sickening ferocity.

30 It was another 15 minutes before the bird weakened and slowed its attack. Thirty minutes later, we quietly opened the door and crept back to the main building.

Questions

(i) For each word given below, choose the correct meaning (as used in the passage) from the options provided.

1. Strolled (line 6)

(a) walk in a leisurely way (b) run
(c) walk with a limp (d) jog slowly

2. Fascination (line 16)

(a) repulsed by something
(b) the desire to want something
(c) attract interest towards something
(d) search for something

3. Foliage (line 30)

(a) the leaves of a plant or tree
(b) forest
(c) a patterned placement of flowers
(d) grassy land

(ii) Answer the following questions briefly in your own words.

(a) What was Pele's wife's first mistake when she saw the bird?

(b) How did the bird react to the lady's third mistake?

(c) What did she do after this reaction of the bird?

(d) Describe the Cassowary.

(e) Why did Pele find the situation amusing at first? Why did he change his attitude?

(iii) With close reference to the last paragraph of the extract and in not more than 50 words, describe how the couple got into their room when they were together.

Answers

(i) 1. (a) walk in a leisurely way

2. (c) attract interest towards something

3. (a) the leaves of a plant or tree

(ii) (a) Pele's wife's first mistake after seeing the bird was to come near it to have a closer look at it.

(b) The bird got more aggressive with the lady's actions and mistakes.

(c) As she saw the bird running aggressively after her, the lady speedily ran towards the dining room and shut its door.

(d) Cassowary is a bird found in Australia's North Queensland rainforests. They weigh 55 kilos or more, stand about 180 centimeters tall and have saber-like toenails that can open a human from chin to groin like a zipper and kill them.

(e) Pele found the situation amusing at first because he felt that his wife was getting scared of a bird which could not harm them in any way.

He changed his attitude when he realised that the bird was not friendly but was hostile to their advances. It aggressively reacted to their presence and was running after them.

(iii)

When	the	couple	encountered	the
cassowary,	it	reacted	aggressively,	hissing
and	stalking	towards	them.	Scared,
Pele	threw	a	rock	but
it	failed	to	stop	the
bird.	Using	a	chair	as
a	shield,	they	ran	to
their	room.	As	it	clawed
the	chair,	Pele	threw	it
and	quickly	shut	the	door.

Q.15 Read the following passage carefully and answer the questions that follow. **(ICSE 2016 Modified)**

1 For some time, Mother had greatly envied us our swimming, both in the daytime and at night, but as she pointed out when we suggested she join us, she was far too old for that sort of thing.

Eventually, however, under constant pressure from us, Mother paid a visit into town and returned to the villa coyly bearing a mysterious parcel. Opening this, she astonished us all by holding up an extraordinary shapeless garment of black cloth, covered from top to bottom with hundreds of frills and pleats and tucks.

2 'Well, what do you think of it?' Mother asked.

3 We started at the odd garment and wondered what it was for.

4 'What is it?' asked Larry at length.

5 'It's a bathing-costume, of course', said Mother. 'What on Earth did you think it was?'

6 'It looks to me like a badly-skinned whale,' said Larry, **peering** at it closely.

7 'You can't possibly wear that, Mother,' said Margo, horrified, 'why, it looks as though it was made in nineteen-twenty.'

8 'What are all those frills and things for?' asked Larry with interest.

9 'Decoration, of course', said Mother indignantly.

10 'What a jolly idea! Don't forget to shake the fish out of them when you come out of the water.'

11 'Well, I like it, anyway,' Mother said firmly, wrapping the monstrosity up again 'and I'm going to wear it.'

12 'You'll have to be careful you don't get waterlogged, with all that cloth around you,' said Leslie seriously.

13 'Mother, it's awful; you can't wear it,' said Margo. 'Why on Earth didn't you get something more up-to-date?'

14 'When you get to my age, dear, you can't go around in a two-piece bathing suit ... you don't have the figure for it.'

15 'I'd love to know what sort of figure that was designed for,' remarked Larry.

16 'You really are hopeless, Mother,' said Margo despairingly.

17 'But I like it ... and I'm not asking you to wear it,' Mother pointed out angrily.

18 'That's right, you do what you want to do,' agreed Larry, 'don't be put off. It'll probably suit you very well if you can grow another three or four legs to go with it.'

19 Mother snorted indignantly and swept upstairs to try on her costume. Presently, she called to us to come and see the effect and we all trooped up to the bedroom. Roger the dog was the first to enter and on being greeted by this strange apparition clad in its voluminous black costume rippling with frills, he retreated hurriedly through the door, backwards, barking **ferociously**.

It was some time before we could persuade him that it really was Mother and even then he kept giving her vaguely uncertain looks from the corner of his eye. However, in spite of all opposition, Mother stuck to her tent-like bathing-suit and in the end we gave up.

20 In order to celebrate her first entry into the sea, we decided to have a moonlight picnic down at the bay, and sent an invitation to Theodore, who was the only stranger that Mother would tolerate on such a great occasion.

The day for the great **immersion** arrived, food and wine were prepared, the boat was cleaned out and filled with cushions and everything was ready when Theodore turned up.

Questions

(i) For each word given below, choose the correct meaning (as used in the passage) from the options provided.

1. Peering (line 18)
(a) stalking (b) looking
(c) nooding (d) scolding

2. Ferociously (line 54)
(a) angrily (b) aggressively
(c) violently (d) All of these

3. Immersion (line 65)
(a) drown (b) put in water
(c) overwhelm (d) confuse

(ii) Answer the following questions briefly in your own words.

(a) Why did mother not join swimming in the beginning?
(b) Briefly describe mother's swimming costume.
(c) What did Larry think it was?
(d) Which sentence tells you that Margo thought it was old-fashioned?
(e) What was Leslie's concern?

(iii) In not more than 50 words, describe what happened after mother went upstairs to try on her costume.

Answers

(i) 1. (b) looking 2. (d) All of these
3. (b) put in water

(ii) (a) Mother did not join swimming in the beginning as she was far too old for that sort of thing.
(b) The swimming costume was an extraordinary shapeless garment of cloth covered from top to bottom with hundreds of frills, pleats and tucks.
(c) Larry thought it was a badly-skinned whale.
(d) The sentence, "Why on Earth didn't you get something more up to date?" tells us that Margo thought it was old-fashioned.
(e) Leslie was concerned that their mother might get waterlogged with all that cloth around her.

(iii)

After	mother	went	upstairs	to
try	on	her	costume,	she
called	them	to	see	the
effect.	Roger,	the	dog,	entered
first	but	was	so	shocked
by	her	appearance	that	he
ran	away,	unrecognising	her.	Despite
opposition	from	the	family,	mother
stuck	to	her	bathing	suit
and	eventually,	they	accepted	it.

Q.16 Read the following passage carefully and answer the questions that follow. **(ICSE 2015 Modified)**

1 Lying in bed, Swami realised with a shudder that it was Monday morning. It looked as though only a moment ago it had been the last period on Friday; already Monday was here. He hoped that an earthquake would reduce the school building to dust but that good building–Albert Mission School had withstood similar prayers for over a hundred years now.

At nine o'clock Swaminathan wailed, "I have a headache." His mother said, "Why don't you go to school in a bullock cart?"

2 "So that I may be completely dead at the other end? Have you any idea what it means to be **jolted** in a cart?"

"Have you any important lessons today?"

3 "Important! Bah! That geography teacher has been teaching the same lesson for over a year now and we have arithmetic, which means for a whole period we are going to be beaten by the teacher.... Important lessons!"

4 And mother generously suggested that Swami might stay at home.

5 At 9:30, when he ought to have been lining up in the school prayer hall, Swami was lying on the bench in Mother's room. Father asked him, "Have you no school today?"

6 "Headache," Swami replied.

7 "Nonsense! Dress up and go."

8 "Headache."

9 "Loaf about less on Sundays and you will be without a headache on Monday."

10 Swami knew how **stubborn** his father could be and changed his tactics. "I cannot go so late to class."

11 "I agree but you' ll have to; it is your own fault. You should have asked me before deciding to stay away."

12 "What will the teacher think if I go so late?"

13 "Tell him you had a headache and so are late."

14 "He will beat me if I say so."

15 "Will he? Let us see. What is his name?"

16 "Mr. Samuel."

17 "Does he beat the boys?"

18 "He is very violent, especially with boys who come late. Some days ago, a boy was made to stay on his knees for a whole period in a corner of the class because he came late and that after getting six cuts from the cane and having his ears twisted, I wouldn't like to go late to Mr. Samuel's class."

19 "If he is so violent, why not tell your headmaster about it?"

20 "They say that even the headmaster is afraid of him. He is such a violent man."

21 And then, Swami gave a lurid account of Samuel's violence; how when he started caning, he would not stop till he saw blood on the boy's hand, which he made the boy press to his forehead like a vermillion marking. Swami hoped that his father would be made to see that he couldn't go to his class late. But Father's behaviour took an unexcepted turn. He became excited. "What do these people mean by beating our children? They must be driven out of service. I will see..."

22 The result was he proposed to send Swami late to his class as a kind of challenge. He was also going to send a letter with Swami to the headmaster. No amount of protest from Swami was of any **avail**. Swami had to go to school.

23 By the time he was ready Father had composed a long letter to the headmaster, put in an envelope and sealed it.

24 "What have you written Father?" Swaminathan asked apprehensively.

25 "Nothing for you. Give it to your headmaster and go to your class."

26 Swami's father did not know the truth, that actually Mr. Samuel was a very kind and gentle man.

Questions

(i) For each word given below, choose the correct meaning (as used in the passage) from the options provided.

1. Jolted (line 12)

(a) shaken (b) doubtful
(c) confused (d) irritated

2. Stubborn (line 31)

(a) angry (b) adamant
(c) accurate (d) admirable

3. Avail (line 64)

(a) join (b) agree
(c) use (d) find

(ii) Answer the following questions briefly in your own words.

(a) What did Swami wish for a Monday morning? Why was his wish unlikely to be answered?

(b) Which sentence tells us that Swami's father was completely unsympathetic to his son's headache?

(c) In what way was Swami's mother's response different from his father's?

(d) Why did Swami give a colourful account of Mr Samuel to his father?

(e) In what way did father's behaviour take an unexpected turn?

(iii) In not more than 50 words, describe how Swami tried to prove that Mr Samuel is a violent man.

Answers

(i) 1. (a) shaken 2. (b) adamant
3. (c) use

(ii) (a) On Monday morning, Swami wished for an earthquake to occur that would completely demolish the school building. For over a hundred years, the students had wished the same for the school but nothing happend. So, his wish was unlikely to be answered.

(b) When Swami told his father that he had a headache, his father said "Nonsense! Dress up and go." This sentence tells that his father was completely unsympathetic to his son's headache.

(c) When Swami informed his mother of his headache, she suggested him to stay at home and miss school. In this way, his mother's response was different from his father's who seemed adamant on sending his son to school.

(d) Swami gave a colourful account of Mr. Samuel to his father in order to skip school for the day. Swami told his father that his teacher Mr. Samuel would beat him with his (Samuel's) cane if he turned up late for class.

(e) Swami had given a false account of his teacher, Mr. Samuel, to his father, thinking that he would allow him to miss school after hearing it. However, his father's behaviour took an unexpected turn when he decided to send Swami late as a challenge. Also, he sent a note to the Headmaster through Swami.

(iii)

Swami	told	his	father	that
if	he	reached	school	late,
his	teacher,	Mr. Samuel,	would	beat
him.	He	described	a	boy
being	punished	for	tardiness,	made
to	kneel	for	a	whole
period.	Only	after	beating	him
with	a	cane	and	painfully
twisting	his	ears	did	Mr. Samuel
finally	allow	him	to	sit.

Q.17 Read the following passage carefully and answer the questions that follow.

Rudyard Kipling, the great achiever of the honourable Nobel Prize for Literature in 1907, was a **versatile** writer with an articulate style of writing. He was an English short story writer, poet and novelist.

He was the first English language writer to receive Nobel Prize for Literature. On one hand, his writings depicted an aureate style of writing. On the other hand, his works have also shown careless and colloquial styles.

Rudyard Kipling was born in Mumbai, on 30th December, 1865 to John Lockwood Kipling and Alice Kipling. His father who was a professor of archaeological sculptor, was appointed curator of the Government Museum in Lahore.

So, his family had to move to Lahore, soon after his birth. At the age of six, he was sent to England for schooling. He did his further education from United Service College, Devon.

When he returned to India, he was a reporter for the Lahore Civil and Military Gazette and the Allahabad Pioneer. After this, he sailed back to England and also travelled through China, Japan and the United States.

Kipling was a versatile personality and had many qualities that made him extremely popular.

He was more than a writer or journalist. His works include stories of Indian people, of children and of animals. His articles also talked about the value of the machine, his belief in progress, benefits of civilisation to the rest of the world. All these things carved him a niche in the hearts of many readers.

He wrote about everything from adventure to supernatural activities, to romance and instilled in everything a special feeling. Although many of his writings were very much different from those of the **contemporary** writers, he won the popularity of readers. He put a new life into the literature of 1890s.

After his daughter's death, Kipling collected stories for what became 'Just so Stories for Little Children' published in 1902. This was the year when he gained highest popularity. Till the first decade of the 20th century, he was at the height of popularity.

One critic described Kipling as "a versatile and **luminous** narrative gift". Henry James, the well known writer once said, "Kipling strikes me personally as the most complete man of genius that I have ever known."

In 1936, when Kipling was 70, he underwent a surgery; a few days after which he died.

Questions

(i) For each word given belows choose the correct meaning (as used in the passage) the option provided.

1. Versatile (line 2)
   (a) all rounder
   (b) very artistic
   (c) able to do many different things
   (d) Both (a) and (c)
2. Contemporary (line 36)
   (a) of or belonging to the same time (or era) as one lives in
   (b) modern time (or era)
   (c) the current time period or age
   (d) a time long gone and forgotten
3. Luminous (line 44)
   (a) easily understood
   (b) complicated or complex
   (c) unnecessary
   (d) None of the above

(ii) Answer the following questions briefly in your own words.

(a) What contrasting features of Rudyard Kipling's writings does the author talk about in the first paragraph?
(b) What are the names of the Kipling's parents?
(c) Why did Kipling's family move to Lahore?
(d) Why, according to you, does the author say that Rudyard Kipling was a versatile personality?
(e) What all was the work of Kipling based on?

(iii) Write the summary of the above passage in your own words. Do not exceed 50 words.

Answers

(i) 1. (d) Both (a) and (c)

2. (a) of or belonging to the same time (or era) as one lives in

3. (a) easily understood

(ii) (a) The author says that some of Kipling's works exhibit a very decorative and expressive style of writing, while a few of his works have been written in informal and careless style.

(b) John Lockwood Kipling and Alice Kipling are the names of Rudyard Kipling's father and mother, respectively.

(c) Kipling's father was appointed curator of the Government Museum of Lahore. Hence, they moved to Lahore from Mumbai.

(d) Rudyard Kipling had many qualities that made him popular. He was not only a writer but also a journalist. His works include short stories, novels and poems all written in different styles of writing. Therefore, the author says he was a versatile personality.

(e) Kipling's works included stories of Indian people, of children and of animals. His works also depicted the value of the machine, benefits of civilisation to the world.

(iii)

Rudyard	Kipling	was	born	in
Mumbai	in	1865	and	his
family	soon	moved	to	Lahore.
Educated	in	England,	he	was
a	prolific	writer	with	a
versatile	personality.	His	works	included
novels,	poetry	and	short	stories
about	Indian	people,	children	and
animals.	The	first	English	Nobel
laureate,	he	died	in	1936.

Q.18 Read the following passage carefully and answer the questions that follow. **(ICSE 2011 Modified)**

I rested for a moment at the door of Anand Bhavan, on Market Road, where coffee drinkers and tiffin eaters at their tables sat **transfixed** uttering low moans on seeing me. I wanted to assure them.

"Don't fear, I am not out to trouble you. Eat your tiffin in peace, don't mind me... You, nearest to me, hugging the cash box, you are craven with fear, afraid even to breathe. Go on, count the cash, if that's your pleasure.

I just want to watch, that's all... If my tail trails down to the street, if I am blocking your threshold : it is because, I'm told, I'm eleven feet tip to tail. I can't help it. I'm not out to kill...I'm too full—found a green pasture teeming with food on the way.

Won't need any for several days to come, won't stir, not until I feel hungry again. Tigers attack only when they feel hungry, unlike human beings who slaughter one another without purpose or hunger..."

To the great delight of children, schools were being hurriedly closed. Children of all ages and sizes were running **helter-skelter** screaming joyously, 'No school, no school, Tiger, tiger!' They were shouting and laughing and even enjoyed being scared. They seemed to welcome me.

I felt like joining them and bounded away from the restaurant door and trotted along with them, at which they gleefully cried, 'The tiger is coming to eat us; let us get back to the school!'

I followed them through their school gate while they ran up and shut themselves in the school hall securely.

I ascended the steps of the school, saw an open door at the far end of a veranda and walked in.

It happened to be the headmaster's room, I believe, as I noticed a very dignified man jumping on his table and heaving himself up into an attic. I walked in and flung myself on the cool floor, having a partiality for cool stone floors, with my head under the large desk—which gave me the feeling of being back in the Mempi cave...

As I drowsed, I was aware of cautious steps and hushed voices all around. I was in no mood to bother about anything. All I wanted was a little moment of sleep; the daylight was dazzling.

In half sleep, I heard the doors of the room being shut and bolted and locked. I didn't care. I slept.

While I slept, a great deal of consultation was going on. I learnt about it later through my master, who was in the crowd—the crowd which had gathered after making sure that I had been properly locked up—and was watching.

The headmaster seems to have remarked some days later, "Never dreamt in my wildest mood that I'd have to yield my place to a tiger ......" A wag had retorted, "Might be one way of maintaining better discipline among the boys."

'Now that this brute is safely locked up, we must decide', began a teacher. At this moment, my master pushed his way through the crowds and **admonished.** 'Never use the words 'beast' or 'brute'. They're ugly words coined by humans in their arrogance. The human being thinks all other creatures are 'beasts', Awful word!

Questions

(i) For each word given below, choose the correct meaning (used in the passage) from the options provided.

1. **Transfixed (line 3)**
(a) unable to move because of great shock
(b) unable to move because of great horror
(c) running around in fear
(d) running around in utter shock

2. **Helter-skelter (line 20)**
(a) now and then
(b) up and down
(c) here and there
(d) right and left

3. **Admonished (line 58)**
(a) reprimanded
(b) shocked and scared
(c) to anger and enfuriate someone
(d) to caution against something

(ii) **Answer the following questions briefly in your own words.**

(a) What reassurance did the tiger give to the coffee drinkers?
(b) In what way are tigers different from human beings?
(c) Why were the children delighted?
(d) What did the headmaster say some days later?
(e) What was the wag's response to the headmaster's words?

(iii) **Describe the tiger's activities from the time it followed the school children till it slept in your own words. Do not exceed 50 words.**

Answers

(i) 1. (b) unable to move because of great horror
2. (c) here and there
3. (d) to caution against something

(ii) (a) The tiger reassured the coffee drinkers that he was there to enjoy the sight and would not trouble them.
(b) Human beings kill one another, even their brethren without any reason or hunger, whereas tigers attack only when they are hungry.
(c) The children were delighted because the schools were being closed hurriedly.
(d) Some days later, the headmaster remarked that he had never dreamt of giving his office up to a tiger.
(e) A wag cracked a joke, saying that the tiger's presence is better for maintaining discipline among the boys.

(iii)

The	tiger	watched	children	cheering,
cherishing	joy	mixed	with	fear.
Hearing	their	joyous	screams,	he
followed	them.	reaching	the	school
steps,	he	saw	an	open
door	and	entered	the	headmaster's
room.	Terrified,	the	headmaster	jumped
into	the	attic.	The	tiger
lay	on	the	cool	floor
under	the	table	and	slept.

Q.19 Read the following passage carefully and answer the questions that follow.

It was a dull autumn day and Jill Pole was crying behind the gym. She was crying because they had been **bullying** her. This is not going to be a school story, so I shall say as little as possible about Jill's school, which is not a pleasant subject.

It was co-educational, a school for both boys and girls, what used to be called a 'mixed' school; some said it was not nearly so mixed as the minds of the people who ran it. These people had the idea that boys and girls should be allowed to do what they liked.

And unfortunately what ten or fifteen of the biggest boys and girls liked best was bullying the others.

All sorts of things, horrid things, went on which at an ordinary school would have been found out and stopped in half a term but at this school they weren't. Or even if they were, the people who did them were not **expelled** or punished. The head said they were interesting psychological cases and sent for them and talked to them for hours. And if you knew the right sort of things to say to the head, the main result was that you became rather a favourite than otherwise.

That was why Jill Pole was crying on that dull autumn day on the damp little path which runs between the back of the gym and the shrubbery.

And she hadn't nearly finished crying when a boy came round the corner of the gym whistling, with his hands in his pockets. He nearly ran into her. "Can't you look where you're going?" said Jill Pole. "All right", said the boy, "you needn't start—" and then he noticed her face, "I say, Jill", he said, "what's up?"

Jill only made faces; the sort you make when you're trying to say something but find that if you speak you'll start crying again. "It's them, I suppose—as usual", said the boy grimly, digging his hands further into his pockets. Jill nodded. There was no need for her to say anything, even if she could have said it. They both knew. "Now, look here", said the boy, "its no use…"

He meant well but he did talk rather like someone beginning a lecture. Jill suddenly flew into a temper (which is quite a likely thing to happen if you have been interrupted in a cry).

"Oh, go away and mind your own business", she said. "Nobody asked you to come **barging** in, did they? And you're a nice person to start telling us what we all ought to do, aren't you? I suppose you mean we ought to spend all our time sucking up to them and currying favour and dancing attendance on them like you do."

'Oh, Lord!' said the boy, sitting down on the grassy bank at the edge of the shrubbery and very quickly getting up again because the grass was soaking wet. His name unfortunately was Eustace Scrubb but he wasn't bad sort.

"Jill!" he said. "Is that fair?"

"I don't know and I don't care," sobbed Jill.

Eustace saw that she wasn't quite herself yet and very sensibly offered her a peppermint. He had one too. Presently Jill began to see things in a clearer light. "I'm sorry, Eustace", she said presently.

Questions

(i) For each word given below, choose the correct meaning (as used in the passage) from the options provided.

1. **Bullying (line 3)**
   (a) to use strength to harm someone
   (b) to intimidate those who are weaker
   (c) to harm people inferior to you
   (d) All of the above
2. **Expelled (line 17)**
   (a) made them take leave
   (b) made them to leave school
   (c) made them to return to school
   (d) None of the above
3. **Barging (line 44)**
   (a) to bump into someone
   (b) to meet someone after long
   (c) to say goodbye to someone
   (d) Both (b) and (c)

(ii) Answer the following questions briefly in your own words.

(a) Why do you think Jill was crying behind the gym?
(b) Who is the 'them' referred to in the line 10.
(c) Why did Jill fly into a temper?
(d) Which sentence tell us that both Jill and Eustace Scrubb had suffered similarly?
(d) When did Jill begin to see things differently?

(iii) What kind of school did the children go to in above passage? Write your answer in your own words and not more than 50 words.

Answers

(i) 1. (d) All of the above
2. (b) made them to leave school
3. (a) to bump into someone

(ii) (a) Jill was crying on the little damp path that ran between the gym and the shrubbery because she was being bullied by malicious students.

(b) 'Them', in line 10 refers to the malicious students of Jill's school who liked to frighten and harm others.

(c) Jill flew into a temper because Eustace seemed to preach her not to be saddened because of those bad students' behaviour.

(d) The sentence "I suppose you mean we ought to spend all our time sucking up to them and currying favour and dancing attendance on them like you do" indicates that both Jill and Eustace had suffered similarly.

(e) Jill began to see things differently when Eustace, understanding the delicacy of the situation, offered her a peppermint. She realised that he was not a bad fellow.

(iii)

The	children	attended	co-educati-onal	school
where	authorities	ignored	student's	problems.
Believing	boys	and	girls	should
do	as	they	pleased,	they
allowed	disorder.	Senior	students	who
enjoyed	harming	and	frightening	others
took	advantage.	Immune	to	expulsion,
they	bulled	freely,	while	other
students	suffered	greatly	from	their
unchecked	cruelty	and	constant	fear.

Q.20 Read the following passage carefully and answer the questions that follow.

A panther was terrorising the Khulna district of Bangladesh, just outside the Sundarbans. It had recently carried off a little girl. She was the seventh person killed in two months by the animal. And it was growing bolder.

The previous victim was a man who had been attacked in broad daylight in his field. The beast dragged him off into the forest and his corpse was later found hanging from a tree. The villagers kept a watch nearby that night, hoping to surprise the panther and kill it but it never appeared.

The Forest Department hired a professional hunter. He set-up a small, hidden platform in a tree near a river where two of the attacks had taken place. A goat was tied to a stake on the river's bank.

The hunter waited several nights. He assumed the panther would be an old, wasted male with worn teeth, incapable of catching anything more difficult than a human. But it was a sleek tiger that stepped into the open one night : a female with a single cub. The goat bleated. Oddly, the cub, who looked to be about three months old, paid little attention to the goat. It raced to the water's edge, where it drank eagerly. Its mother followed it. Of hunger and thirst, thirst is the greater urge. Only once the tiger had **quenched** her thirst did she turn to the goat to satisfy her hunger.

The hunter had two rifles with him : one with real bullets, the other with immobilising darts. This animal was not the man-eater, but so close to human habitation she might pose a threat to the villagers, especially as she was with a cub. He picked up the gun with the darts. He fired as the tiger was about to attack the goat.

The tiger **reared** up and snarled and raced away. But immobilising darts don't bring on sleep gently-they knock the creature out without warning. A burst of activity on the animal's part makes it act all the faster. The hunter called his assistants on the radio. They found the tiger about two hundred yards from the river. She was still conscious. Her back legs had given way and her balance on her front legs was shaky. When the men got close, she tried to get away but could not manage it.

She turned on them, lifting a paw that was meant to kill. It only made her lose her balance. She collapsed and the Pondicherry zoo had two new tigers. The cub was found in a bush close by, meowing with fear.

The hunter, whose name was Richard Parker, picked it up with his bare hands and remembering how it had rushed to drink in the river, named it Thirsty. But the shipping clerk at the Howrah train station was evidently a man both confused and diligent.

All the papers received with the cub clearly stated that its name was Richard Parker, that the hunter's first name was Thirsty and that his family name was none given. Richard Parker's name stuck. don't know if the hunter was ever called Thirsty None Given!

Questions

(i) For each word given below, choose the correct meaning (as used in the passage) from the options provided.

1. Corpse (line 8)

(a) dead animal

(b) decomposed human

(c) dead body

(d) decomposed insects

2. Quenched (line 25)

(a) thirst (b) increased

(c) satisfied (d) decreased

3. Reared (line 34)

(a) to put down

(b) to raise itself upright on its hind legs

(c) to fall down

(d) None of the above

(ii) Answer the following questions briefly in your own words.

(a) Why does the author say that the panther 'was getting bolder'?

(b) Why did the Forest Department hire a professional hunter?

(c) What did the hunter expect to encounter? What did he actually encounter?

(d) What did the tiger do before turning to attack the goat? Why did it do that?

(e) What name did the hunter give to the cub? Why?

(iii) Narrate how the hunter and his assistants captured the tiger and her cub, in your own words and not more than 50 words.

Answers

(i) 1. (c) dead body

2. (c) satisfied

3. (b) (of an animal) to raise itself upright on its hind legs

(ii) (a) The panther was getting bolder as it had killed seven people in two months. Very recently, it carried off a little girl and the previous victim had been a man who was attacked in broad daylight in his field.

(b) The villagers kept a watch for the panther hoping to surprise and kill it but it never appeared. So, the Forest Department hired a professional hunter to track and kill it.

(c) The hunter expected that the panther would be an old, wasted male with worn teeth, incapable of catching anything more difficult than a human. But what he actually encountered was a sleek tigress with a cub.

(d) The tiger followed the cub to the water's edge and drank water before she turned to the goat to satisfy her hunger because thirst is a greater urge than hunger.

(e) The hunter named the cub 'Thirsty' as he remembered how the cub had rushed to drink water in the river.

(iii)

The	hunter	shot	at	the
tiger	as	she	was	about
to	attack	the	goat.	The
tiger	rose	and	ran	away.
The	hunter	called	his	assistants.
They	found	the	tiger	about
two	hundred	yards	from	the
river.	She	tried	to	attack
as	they	got	close	but
collapsed.	The	men	captured	her.

Q.21 Read the following passage carefully and answer the questions that follow.

There were other boys in Manjari village but Bisnu was the only one who went to school. His mother would not have fussed if he had stayed at home and worked in the fields.

That was what the other boys did; all except lazy Chittru, who preferred fishing in the stream or helping himself to the fruit of other people's trees. But Bisnu went to school. He went because he wanted to. No one could force him to go and no one could stop him from going.

He had set his heart on receiving good schooling. He wanted to read and write as well as anyone in the big world and so he walked to school everyday.

A colony of langoors lived in the forest. They fed on oak leaves, acorns and other green things and usually remained in the trees, coming down to the ground only to play or sun themselves.

They were beautiful, supple-limbed animals, with black faces and silver-grey coats and long, sensitive tails. They leapt from tree to tree with great **agility**. The young ones wrestled on the grass like boys.

A dignified community, the langoors did not have the cheekiness or dishonest habits of the red monkeys of the plains; they did not approach dogs or humans.

But they had grown used to Bisnu's comings and goings, and did not fear him. Some of the older ones would watch him quietly, a little puzzled. They did not go near the town; because the boys threw stones at them. And anyway, the forest gave them all the food they required.

Coming from another direction was a second path and at the junction of the two paths Sarru was waiting for him. Sarru came from a small village about three miles from Bisnu's and closer to the town.

They **hailed** each other and walked along. They often met at this spot, keeping each other company for the remaining two miles.

'There was a panther in our village last night,' said Sarru.

This information interested but did not excite Bisnu.

Panthers were common enough in the hills and did not usually present a problem except during the winter months, when their natural prey was scarce.

'Did you lose any animals?' asked Bisnu. 'No, It tried to get into the cowshed but the dogs set off the alarm. We drove it off.'

'It must be the same one that came around last winter. We lost a calf and two dogs in our village.'

'Wasn't that the one the shikaris wounded? I hope it hasn't become a cattle-lifter.'

'It could be the same. It has a bullet in its leg. These hunters are the people who cause all the trouble. They think it's easy to shoot a panther. It would be better if they missed altogether but they usually wound it.'

...............'And then the panther's too slow to catch the barking-deer and starts on our own animals'.

We're lucky it didn't become a man-eater. Do you remember the man-eater six years ago? I was very small then. My father told me all about it. Ten people were killed in our valley alone.'

'What happened to it?'

'I don't know. Some say it poisoned itself when it ate the headman of the village.' Bisnu laughed. No one liked that old **villain**. They linked arms and scrambled up the stony path to school.

Questions

(i) For each word given below, choose the correct meaning (as used in the passage) from the options provided.

1. Agility (line 20)

(a) to move around slowly

(b) the ability to move about quickly and easily

(c) to stay stationary for a long time

(d) All of the above

2. Hailed (line 35)

(a) to call and attract attention of someone

(b) to enchant someone in a spell

(c) to praise someone without stopping

(d) All of the above

3. Villain (line 64)

(a) a joyous hero (b) an anti-hero

(c) a murderer (d) a wicked man

(ii) Answer the following questions briefly in your own words.

(a) How was Chittru different from other boys?

(b) What was Bisnu's ambition?

(c) What information did Sarru give Bisnu?
(d) How did the information affect Bisnu?
(e) What joke did Sarru make?

(iii) Describe what the narrator tells us about the behaviour of the langoors, in your own words and not more than 50 words.

Answers

(i) 1. (b) the ability to move about quickly and easily
2. (a) to call and attract attention of someone
3. (d) a wicked man

(ii) (a) While other boys worked in the fields, Chittru did fishing in the stream or engaged himself in plucking fruits from other people's trees. This is how he was different from other boys.

(b) Bisnu aspired to receive good schooling. He wanted to be known in the big world. So, he went to school regularly.

(c) Sarru informed Bisnu that a panther had entered his village the previous night. He also told that they didn't lose any animal.

(d) The information interested Bisnu but did not excite him. This was so because panthers were common in the hills and they did not present any problem except during the winter months, when their natural prey was scarce.

(e) Bisnu asked Sarru what happened to the panther that purportedly killed ten people. Sarru joked that it ate the headman of his village and got poisoned to death.

(iii)

A	colony	of	langoors	lived
in	the	forest,	feeding	on
oak	leaves,	acorn	and	greens.
they	stayed	in	trees,	moving
swiftly	between	branches,	descending	only
to	play.	Young	langoors	wrestled
like	boys	on	the	grass.
Honest	and	wary,	they	avoided
dogs	and	humans	but	silently
watched	Bisnu	as	he	passed.

10

TENSES (VERB FORMS)

Present Tense

1. Simple Present Tense

The Simple Present Tense is used to state an action that is a happening at the moment, a habit or a universal fact.

Type of Sentence	Structure	Example
Affirmative	Singular Subject + V1 + s/es + Object I/Plural Subject + V1 + Object	She goes for a walk. They go for a walk.
Negative	Singular Subject + does not + V1 + Object I/Plural Subject + do not + V1 + Object	She does not go for a walk. They do not go for a walk.
Interrogative	Does + Singular Subject + V1 + Object? Do + I/Plural Subject + V1 + Object?	Does she go for a walk? Do they go for a walk?

2. Present Continuous Tense

The Present Continuous Tense form of a verb tells us that an action is in progress at the time of speaking.

Type of Sentence	Structure	Example
Affirmative	Singular Subject + is/am + V1 + -ing + Object Plural Subject + are + V1 + -ing + Object	She is going for a walk. They are going for a walk.
Negative	Singular Subject + is/am + not + V1 + -ing + Object Plural Subject + are + not + V1 + -ing + Object	She is not going for a walk. They are not going for a walk.
Interrogative	Is/Am + Singular Subject + V1 + -ing + Object? Are + Plural Subject + V1 + -ing + Object?	Is she going for a walk? Are they going for a walk?

3. Present Perfect Tense

The Present Perfect Tense form of a verb tells us about an action that began in the past and has been completed recently.

Type of Sentence	Structure	Example
Affirmative	Singular Subject + has + V3 + Object I/ Plural Subject+ have + V3 + Object	She has gone for a walk. They have gone for a walk.
Negative	Singular Subject + has + not + V3 + Object I/Plural Subject+ have + not + V3 + Object	She has not gone for a walk. They have not gone for a walk.
Interrogative	Has + Singular Subject + V3 + Object? Have + I/ Plural Subject+ V3 + Object?	Has she gone for a walk? Have they gone for a walk?

4. Present Perfect Continuous Tense

The Present Perfect Continuous Tense form of a verb is used to talk about an action that started in the past and is still continuing in the present.

Type of Sentence	Structure	Example
Affirmative	Singular Subject + has been + V1 + -ing + Object I/ Plural Subject+ have been + V1 + -ing + Object	She has been going for a walk. They have been going for a walk.
Negative	Singular Subject + has + not + been + V1 + -ing + Object I/ Plural Subject+ have + not + been + V1 + -ing + Object	She has not been going for a walk. They have not been going for a walk.
Interrogative	Has + Singular Subject + been + V1 + -ing + Object? Have + I/ Plural Subject + been + V1 + -ing + Object?	Has she been going for a walk? Have they been going for a walk?

Past Tense

1. Simple Past Tense

The Simple Past Tense is used to show an action that had started and was completed at a specified time in the past.

Type of Sentence	Structure	Example
Affirmative	Singular/ Plural Subject + V2 + Object	She went for a walk.
Negative	Singular/ Plural Subject + did not + V1 + Object	They did not go for a walk.
Interrogative	Did + Singular/ Plural Subject + V1 + Object?	Did they go for a walk?

2. Past Continuous Tense

The Past Continuous Tense form of a verb tells us that an action was in progress at some point in the past.

Type of Sentence	Structure	Example
Affirmative	Singular Subject + was + V1 + -ing + Object Plural Subject+ were + V1 + -ing + Object	She was going for a walk. They were going for a walk.
Negative	Singular Subject + was + not + V1 + -ing + Object Plural Subject+ were + not + V1 + -ing + Object	She was not going for a walk. They were not going for a walk.
Interrogative	Was + Singular Subject + V1 + -ing + Object? Were + Plural Subject+ V1 + -ing + Object?	Was she going for a walk? Were they going for a walk?

3. Past Perfect Tense

The Past Perfect Tense form of a verb tells us that an action was complete before another action began in the past.

Type of Sentence	Structure	Example
Affirmative	Singular/ Plural Subject + had + V3 + Object	They had gone for a walk.
Negative	Singular/ Plural Subject + had + not + V3 + Object	She had not gone for a walk.
Interrogative	Had + Singular/ Plural Subject + V3 + Object?	Had they gone for a walk?

4. Past Perfect Continuous Tense

The Past Perfect Continuous Tense denotes an action that had continued for some time in the past before being completed at some other point in the past itself.

Type of Sentence	Structure	Example
Affirmative	Singular/ Plural Subject + had been + V1 + -ing + Object	She had been going for a walk.
Negative	Singular/ Plural Subject + had + not + been + V1 + -ing + Object	They had not been going for a walk.
Interrogative	Had + Singular/ Plural Subject + been + V1 + -ing + Object?	Had they been going for a walk?

Future Tense

1. Simple Future Tense

The Simple Future Tense tells us that an action will take place in the future.

Type of Sentence	Structure	Example
Affirmative	Singular/ Plural Subject + will/ shall + V1 + Object	She will go for a walk.
Negative	Singular/ Plural Subject + will/ shall + not + V1 + Object	They will not go for a walk.
Interrogative	Will/ Shall + Singular/ Plural Subject + V1 + Object?	Will they go for a walk?

2. Future Continuous Tense

The Future Continuous Tense form of a verb tells us that an action will start in the future and continue for some time in the future.

Type of Sentence	Structure	Example
Affirmative	Singular/ Plural Subject + will/ shall be + V1 + -ing + Object	They will be going for a walk.
Negative	Singular/ Plural Subject + will/ shall not be + V1 + -ing + Object	She will not be going for a walk.
Interrogative	Will/ Shall + Singular/ Plural Subject + be + V1 + -ing + Object	Will they be going for a walk?

3. Future Perfect Tense

The Future Perfect Tense form of a verb denotes that an action will complete before a point of time in future.

Type of Sentence	Structure	Example
Affirmative	Singular/ Plural Subject + will/ shall have + V3 + Object	She will have gone for a walk.
Negative	Singular/ Plural Subject + will/ shall + not + have + V3 + Object	They will not have gone for a walk.
Interrogative	Will/ Shall + Singular/ Plural Subject + have + V3 + Object?	Will she have gone for a walk?

4. Future Perfect Continuous Tense

The Future Perfect Continuous Tense denotes an action that will continue till a specific point of time in the future.

Type of Sentence	Structure	Example
Affirmative	Singular/ Plural Subject + will/shall have been + V1+ -ing + Object	They will have been going for a walk.
Negative	Singular/ Plural Subject + will/ shall + not + have been + V1 + -ing + Object	She will not have been going for a walk.
Interrogative	Will/ Shall + Singular/ Plural Subject + have been + V1 + -ing + Object?	Will they have been going for a walk?

EXAM ORIENTED QUESTIONS

Q.1 Fill in each of the numbered blanks with the correct form of the word given in brackets. Do not copy the passage but write in correct serial order the word or phrase appropriate to the blank space. **(ICSE 2025)**

Example

One day we **(0)** .... (lift) the box up.

Answer (0) lifted

We **(1)** .... (find) a dead mouse **(2)** .... (lie) among our treasures. It **(3)** .... (be) an exciting discovery. A boy took it up by its tail and **(4)** .... (wave) it in front of our faces.

"What shall we do with it?" he **(5)** .... (cry). "It stinks!" someone **(6)** .... (shout).

"Throw it out of the window quick!"

He **(7)** .... (hesitate). They all **(8)** .... (look) at me.

Ans. 1. found 2. lying
3. was 4. waved
5. cried 6. shouted
7. hesitated 8. looked

Q.2 Fill in each of the numbered blanks with the correct form of the word given in brackets. Do not copy the passage but write in correct serial order the word or phrase appropriate to the blank space. **(ICSE Specimen 2025)**

Example

The Sun **(0)** .... (shine) bright outside.

Answer (0) shone

It was hot in the railway compartment and the fan **(1)** .... (not work). The elderly lady **(2)** .... (use) up all her water because she had cheerfully shared it with her fellow passengers. She knew that the train **(3)** .... (halt) at the station for only three minutes. Calling a shoeshine boy she said, 'Will you help me? I **(4)** .... (need) a bottle of cold water and here is the money,' and she put a twenty rupee note in his hand. The boy snatched the money and **(5)** .... (disappear) into the crowd on the platform. A fellow passenger **(6)** .... (cannot believe) what he had witnessed. 'What **(7)** .... (you do)?" He said, 'You **(8)** .... (never see) your money again.' Just then the whistle was heard and the train began to move. At that moment the child appeared at the window with the water. 'You water,' he gasped, out of breath. 'And the change.'

Ans. 1. was not working 2. had used
3. would halt 4. need
5. disappeared 6. could not believe
7. are you doing 8. will never see

Q.3 Fill in the blanks with the right form of the verb forms for the words given in the brackets. **(Competency Based Que.)**

1. She .... (go) to school by bus when the naughty boy hit her.
2. My brother .... (drink) coffee every morning while I like tea.
3. The boy got up late and .... (miss) the bus.
4. The library .... (close) for the winter break.
5. The patient .... (recover) before you arrive to see her.
6. Have you .... (read) Pride and Prejudice?
7. Mrs. Bose .... (teach) for ten years next month.
8. The train has just .... (leave) the station.
9. The baby .... (eat) all the cookies.
10. The boat .... (sail) yesterday.
11. My sister .... (graduate) from college last year.
12. I .... (move) to Delhi soon.
13. Shruti .... (complete) her homework when her parents came back.
14. The disappointed student .... (sob) for hours over her inability to score good marks.
15. We .... (watch) a wonderful movie yesterday.
16. When I reached, Gullu .... (play) video games.
17. I .... (finish) my assignment when the call came.
18. We .... (go) to school yesterday.
19. They .... (know) each other for a long time.

Ans. 1. was going 2. drinks 3. missed
4. is closed/ will be closed
5. will have recovered 6. read
7. will have been teaching
8. left 9. has eaten 10. sailed
11. graduated 12. will move
13. had completed 14. sobbed 15. watched
16. was playing 17. had finished 18. went
19. have known

Q.4 Fill in each of the numbered blanks with the correct form of the word given in brackets. Do not copy the passage but write in correct serial order the word or phrase appropriate to the blank space. **(ICSE 2024)**

Example

Next day my uncle **(0)** .... (spend) a lot of time.

Answer (0) spent

He **(1)** .... (select) clothes for me and my aunt **(2)** .... (give) my face a scrub and **(3)** .... (groom) me. My uncle **(4)** .... (follow) me about **(5)** .... (utter) several pieces of advice before **(6)** .... (let) me out. 'You must never scowl even if the Sun **(7)** .... (hit) you in the eyes. You must try **(8)** .... (look) pleasant.'

Ans. 1. selected 2. gave 3. groomed 4. followed 5. uttering 6. letting 7. hits 8. to look

Q.5 Fill in each of the numbered blanks with the correct form of the word given in brackets. Do not copy the passage but write in correct serial order the word or phrase appropriate to the blank space. **(ICSE Specimen 2024)**

Example

Rikki-tikki **(0)** .... (know) better than to waste time in staring.

Answer (0) knew

Rikki-tikki was angry. He sat back on his tail and hind legs, and **(1)** .... (look) all round him, **(2)** .... (chatter) with rage. But Nag and Nagaina **(3)** .... (disappear) already into the grass. When a snake misses its stroke, it never **(4)** .... (say) anything or **(5)** .... (give) any sign of what it means to do next. Rikki-tikki did not care to follow them, for he did not **(6)** .... (feel) sure that he **(7)** .... (can) manage two snakes at once.

So, he trotted off to the gravel path, and sat down to think. It **(8)** .... (is) a serious matter for him.

Ans. 1. looked 2. chattering 3. had disappeared 4. says 5. gives 6. feel 7. could 8. was

Q.6 Fill in each of the numbered blanks with the correct form of the word given in brackets. Do not copy the passage but write in correct serial order the word or phrase appropriate to the blank space. **(ICSE 2023)**

Example

One night four college students **(0)** .... (be) out partying late and did not study for the test scheduled for the next day.

Answer (0) were

In the morning, they **(1)** .... (think) of a plan. They **(2)** .... (make) themselves look dirty with grease and dirt. Then they **(3)** .... (go) to the Dean and **(4)** .... (say) they **(5)** .... (go) out to a wedding last night and on their way back the tyre of their car burst and they had to push the car all the way back.

The Dean thought for a minute and said that they could have the re-test after three days. They **(6)** ...... (thank) him and said they would be ready. On the day of the test, they were made to sit in separate rooms. They agreed as they **(7)** .... (prepare) well. But they **(8)** .... (get) a rude shock!

Ans. 1. thought 2. made 3. went 4. said 5. had gone 6. thanked 7. had prepared 8. got

Q.7 Fill in each of the numbered blanks with the correct form of the word given in brackets. Do not copy the passage but write in correct serial order the word or phrase appropriate to the blank space. **(ICSE Specimen 2023, ICSE 2019)**

Example

I **(0)** .... (slow) the car as I saw the new house.

Answer (0) slowed

I **(1)** .... (pull) up into the driveway **(2)** .... (observe) the way they had **(3)** .... (build) up the balcony. I **(4)** .... (forgot) that the bricks of the house **(5)** .... (be) chocolate brown. The new people **(6)** .... (make) the tiny balcony into a study room. I **(7)** .... (stare) at this house, **(8)** .... (remember) my childhood there.

Ans. 1. pulled 2. to observe 3. built 4. had forgotten 5. were 6. had made 7. stared 8. remembering

Q.8 Fill in the blanks with the correct forms of the words provided after the blanks. **(ICSE Specimen, 2022 Sem II)**

When Ranji **(0)** .... (see) the pool, he did not hesitate to **(1)** .... (get) into it. He had often **(2)** .... (go) swimming, alone or with friends, when he had **(3)** .... (live) with his parents in a thirsty town in the middle of the Rajputana Desert. There, he had **(4)** .... (know) only sticky, muddy pools where buffaloes wallowed and women washed clothes.

Example (0) saw

Ans. 1. get 2. gone 3. lived 4. known

Q.9 Fill in each of the numbered blanks with the correct form of the word given brackets. Do not copy the passage but write in correct serial order the word phrase appropriate to the blank space. **(ICSE 2020 Modified)**

By the time she was three, Matilda had **(0)** .... (teach) her to read by **(1)** .... (study) newspapers and magazines **(2)** .... (throw) around the house. At the age of four, she **(3)** .... (read) fast and well and she naturally began **(4)** .... (hanker) after books. The only book in the whole of enlightened household was something called Easy Cooking, **(5)** .... (belong) to her mother, and when she had read this cover-to-cover and had **(6)** .... (learn) all the recipes by heart, she **(7)** .... (decide) she **(8)** .... (want) something interesting.

Example (0) taught

Ans.

1. studying	2. thrown
3. read	4. hankering
5. belonging	6. learnt
7. decided	8. wanted

Q.10 Fill in each of the numbered blanks with the correct form of the word given in brackets. Do not copy the passage but write in correct serial order the word or phrase appropriate to the blank space. **(ICSE 2019)**

Once upon a time, in the days when genies and giants **(0)** .... (roam) the land, there **(1)** .... (live) a farmer **(2)** .... (name) Baba Ayub. He lived with his family in a little village by the name of Maidan Sabz. Because he had a large family to feed, Baba Ayub **(3)** .... (see) his days **(4)** .... (consume) by hard work. Every day, he **(5)** .... (labour) from dawn to sundown, **(6)** .... (plough) his field and **(7)** .... (turn) the soil and **(8)** .... (tend) to his meagre pistachio trees.

Example (0) roamed

Ans.

1. lived	2. named	3. saw
4. consumed	5. laboured	6. ploughing
7. turning	8. tending	

Q.11 Fill in each of the numbered blanks with the correct form of the word given in brackets. Do not copy the passage but write in correct serial order the word or phrase appropriate to the blank space. **(ICSE 2018)**

Alice was **(0)** .... (begin) to get very tired of **(1)** .... (sit) by her sister on the bank and of having nothing to do. Once or twice, she had **(2)** .... (peep) into the book her sister was reading, but it **(3)** .... (have) no pictures or conversations in it, "and what is the use of a book," **(4)** .... (think) Alice, "without pictures or conversations?" Alice wondered whether the pleasure of **(5)** .... (make) a daisy- chain would be worth the trouble of getting up and picking the daisies, when suddenly a white rabbit with pink eyes **(6)** .... (run) close by her. Alice did not think this was very remarkable, until the rabbit actually **(7)** .... (take) a watch out of its waistcoat-pocket, and **(8)** .... (look) at it, and then hurried on.

Example (0) beginning

Ans.

1. sitting	2. peeped
3. had	4. thought
5. making	6. ran
7. took	8. looked

Q.12 Fill in each of the numbered blanks with the correct form of the word given in brackets. Do not copy the passage but write in correct serial order the word or phrase appropriate to the blank space. **(ICSE 2017)**

My mother **(0)** .... (start) school when she **(1)** .... (be) six and **(2)** .... (stop) the same term. She was unusual in the village as she had a father and brother who **(3)** .... (encourage) her to go to school. She was the only girl in a class full of boys and claims she was brighter than the boys. But every day, she **(4)** .... (will) leave behind her girl cousins **(5)** .... (play) at home and she **(6)** .... (envy) them. There **(7)** .... (seem) to be no point in **(8)** .... (go) to school just to end up doing housework.

Example (0) started

Ans.

1. was	2. stopped
3. had encouraged	4. would
5. playing	6. would envy
7. seemed	8. going

Q.13 Fill in each of the numbered blanks with the correct form of the word given in brackets. Do not copy the passage but write in correct serial order the word or phrase appropriate to the blank space. **(ICSE Specimen 2017)**

The other day we **(0)** .... (discuss) the attitudes of people in our country. "Why **(1)** .... (be) most of them rude and aggressive?" Pritam asked. Sanjana **(2)** .... (say) that it **(3)** .... (be) because there **(4)** .... (be) too many people and one had to fight for everything. Nirode **(5)** .... (insist) that it **(6)** .... (be) the climate. We **(7)** .... (be) as efficient and polite as Europeans if only our weather **(8)** .... (be) better.

Example (0) discussed

Ans. 1. are 2. said 3. was
4. were 5. insisted 6. was
7. will be 8. is

Q.14 One morning, I **(0) saw** (see) a python curled up on the dressing table. It was **(1)** .... (gaze) at its own reflection in the mirror. I **(2)** .... (go) for grandfather but by the time we **(3)** .... (return) to the room, the python **(4)** .... (move) on. He was seen in the garden and once the cook saw him **(5)** .... (crawl) up the ladder to the roof. Then, we **(6)** .... (find) him on the dressing table again **(7)** .... (admire) himself in the mirror. "He's trying to look better for Aunt Mabel", I said. I **(8)** .... (regret) this remark immediately because grandmother overheard and held up my pocket money for the rest of the week! **(ICSE 2015)**

Ans. 1. gazing 2. went
3. returned 4. had moved
5. crawling 6. found
7. admiring 8. regretted

Q.15 From his perch behind the clock, Hugo could **(0) see** (see) everything. He rubbed his fingers nervously against the small notebook in his pocket and **(1)** .... (tell) himself to be patient. The old man in the toy booth **(2)** .... (argue) with the girl. She **(3)** ....(be) about Hugo's age and he often saw her go into the booth and **(4)** .... (disappear) behind the counter. The old man **(5)** .... (look) agitated today. Had he figured out that some of his toys were **(6)** .... (miss)? Well, there was nothing to be **(7)** .... (do) about that now. The old man and the girl argued some more and finally she closed her book and **(8)** ....(run) off.

Ans. 1. told 2. was arguing
3. was 4. disappear
5. looked 6. missing
7. done 8. ran

Q.16 A woman **(0) was waiting** (wait) at an airport one night, with several long hours before her flight. She **(1)** .... (hunt) for a book in the airport shops, **(2)** .... (buy) a bag of cookies and found a place to sit. She **(3)** .... (engross) in her book, when she happened to see that the man sitting beside her, bold as could be, grabbed a cookie or two from the bag in between, which she tried to ignore to avoid a scene. So, she **(4)** .... (munch) on the cookies and watched the clock, as the gutsy thief diminished her stock. She **(5)** .... (get) more irritated as the minutes ticked by, thinking, "If I wasn't so nice, I **(6)** .... (blacken) his eye." With each cookie she took, he took one too. When only one was left, she wondered what he would do. With a smile on his face, a nervous laugh, he **(7)** .... (take) the last cookie and broke it in half. He offered her half, as he ate the other. She had never known she could be so angry and turned to gather her belongings. As she reached for her baggage, she gasped with surprise, there was her bag of cookies, in front of her eyes. If mine are here, she moaned in despair, the other were his, he **(8)** .... (try) to share.

Ans. 1. hunted 2. bought
3. was engrossed 4. munched
5. was getting 6. would blacken
7. took 8. was trying

Q.17 My guide **(0) told** (tell) me that if I wanted to meet these people, I would have to walk two miles. We finally **(1)** .... (reach) a village where I **(2)** .... (meet) a lady whose age I **(3)** .... (can) not immediately make out. My translator **(4)** .... (find) it difficult to interpret the lady's words because her dialect was quite different. She **(5)** .... (be) a dark-skinned and dark-haired lady. She must have been around 70 years old, but there was no grey in her hair. She obviously could not afford to dye her hair. So, what was her secret? Nobody **(6)** .... (know). It must have been a 'secret' common to all for not one person in that whole village **(7)** .... (has) a trace of grey hair! I **(8)** .... (think) about it for a long time.

Ans. 1. reached 2. met
3. could 4. found
5. was 6. knew
7. had 8. thought

Q.18 We were not **(0) allowed** (allow) to talk during the lecture. The children **(1)** .... (sit) in a neat circle and **(2)** .... (begin) **(3)**......... (copy) their multiplication tables. Most **(4)** .... (scratch) in the dirt with sticks they had **(5)** .... (bring) for that purpose. The more fortunate **(6)** ....(has) slate boards that they **(7)** .... (write) on with sticks **(8)** .... (dip) in a mixture of mud and water.

Ans. 1. sat 2. began
3. copying 4. were scratching
5. brought 6. had
7. were writing 8. dipped

Q.19 But just when I had almost **(0) given** (give) up hope, I was **(1)** .... (strike) with a brilliant idea : my birthday was due fairly soon and if I **(2)** .... (deal) with the family skilfully, I **(3)** .... (feel) sure, I could not only get a boat but a lot of other equipments as well. I **(4)** .... (suggest) to the family that, instead of **(5)** .... (let) them choose my presents, I **(6)** .... (may) tell them the things that I **(7)** .... (want) most. In this way, they could be sure of not **(8)** .... (disappoint) me.

Ans. 1. struck 2. dealt
3. felt 4. suggested
5. letting 6. might
7. wanted 8. disappointing

Q.20 As she **(0) spoke** (speak), I **(1)** .... (rise) and **(2)** .... (go) to the centre blackboard. I **(3)** .... (find) the chalk **(4)** .... (write) in block letters the title of the book. Then, I **(5)** .... (put) the chalk down and went to **(6)** .... (sit) beside her, to **(7)** .... (hold) her hand. The day had barely **(8)** .... (begin).

Ans. 1. rose 2. went
3. found 4. to write
5. put 6. sit
7. hold 8. begun

Q.21 I **(0) am convinced** (convince) that my father **(1)** .... (remember) by all those who value integrity. He **(2)** .... (be) a man of learning and also saw to it that he **(3)** .... (teach) his pupils with passion and patience. He, at times, **(4)** .... (use) to lose his temper but that was because he always **(5)** .... (want) his pupils to learn and learn well.
As a person, he was honest and simple.
His greatness **(6)** .... (lie) in the fact that he **(7)** .... (have) a pure heart, devoid of malice. Such a man is always valued and **(8)** .... (be) very rare to find. **(ICSE 2010)**

Ans. 1. will be remembered 2. was
3. taught 4. used
5. wanted 6. lay
7. had 8. is

Q.22 The man **(0) called** (to call) Boone, **(1)** .... (to wake) up at the crack of dawn and **(2)** .... (to make) his way to the pier. His assistant was already **(3)** .... (to pack) the fishing net as the boat gently **(4)** .... (to bob) in the calm waters. "What **(5)** .... (to do) it look like Jon?", **(6)** .... (to ask) Boone. "The forecast **(7)** .... (to mention) a quiet start to the day with a spell of rain **(8)** .... (to come) later on in the afternoon." "Well, let's set off then as soon as you are done."

Ans. 1. woke 2. made
3. packing 4. bobbed
5. does 6. asked
7. mentioned 8. to come

Q.23 I **(1)** .... (realise) that I **(2)** .... (know) one of the two men by sight, and I **(3)** .... (spend) a few seconds thinking why he **(4)** .... (seek) me out on a Sunday afternoon. **(5)** .... (walk) up the passage from the house behind me, **(6)** .... (thread) a way around me and the two men outside, and silently **(7)** .... (climb) like cats up into a tree in the middle of the lawn outside. There, the three figures **(8)** .... (rest).

Ans. 1. realised 2. knew
3. spent 4. sought
5. walked 6. threading
7. climbed 8. rested

11

PREPOSITIONS

A preposition is a word which shows the relationship of the nouns (or the pronouns) with the other words in the sentence.

Role of a Preposition

Prepositions are important when constructing sentences. Prepositions are usually short words and are generally placed directly in front of nouns. For example,

1. He kept the water bottle on the table.
   (The preposition 'on' shows the relationship between *water bottle* and *table.*)
2. The school is between the church and the confectionary shop.
   (The preposition 'between' shows the relationship between *the church* and *the confectionary shop.*)

Some Prepositions and Their Uses

Common Prepositions	Their Uses	Examples
On	• to refer to specific days and dates (time) • to refer to a surface (place) • to refer to devices (agent)	• He will meet you after dance class on Monday. • The kitten is sleeping on the ground. • Right now, she is watching her favourite show on the TV.
At	• to refer to a specific time • to indicate a place	• He called me at 8 o'clock yesterday. • I will see you at the venue.
In	• to specify day, month, season, year (time) • to indicate a location (place) • used while doing something (agent) • to indicate color, shape and size	• The session will begin in March. • Your dog is running in the park. • She went to Chennai in a hurry. • This shirt comes in four colours.
To	• to refer to a time period • to indicate the direction	• You have to be there from 1 p.m. to 2:30 pm. • My cousins went to watch a game.
For	• to indicate the duration or time • to indicate the receiver • to indicate the purpose of an action	• We walked around for an hour. • She bought this bag for me. • We use the hall for dance practice.
With	• to indicate agent • to indicate being together	• I wrote to her with my favourite pencil. • He ordered a coffee with the brownie.

Common Prepositions	Their Uses	Examples
By	• to indicate an end point of time • to indicate proximity (place) • to indicate means or a method (agent)	• They should arrive by tomorrow. • She was standing by her brother. • I request you to send this file by mail.
Since	• to indicate that something started in the past and continues till now	• No one has seen him since the last weekend.
From	• to show the time or point in time when something starts. • to show who sent something/somebody • to show the range of something	• Tickets for the game are available from this week. • He received a mail from his estranged father. • The store sells everything from pins to computers.
After	• to refer to a later time • to indicate place next to • following somebody	• She will arrive home after a month. • My name comes after his in the list. • He ran after her when she left.
Before	• to refer to timed events • to refer to place	• I like to practice my violin before the evening tea. • Remember to get off the bus before the school.
Until/till	• to show when something will happen, begin or end	• Until I see it, I won't believe it.
During	• to denote the length of time in which something happens	• During the holidays, I wrote many poems.
Beside	• means next to or at the side of	• The building beside the school is being demolished today.
Besides	• means in addition to	• Besides him, who did you tell?
Of	• to indicate relating to, belonging to • to indicate measurement • to indicate being part of something	• The poet is a close acquaintance of mine. • The cost of 2 kgs of onion is 50 rupees. • The lid of the box has fallen down.

EXAM ORIENTED QUESTIONS

Q.1 Fill in the blanks with an appropriate words.

(i) My best friend, John is named .... his grandfather.

(ii) A grey mist hung .... the fields.

(iii) The little girl spoke .... against the bully.

(iv) They accused him .... theft.

(v) The police got the fire .... control.

(vi) There is a bridge .... the river.

(vii) The driver jumped .... the car.

(viii) I have not seen my uncle .... last summer.

Ans. (i) after (ii) over (iii) out
(iv) of (v) under (vi) over
(vii) out of (viii) since

Q.2 Fill in the blanks with an appropriate word. **(ICSE Specimen 2025)**

(i) We can cut .... this field instead of taking the main road.

(ii) Passangers are advised .... standing on the footboard of a moving bus.

(iii) They have been working on the project .... years now.

(iv) Ever .... the accident, he has been afraid of boarding buses.

(v) It is a hard climb .... the hill.

(vi) She turned .... the offer because she did not like the terms and conditions.

(vii) I will need to speak .... my parents before I sign up for the school trip.

(viii) The sports teacher was taken .... when he heard how enthusiastic the team was.

Ans. (i) across (ii) against (iii) for
(iv) since (v) up (vi) down
(vii) to (viii) aback

Q.3 Fill in each blank with an appropriate word. **(Competency Based Que.)**

(i) The jumble sale will be held .... the weekend.

(ii) We can rummage .... these old clothes and we are sure to find something useful to sell.

(iii) The senior students have been hard at work .... yesterday.

(iv) Stalls will also be put .... selling craftwork students have made.

(v) The proceeds will go .... charity.

(vi) Volunteer students will be placed .... duty at important junctions.

(vii) I will need to wait .... my parents agree before I sign up as a volunteer.

(viii) Everyone is excited .... the thought of being able to participate.

(ix) The young man jumped .... the running bus.

(x) The soldier succumbed .... his injuries.

(xi) The boy takes .... his father.

(xii) Suman was leaning .... the wall when the earthquake struck.

(xiii) The dog hid .... the bed when the storm began.

(xiv) We must abide .... the laws of the country.

(xv) The Supreme Court set .... the decree of the High Court.

(xvi) I will go .... the notes once more before the examination.

Ans. (i) during (ii) through (iii) since
(iv) up (v) to (vi) on
(vii) till (viii) at (ix) off
(x) to (xi) after (xii) against
(xiii) under/behind (xiv) by (xv) aside
(xvi) through

Q.4 Fill in the blanks with an appropriate words. **(ICSE 2024)**

(i) There's a black cat sitting .... the wall.

(ii) The horse jumped .... the hedge.

(iii) Mother goes .... the market every day.

(iv) Several people have climbed Mount Everest .... recent years.

(v) I often go to school .... my friend.

(vi) I have left my keys .... home.

(vii) Instead of talking, prove your worth .... doing something.

(viii) I have not slept .... yesterday.

Ans. (i) on (ii) over (iii) to
(iv) in (v) with (vi) at
(vii) by (viii) since

Q.5 Fill in the blanks with an appropriate word. **(ICSE Specimen 2024)**

(i) My sister and I get .... very well with each other.

(ii) Mini plays basketball .... her friends every day.

(iii) It has been twenty years .... she graduated from college.

(iv) Growing up, we were looked .... and brought up by our grandparents.

(v) Most students take the bus .... school as it reaches the premises on time.

(vi) The cricket match was put .... because of torrential rains.

(vii) Roy backed .... of the competition at the last minute.

(viii) I have been training under her .... the past two years.

Ans. (i) along (ii) with (iii) since (iv) after (v) to (vi) off (vii) out (viii) for

Q.6 Fill in the blanks with an appropriate words. **(ICSE 2023)**

(i) A bird .... hand is worth two in the bush.

(ii) The boy is crazy .... football.

(iii) She was tired .... fighting and struggling all the time.

(iv) He opted .... of the race.

(v) We borrowed the bikes .... our uncle.

(vi) The police station is .... the right.

(vii) I looked at the stars .... the telescope.

(viii) There was an accident .... the crossroads.

Ans. (i) in (ii) about (iii) of (iv) out (v) from (vi) on (vii) through (viii) at

Q.7 Fill in the blanks with an appropriate word. **(ICSE Specimen 2023)**

(i) Please wash .... the curry stain from your dress.

(ii) She turned .... the offer to work at the factory.

(iii) The burglars broke .... the house when the family was away.

(iv) I shall compete .... him.

(v) She agreed .... my proposal.

(vi) She would like to come .... foot.

(vii) The Vishwas Group of Companies has taken .... the cosmetic market completely.

(viii) He agreed to carry .... the manager's orders.

Ans. (i) away (ii) down (iii) into (iv) with (v) to (vi) on (vii) over (viii) out

Q.8 Choose the correct option to fill in the blanks. **(ICSE Specimen 2022 Sem II Modified)**

(i) He was frightened so he hid .... the cupboard.

(ii) They built a bridge .... a turbulent stream.

(iii) His intelligence will carry him .... all his difficulties.

(iv) She called .... her teacher to help her to sort out her difficulties.

Ans. (i) behind/inside (ii) across (iii) through (iv) up

Q.9 Fill in the blanks with an appropriate word. **(ICSE 2020)**

(i) It has been raining .... two hours.

(ii) He just scrapped .... his examination.

(iii) Mrs. Kapoor was bent .... attending the meeting.

(iv) She is proud and looks .... on her colleagues.

(v) Rahul plays football .... his grandfather.

(vi) The mother was sitting .... the sick child all night.

(vii) Monica is leaning .... the wall.

(viii) Rosie is very good .... art and craft.

Ans. (i) for (ii) through (iii) upon (iv) down (v) with (vi) beside (vii) against (viii) at

Q.10 Fill in each blank with an appropriate word. **(ICSE 2019)**

(i) The puppy was hiding .... the sofa.

(ii) Stop worrying .... your future.

(iii) When I stepped .... the lift, I found it had stopped working.

(iv) We had to use a bridge to go .... the river.

(v) I have lived in this town .... ten years.

(vi) Please switch .... all lights and fans when you leave the room.

(vii) Ronnie is married .... my cousin.

(viii) The gift came .... a birthday card.

Ans. (i) beneath (ii) about (iii) into (iv) across (v) for (vi) off (vii) to (viii) with

Q.11 Fill in each blank with an appropriate word. **(ICSE Specimen 2019)**

(i) He hid the stolen goods .... the floor boards.

(ii) The teacher knew all .... the problem.

(iii) The boy sat still .... the night waiting to be called.

(iv) My grandmother would have fallen .... if I had not caught her hand.

(v) The sailor held on to the mast of the boat for fear of being blown .... in the storm.

(vi) All the boarders were taken .... a walk today.

(vii) Even though she slept .... several mattresses, she still felt the hard pea.

(viii) Anup and Arun have quarrelled .... a silly matter.

Ans. (i) under (ii) about (iii) throughout
(iv) off (v) away (vi) on
(vii) on (viii) over

Q.12 Fill in each blank with an appropriate word. **(ICSE 2018)**

(i) The poet's mother was stung .... a scorpion.

(ii) "Please write .... what I tell you; otherwise, you will forget," the teacher said.

(iii) The dog was hiding .... the bed, barking at the stranger.

(iv) Sheila's grandmother found it difficult to climb .... the steep staircase.

(v) The soldier fought bravely .... his country.

(vi) There is no use crying .... split milk.

(vii) I don't know what they were arguing .... but I could hear angry voices.

(viii) The school playground is out .... bounds for the pupils of the primary school.

Ans. (i) by (ii) down (iii) under
(iv) up (v) for (vi) over
(vii) about (viii) of

Q.13 Fill in each blank with an appropriate word. **(ICSE 2017)**

(i) She shouted angrily .... the disobedient boy.

(ii) I asked them to provide us .... a guide.

(iii) The tree grew at a dangerous slant and had to be cut ....

(iv) My daughter believes .... fairies.

(v) He drew a beautiful diagram .... the board.

(vi) She battled her way .... the crowd.

(vii) We were asked to gather .... the teacher.

(viii) They had to climb .... the steep pathway to reach the top.

Ans. (i) at (ii) with (iii) down
(iv) in (v) on (vi) through
(vii) around (viii) up

Q.14 Fill in the blanks with an appropriate word.
(ICSE Specimen 2017)

(i) Her parents live .... New Delhi.

(ii) Joe's parents are sick .... his behaviour.

(iii) Colonel Gurmeet congratulated the soldiers .... their victory.

(iv) The planet was seen .... the telescope.

(v) The news of his promotion came .... the next day.

(vi) He is not afraid .... the consequences.

(vii) He rushed .... the class as he was late.

(viii) The school is famous .... its sports achievements.

Ans. (i) in (ii) of (iii) on
(iv) through (v) on (vi) of
(vii) to (viii) for

Q.15 Fill in each blank with an appropriate word. **(ICSE 2016)**

(i) There was a steep rise .... onion prices.

(ii) Air pollution is responsible for the spread .... bronchitis.

(iii) He was .... pressure to complete the work.

(iv) John jumped .... the river to rescue the child.

(v) His teacher is very pleased .... him.

(vi) Ali took .... his cap and wiped his face.

(vii) The old woman could not get .... the shock.

(viii) He should not get .... with such rudeness.

Ans. (i) in (ii) of (iii) under
(iv) into (v) with (vi) off
(vii) over (viii) away

Q.16 Fill in the blanks with an appropriate word. **(ICSE 2015)**

(i) He found the key just .... the front door.

(ii) I could not accompany my cousin .... the trip because I had fever.

(iii) The noise prevented us .... sleeping.

(iv) The young man put the flute .... his lips and began to play.

(v) Ashok leaned .... the wall tiredly.

(vi) The paper dart went gliding .... the air.

(vii) The cyclist rode quickly .... the path.

(viii) The young child carried the heavy bucket .... the stairs.

Ans. (i) near (ii) on (iii) from
(iv) to (v) against (vi) into
(vii) on (viii) up

Q.17 Fill in the blanks with an appropriate word. **(ICSE 2011)**

(i) He congratulated me .... my great achievement.

(ii) The poor man is afflicted .... arthritis.

(iii) She is blind .... the faults of her husband.

(iv) The boss had many complaints .... Shyam.

(v) You must prepare .... the examinations.
(vi) She is not aware .... the danger.
(vii) Ravi was accurate .... his calculations.
(viii) They hid the money .... the carpet.

Ans. (i) on (ii) with
(iii) to (iv) against
(v) for (vi) of
(vii) with (viii) under

Q.18 Fill in the blanks with an appropriate word. **(ICSE 2010)**
(i) I refrained .... telling Reeta the truth.
(ii) The leader counted .... the cooperation of his colleagues.
(iii) The public was cautioned .... pickpockets.
(iv) Janaki escorted her daughter to the cinema theatre as she was anxious .... her safety.
(v) The path was beset .... difficulties yet they succeeded.
(vi) The mouse crept stealthily .... the cheese.
(vii) It was good .... you to invite Sheila for the picnic.
(viii) Smoking .... public places is banned now.

Ans. (i) from (ii) on
(iii) against (iv) about
(v) with (vi) towards
(vii) of (viii) in

Q.19 Fill in the blanks with an appropriate word. **(ICSE 2009)**
(i) I prevailed .... him to join the gymnasium.
(ii) The curious child eagerly begged .... an answer to the riddle.
(iii) He was bent .... coming first in the examination.
(iv) The theory exam was followed .... a group discussion.
(v) I ran .... my teacher at the show last night.
(vi) She is extremely anxious .... the interview next week.
(vii) What a contrast .... the two siblings!
(viii) The brothers fought .... their father's property.

Ans. (i) upon (ii) for
(iii) on/upon (iv) by
(v) into (vi) about
(vii) between (viii) over/for

Q.20 Fill in the blanks with an appropriate word. **(ICSE 2008)**
(i) The elderly man prepared himself for a life .... retirement.
(ii) Do you take his word .... mine?
(iii) Rohini is very concerned .... her father's health.
(iv) Altaf had many books and papers scattered all .... the room.
(v) The phoenix is a legendry bird that rises ...... its ashes.
(vi) The police pulled the briefcase from ...... the table.
(vii) The mob rushed onto the pavement, everyone seemed angry .... everyone else.
(viii) The old woman looked .... the cupboard, searching for the photograph.

Ans. (i) after (ii) over
(iii) about (iv) over
(v) from (vi) under
(vii) with (viii) inside/into

Q.21 Fill in the blanks with an appropriate word.
(i) Truth always prevails .... the long-run.
(ii) Sujata stood ..... the river and saw the ship pass by.
(iii) She took some money .... her father to buy a video game.
(iv) Shilpa gave me a rare gift .... my birthday.
(v) Deepak was very upset .... me.
(vi) Michelle is longing .... meet me.
(vii) It has been a long time .... I met my sister.
(viii) The worker asked .... his wages.

Ans. (i) in (ii) beside
(iii) from (iv) for
(v) with (vi) to
(vii) since (viii) for

12

CONJUNCTION AND COMBINATION OF SENTENCES

Conjunctions

Conjunctions are one or more words used to join phrases, clauses or sentences to form new sentences.

Conjunctions can be divided into four categories. They are

1. Coordinating Conjunctions

Coordinating conjunctions are used to join two words, clauses or sentences of equal importance. There are seven coordinating conjunctions, which are and, but, for, or, yet, so, nor.

Use of Coordinating Conjunctions

Coordinating Conjunction	Uses	Sentences	Sentences Combined Using Conjunctions
For	Used when we have to express a reason or a cause	I could not attend the wedding. I had a fever.	I could not attend the wedding for I had a fever.
And	To join together two sentences or words	She called me. She told me about her situation.	She called me and told me about her situation.
Nor	To introduce further negative sentence	The teacher did not smile. She did not speak to the class.	The teacher did not smile, nor did she speak to the class.
But	To join words or sentences which have opposite ideas	He put too much sugar in the dessert. The dessert turned out delicious.	He put too much sugar in the dessert but it turned out delicious.
Or	To join words or sentences which offer a choice	Do the chores of the house. Clean your room.	Do the chores of the house or clean your room.
Yet	To join words or sentences those have opposite ideas	They were poor. They were happy.	They were poor, yet happy.
So	To express result	Manisha broke her arm. She won't come to school.	Manisha broke her arm so she won't come to school.

2. Subordinating Conjunctions

A subordinating conjunction introduces the subordinate clause in a sentence and joins it with the main clause.

Some common subordinating conjunctions are though, although, since, after, as, because, before, lest, than, till, until, if, while, when, whether.

Use of Subordinate Conjunctions

Subordinating Conjunction	Uses	Sentences	Sentences Combined Using Conjunctions
Although/Though	To join words or sentences those have opposite ideas	She lives far away. She always comes on time.	Although she lives far away, she always comes on time.
Because	Used when we have to express a reason or a cause	Lata Mangeshkar is my favourite singer. I love her voice.	Lata Mangeshkar is my favourite singer because I love her voice.
As	Use when we have to express reason, time, comparison or a condition	You should take an umbrella. It is going to rain today.	You should take an umbrella as it is going to rain today.
If	Used when there is a condition	You work hard for the prize. You will win the prize.	You will win the prize if you work hard for it.
Unless		It is raining outside. You have to go to school.	Unless it is raining outside, you have to go to school.
As soon as	To indicate that an action will happen immediately after another action.	I will call you immediately after reaching home.	As soon as I reach home, I will call you.
Where	To indicate place or location	I will meet you there. The place where we always used to meet.	I will meet you where we always used to meet.
Before	To indicate time or duration	Please come home. It will get dark soon.	Please come home before it gets dark.
After		I got a call from Sona. You'd left.	After you'd left, I got a phone call from Sona.
Till		He stayed in the classroom. He finished the work.	He stayed in the classroom till he finished the work.
Since		I have played in this park. I was a child.	I have played in this park since I was a child.

3. Correlative Conjunctions

A correlative conjunction is a pair of words that is used to join two or more clauses or sentences of equal importance.

Some common correlative conjunctions are both...and, not only...but also, either...or, neither...nor, no sooner...than, hardly...when, such...that.

Use of Correlative Conjunctions

Correlative Conjunction	Uses	Sentences	Sentences Combined Using Conjunctions
Both....and	To express a statement together or two qualities	Kenneth scores well because he is hardworking. He scores well because he is intelligent.	Kenneth scores well because he is both hardworking and intelligent.
Either....or	To express a choice	I want to travel to Manali. I want to travel to Ladakh.	I want to travel to either Manali or Ladakh.
Neither…nor	To express that none of the choices can be taken	Meenal doesn't want to go into that room. Sheela doesn't want to go into that room.	Neither Meenal nor Sheela wants to go into that room.
Not only…but also	Referring to two actions/things/people	Her dress is extraordinary. Her jewellery is extraordinary.	Not only her dress but also her jewellery is extraordinary.
No sooner…than	To show that one action immediately followed another action	They had completed the work. They demanded the wages.	No sooner had they completed the work than they demanded the wages.
Such…that	To show a cause and effect relationship between two actions	The man spoke with passion. All the listeners were moved to tears.	The man spoke with such passion that all the listeners were moved to tears.
Whether..or	To introduce a choice between two alternatives.	She may or may not come to the party. I don't know.	I don't know whether she will come to the party or not.
As much..as	To make comparisons indicating equality.	He loves basketball. He loves football.	He loves basketball as much as he loves football.

EXAM ORIENTED QUESTIONS

Q.1 Choose the correct option to make one complete sentence **without using <u>and, but</u>** or **<u>so</u>**. **(ICSE 2025, 4 M)**

(i) **These are fresh mangoes. I bought them yesterday.**

(a) These are fresh mangoes which I bought yesterday.

(b) These mangoes were fresher when I bought them yesterday.

(c) These are fresh mangoes which were bought yesterday.

(d) These are fresh mangoes brought by me yesterday.

(ii) **The debating teams were very happy. They were declared joint champions.**

(a) The debating teams were very happy as they have been declared joint champions.

(b) The debating teams are very happy as they are declared joint champions.

(c) The debating teams were very happy as they had been declared joint champions.

(d) The debating teams will be very happy as they will be declared joint champions.

(iii) **The rain came down. All the people ran away.**

(a) When the rain came down, all the people ran away.

(b) When it rained, the people ran away.

(c) The rain had come down all the people ran away.

(d) The The rain having come, all the people ran away.

(iv) **The disciple was wise. The teacher did not trust him.**

(a) Although the disciple was wise yet the teacher trusted him.

(b) Although the disciple was not wise the teacher trusted him.

(c) Although the disciple is wise, the teacher trusted him.

(d) Although the disciple was wise, the teacher did not trust him.

Ans. (i) (a) (ii) (c) (iii) (a) (iv) (d)

Q.2 Join the following sentences to make one complete sentence without using and, but or so. Choose the correct option. **(ICSE Specimen 2025)**

(i) **Stay still. We cannot take your photograph otherwise.**

(a) Stay still, else we cannot take your photograph otherwise.

(b) Stay still because we can take your photograph otherwise.

(c) Unless you stay still, we cannot take your photograph.

(d) If you stay still we cannot take your photograph.

(ii) **Roy's mother rang up the school office. She wanted to enquire about the swimming classes at the summer camp.**

(a) Roy's mother rang up the school office as she want to enquire about the swimming classes at the summer camp.

(b) Roy's mother rang up the school office to enquire about the swimming classes at the summer camp.

(c) Roy's mother has rung up the school office to enquire about the swimming classes at the summer camp.

(d) Roy's mother rang up the school office wanting enquiry about the swimming classes at the summer camp.

(iii) **I left my keys somewhere. Do you know where they are?**

(a) Do you know where I had left my keys?

(b) Do you know where my keys were left behind?

(c) Do you know where I left my keys?

(d) Do you know where I would have left my keys?

(iv) **The captain should not be blamed for the team's defeat. The players should not be blamed for the team's defeat.**

(a) The captain should neither be blamed nor the players should be blamed for the team's defeat.

(b) Neither the captain nor the players should be blamed for the team's defeat.

(c) The captain should not be blamed for the team's defeat as the players should not be blamed for the team's defeat.

(d) The captain should not be blamed for the team's defeat but the players too should not be blamed for the team's defeat.

Ans. (i) (c) (ii) (b) (iii) (c) (iv) (b)

Q.3 Join the sentences to make one complete sentence without using and, but or so. Choose the correct option. **(Competency Based Que.)**

(i) The fans were on. It felt hot and humid.
(a) In spite of the fans being on, it was feeling hot and humid.
(b) It felt hot and humid, but the fans were on.
(c) It felt hot and humid despite the fans being on.
(d) Due to it feeling hot and humid, the fans were being put on.

(ii) You may get lost. Follow the guide.
(a) Follow the guide if you don't want to get lost forever.
(b) You may get lost unless you follow the guide
(c) You may follow the guide and get lost
(d) You should not get lost, do follow the guide.

(iii) It is very hot. I can't go out now.
(a) It is very hot, so I can't go out now.
(b) It is too hot, and I can't go out now.
(c) It was very hot to go out now.
(d) It is so hot that I can't go out now.

(iv) I bought these mangoes yesterday. They are very sweet.
(a) I bought these mangoes yesterday which are very sweet.
(b) These mangoes which I bought yesterday are very sweet.
(c) I bought these mangoes yesterday because they are very sweet.
(d) Since I bought these mangoes yesterday, they are very sweet.

(v) Jack took a holiday. He wanted to visit his grandmother.
(a) Jack took a holiday when he wanted to visit his grandmother.
(b) Jack took a holiday as because he wanted to visit his grandmother.
(c) Jack took a holiday to visit his grandmother.
(d) Jack wanted to visit his grandmother, so he took a holiday.

(vi) The baby ate his breakfast. He went to sleep.
(a) Having eaten his breakfast, the baby went to sleep.
(b) By eating his breakfast, the baby went to sleep.
(c) Having eaten his breakfast, he went to sleep.
(d) Eating his breakfast, the boy went off to sleep.

(vii) Tanya plays the guitar. Soham plays the guitar.
(a) Both Tanya and Soham play the guitar.
(b) Both Tanya and Soham play the guitar.
(c) Tanya, as well as Soham, play the guitar
(d) Tanya, as well as Soham, plays the guitar.

(viii) Ravi did not lock the house. Ravi did not lock the gates.
(a) Neither Ravi locked the house nor the gates.
(b) Ravi locked neither the house nor the gates.
(c) Neither did Ravi lock the house or the gates.
(d) Neither the house nor the gates did Ravi lock.

Ans. (i) (c) (ii) (b) (iii) (d) (iv) (b)
(v) (c) (vi) (a) (vii) (d) (viii) (b)

Q.4 Choose the correct option to make one complete sentence without using and, but or so. **(ICSE 2024)**

(i) The magician took pity on the mouse. He turned it into a cat.
(a) Showing pity on the mouse he turned it into a cat.
(b) Taking pity on the mouse he turned it into a cat.
(c) The magician turned the mouse into a cat by taking pity.
(d) Taking pity on the mouse the magician turned it into a cat.

(ii) This work must be completed. There is a deadline.
(a) Since this work must be completed, there is a deadline.
(b) This work must be completed because there is a deadline.
(c) This work must be completed though there is a deadline.
(d) This work must be completed when there is a deadline.

(iii) He fled somewhere. His pursuers could not follow him.
(a) He fled where his pursuers could not follow him
(b) He pursued somewhere his followers could not flee.
(c) He fled somewhere when his pursuers could not follow him.
(d) He fled where his pursuers cannot follow him.

(iv) He began late. He finished first.
(a) He finished first and began late.
(b) He began first but finished late.
(c) Though he finished late, he began first.
(d) Though he began late, he finished first.

Ans. (i) (d) (ii) (b) (iii) (a) (iv) (d)

Q.5 Join the following sentences to make one complete sentence without using and, but or so. Choose the correct option. **(ICSE Specimen 2024)**

(i) We placed our order late. We received the food on time.
(a) Despite placed our order late, the food was received on time.
(b) Despite placing our order late, we received the food on time.

(c) Despite we placed our order late, the food was received on time.
(d) Despite of us placing our order late, we receiving the food on time.

(ii) **The music stopped. The audience left the auditorium.**
(a) Hardly had the music stopped so the audience left the auditorium.
(b) Hardly had the music stopped then the audience left the auditorium.
(c) Hardly had the music stopped since the audience left the auditorium.
(d) Hardly had the music stopped when the audience left the auditorium

(iii) **You cannot enter the club. You do not have a membership.**
(a) You cannot enter the club unless you have a membership.
(b) You cannot enter the club since you have a membership.
(c) You cannot enter the club whereas you have a membership.
(d) You cannot enter the club if you have a membership.

(iv) **She was very late. She could not catch the train.**
(a) She was to late to catch the train.
(b) She was so late to catch the train.
(c) She was too late to catch the train.
(d) She was as late so as to catch the train.

Ans. (i) (b) (ii) (d) (iii) (a) (iv) (c)

Q.6 **Join the following sentences to make one complete sentence without using and, but or so. Choose the correct option.** **(ICSE 2023)**

(i) **He jumped up. He ran away.**
(a) He jumped up before he ran away.
(b) Jumping up, he ran away.
(c) He ran away after jumping.
(d) He ran away because he jumped up.

(ii) **He has failed many time. Still, he hopes to succeed.**
(a) He succeeds after he failed many times.
(b) Despite of failing, he hopes to succeed.
(c) In spite of many failures, he hopes to succeed.
(d) He failed many times even though he hopes to succeed.

(iii) **Do not be a jeweller. Do not be a goldsmith.**
(a) Be neither a jeweller nor a goldsmith.
(b) Be both a jeweller and a goldsmith.
(c) Either be a jeweller or a goldsmith.
(d) Be a jeweller as well as a goldsmith.

(iv) **A cottager and his wife had a hen. The hen had an egg every day.**
(a) Everyday, a hen laid an egg for a cottager and his wife.
(b) A cottager and his wife had a hen who laid an egg every day.
(c) The cottager and his wife had an egg every day because they had a hen.
(d) A cottager and his wife had a hen which laid an egg every day.

Ans. (i) (c) (ii) (c) (iii) (a) (iv) (d)

Q.7 **Choose the correct option to join the following sentences without using and, but or so.** **(ICSE Specimen 2022 Sem II)**

(i) **He plays cricket. He plays tennis.**
(a) He plays not only cricket but also tennis.
(b) He plays either cricket or tennis.
(c) He plays cricket as well as tennis.
(d) He plays neither cricket nor tennis.

(ii) **Submit your project. Only then can you appear for the test.**
(a) Until you submit your project, you can appear for the test.
(b) Until you appear for the test, you cannot submit your project.
(c) Unless you submit your project, you can appear for the test.
(d) Unless you submit your project, you cannot appear for the test.

(iii) **The man was running fast. The police caught him.**
(a) Although the man was running fast, the police caught him.
(b) The police caught the man in spite he was running fast.
(c) Despite his running fast, the man caught the police.
(d) The man was running fast although the police caught him.

(iv) **Sheena drew a picture. Her mother put it up on the fridge.**
(a) Her mother put a picture on the fridge that Sheena drew.
(b) Sheena drew a picture that her mother put on the fridge.
(c) He mother drew a picture that Sheena put on the fridge.
(d) Her mother put on the picture that Sheena drew.

Ans. (i) (c) (ii) (d) (iii) (a) (iv) (b)

Q.8 Choose the correct option to join the following sentences without using and, but or so. Choose the correct option. **(ICSE 2021)**

(i) **He will be late. It is certain.**
 (a) He is certainly late.
 (b) It is late he will be certain.
 (c) He is certain to be late.
 (d) He is certain that he will be late.

(ii) **She keeps her money in the purse. This is the purse.**
 (a) She keeps the purse with the money.
 (b) This is the purse where she keeps her money.
 (c) This is the money which she keeps in the purse.
 (d) The money in the purse is here.

(iii) **He said something. I did not hear.**
 (a) I hear he said something.
 (b) I heard something what he said.
 (c) I did not hear what he said.
 (d) I did hear what he said.

(iv) **He may be blunt. He is at least honest.**
 (a) Although he is blunt, he is at least honest.
 (b) He may be blunt and honest at least.
 (c) He is blunt and at least honest.
 (d) He is at least blunt and honest.

Ans. (i) (c) (ii) (b) (iii) (c) (iv) (a)

Q.9 Join the following sentences to make one complete sentence without using and, but or so. **(ICSE 2020 Modified)**

(i) **Sarah and Tyra are twins. They look exactly alike.**
 (a) Sarah and Tyra look exactly alike, as they are twins.
 (b) They are twins, hence, Sarah and Tyra look exactly alike.
 (c) For they are twins, Sarah and Tyra look exactly alike.
 (d) Given that they are twins, Sarah and Tyra look exactly alike.

(ii) **Rohan does not like to play cricket. He does not like to play hockey either.**
 (a) Rohan neither likes to play cricket or hockey.
 (b) Rohan neither like to play cricket nor hockey.
 (c) Rohan does not like to play either cricket or hockey.
 (d) Rohan likes to play neither cricket or hockey.

(iii) **Sania pushed as hard as she could. The door would not open.**
 (a) Though Sania pushed as hard as she could yet, the door would not open.
 (b) Though Sania pushed as hard as she could, she could not open the door.
 (c) Though Sania pushed as hard as she could, the door would not open.
 (d) Though Sania pushed as hard as she could, the door did not open.

(iv) **The school bus drove through the gate. The clock was striking eight at that moment.**
 (a) When the bus drove through the gate, the clock struck eight.
 (b) As soon as the bus drove through the gate, the clock struck eight.
 (c) After the bus drove through the gate, the clock struck eight.
 (d) Both (a) and (b)

Ans. (i) (a) (ii) (d) (iii) (c) (iv) (a)

Q.10 Join the following sentences to make one complete sentence without using and, but or so. **(ICSE 2020 Modified)**

(i) **He was very ill. He did not take any medicine.**
 (a) Even when ill, he did not take medicine.
 (b) Although he was very ill, he did not take any medicine.
 (c) He was very ill yet he did not take any medicine.
 (d) Both (a) and (c)

(ii) **You come back from your holiday. We will discuss the problem.**
 (a) When you come back from your holiday, we will discuss the problem.
 (b) As soon as you came back from your holiday, we will discuss the problem.
 (c) When you came back from your holiday, we will discuss the problem.
 (d) We will discuss the problem after you come back holidays.

(iii) **He remained absent on Friday. It was foolish of him.**
 (a) It is foolish of him to be absent on Friday.
 (b) It was foolish of him to remain absent on Friday.
 (c) It was considered foolish of him that he remained absent on Friday.
 (d) It was foolish of him to be absent.

(iv) **Rahul ran all the way to the bus stop. He missed the bus.**
 (a) When Rahul ran all the way to the bus stop, he missed the bus.
 (b) Although Rahul ran all the way to the bus stop, he missed the bus.
 (c) Even if Rahul runs all the way to the bus stop, he will miss the bus.
 (d) When Rahul runs all the way to the bus stop, he misses the bus.

Ans. (i) (b) (ii) (d) (iii) (b) (iv) (b)

Q.11 Join the following sentences to make one complete sentence without using and, but or so.
(ICSE 2018 Modified)

(i) **They have to go to bed early every night. They are allowed to stay up late on Saturdays.**
 (a) They have to go to bed every night except on Saturdays.
 (b) On Saturday, they are allowed to stay up late or otherwise they have to go to bed every night.
 (c) They have to go to bed early every night except Saturdays, when they are allowed to stay up late.
 (d) None of the above

(ii) **The children were delighted. The exams had been cancelled.**
 (a) The children were delighted because the exams had been cancelled.
 (b) The exams had been cancelled because the children were delighted.
 (c) The children were delighted that the exams had been cancelled.
 (d) The exams had been cancelled as if the children were delighted.

(iii) **We are not allowed to play in the Sun. We are not allowed to play in the rain.**
 (a) We are not allowed to play in the Sun or the rain.
 (b) We are neither allowed to play in the Sun or in the rain.
 (c) And in the rain, we are not allowed to play or in the Sun.
 (d) In the rain and in the Sun, we are allowed to play.

(iv) **This is the place. The dog was rescued from its cruel owner.**
 (a) This is the place when the dog was rescued from its cruel owner.
 (b) This is the place where the dog was rescued from its cruel owner.
 (c) The dog was rescued from this place from its cruel owner.
 (d) All of the above

Ans. (i) (a) (ii) (a) (iii) (b) (iv) (b)

Q.12 Join the following sentences to make one complete sentence without using and, but or so.
(ICSE 2017 Modified)

(i) **This is the hospital. I was born here.**
 (a) This is the hospital where I was born.
 (b) I was born in this hospital.
 (c) I was born in that hospital.
 (d) Both (a) and (b)

(ii) **The children have been sick for a week. They were unable to go to school.**
 (a) The children were unable to go to school as they were sick.
 (b) Being sick for a week, the children didn't go to school.
 (c) Having been sick for a week, the children were unable to go to school.
 (d) Having been sick for a week, that the children were unable to go to school.

(iii) **Mrs. Kumar has been a teacher for thirty years. She will now retire.**
 (a) As Mrs. Kumar has been a teacher for thirty years, she will now retire.
 (b) Mrs. Kumar who has been a teacher for thirty years will now retire.
 (c) It is time for Mrs. Kumar to retire.
 (d) Mrs. Kumar has been a teacher for thirty years for now she will retire.

(iv) **We have had no respect for nature. Now, we are suffering from the effects of global warming.**
 (a) Since we have no respect for nature, we are suffering from the effects of global warming.
 (b) Because we have no respect for nature, we are suffering from the effects of global warming.
 (c) As we have no respect for nature, we are suffering from the effects of global warming.
 (d) All of the above

Ans. (i) (d) (ii) (c) (iii) (b) (iv) (d)

Q.13 Join the following sentences to make one complete sentence without using and, but or so. Choose the correct option.

(i) **He is good at gymnastics. His handwriting is beautiful.**
 (a) Not only is he good at gymnastics but his handwriting is also beautiful.
 (b) Not only is he good at gymnastics but his handwriting is beautiful.
 (c) Both (a) and (b)
 (d) None of the above

(ii) **Her grandfather gifted her a paint box. He knew she was good at art.**
 (a) He knew she was good at art because her grandfather gifted her a paint box.
 (b) Her grandfather gifted her a paint box because he knew she was good at art.
 (c) Though her grandfather gifted her a paint box, he knew she was good at art.
 (d) Though he knew she was good at art, her grandfather gifted her a paint box.

(iii) **Ravi fractured his arm. He insisted on playing the match.**
(a) Even though he fractured his arm, Ravi insisted on playing the match.
(b) Ravi insisted on playing the match despite having his arm fractured.
(c) Both (a) and (b)
(d) None of the above

(iv) **Mona has been ill for a month. She stood first in the examination.**
(a) Mona has been ill for a month because she stood first in the examination.
(b) Mona stood first in the examination despite having been ill for a month.
(c) Mona stood first in the examination despite of having been ill for a month.
(d) Mona stood first in the examination inspite being ill for a month.

Ans. (i) (a) (ii) (b) (iii) (c) (iv) (b)

Q.14 Join the following sentences to make one complete sentence without using and, but or so. Choose the correct option.

(i) **We had better got ready now. We may not have time to reach the airport.**
(a) We had better get ready now; otherwise, we might not have time to reach the airport.
(b) We had better get ready now and we might not have time to reach the airport.
(c) We might not have time to reach the airport because we had better get ready.
(d) None of the above

(ii) **Mr. Liew has been sick. He has been so since he came back from Japan.**
(a) Mr. Liew has been sick since he came back from Japan.
(b) Mr. Liew has been sick when he came back from Japan.
(c) Mr. Liew has been sick and he has been so since he came back from Japan.
(d) Mr. Liew has been sick because he came back from Japan.

(iii) **The debating teams were very happy. Both were declared joint-champions.**
(a) Both the debating teams were very happy and they were declared joint-champions.
(b) Both the debating teams were very happy; however, they were declared joint-champions.
(c) Both the debating teams were very happy after they were declared joint-champions.
(d) Both the debating teams were very happy as they were declared joint-champions.

(iv) **He escaped from the prison. He looked for a place where he could hide.**
(a) While he escaped from the prison, he looked for a place where he could hide.
(b) He escaped from the prison because he looked for a place where he could hide.
(c) As he escaped from the prison, he looked for a place where he could hide.
(d) Therefore, he escaped from the prison, he looked for a place where he could hide.

Ans. (i) (a) (ii) (a) (iii) (d) (iv) (c)

Q.15 Join the following sentences to make one complete sentence without using and, but or so. Choose the correct option.

(i) **He lived in the city for many years. He could not find his way out.**
(a) Although he lived in the city for many years, yet he could not find his way out.
(b) Although he lived in the city for many years, but he could not find his way out.
(c) Although he lived in the city for many years, he could not find his way out.
(d) None of the above

(ii) **She complained that her brother did not know anything. Her brother claimed he knew everything.**
(a) She complained that her brother did not know anything before her brother claimed he knew everything.
(b) She complained that her brother did not know anything whereas her brother claimed he knew everything.
(c) She complained that her brother did not know anything when her brother claimed he knew everything.
(d) She complained that her brother did not know anything after her brother claimed he knew everything.

(iii) **The coffee isn't strong. It won't keep us awake.**
(a) The coffee isn't strong enough to keep us awake.
(b) The coffee isn't strong for keeping us awake.
(c) The coffee isn't strong because it will keep us awake.
(d) The coffee isn't strong and it won't keep us awake.

(iv) **I finished my homework. I switched on the TV.**
(a) I switched on the TV as I finished my homework.
(b) I switched on the TV while I finished my homework.
(c) I switched on the TV as soon as I finished my homework.
(d) I switched on the TV while I was finishing my homework.

Ans. (i) (c) (ii) (b) (iii) (a) (iv) (c)

13

TRANSFORMATION OF SENTENCES

Transformation means to change the sentence from one grammatical form to another without altering its original sense. There are different ways of transforming a sentence form into another.

Sentence containing Adverb 'Too'

Adding Adverb 'Too'

Adverb 'too' can be added alongwith the infinitive 'to + verb base form' to replace so...that in a sentence.

e.g. (i) Manpreet is so humble that she cannot disobey her mother. (Add 'too')

Manpreet is too humble to disobey her mother.

Removal of Adverb 'Too'

The adverb too can be removed by replacing it with 'so'. The infinitive is replaced by a subordinating clause.

e.g. (i) These apples are too cheap to be good. (Remove too)

These apples are so cheap that they cannot be good.

Interchange of the Degrees of Adjectives

Adjectives not only describe a noun but also to make a comparison between two or more nouns.

When we use an adjective to compare the qualities of two or more nouns, we use degrees of comparison.

There are three forms of degree of comparison. These are

1. Positive Degree of Comparison

The simple from of the adjective is called the positive degree.

e.g. good, rich, tall, young, etc. It states a quality without any comparison.

For example

- This chocolate is <u>sweet</u>.
- Lekha is <u>good</u> at cooking rice.

2. Comparative Degree of Comparison

A comparative degree of an adjective is used to compare the quality between two nouns,

e.g. better, richer, taller, younger, etc.

We always use the word <u>'than'</u> to show the comparison.

For example

- This chocolate is <u>sweeter than</u> the other one.
- Sulekha is <u>worse</u> at cooking rice <u>than</u> Lekha.

3. Superlative Degree of Comparison

A superlative degree of an adjective is used to compare the quality among three or more nouns.

e.g. best, richest, tallest, youngest, etc. It indicates the highest degree of quality.

For example

- This chocolate tastes the <u>sweetest</u>.
- Rekha is the <u>worst</u> at cooking rice.

Superlative to Positive and Comparative Degree

When an object has the highest degree of a quality, it's in the superlative degree.

To transform it into

- **Positive** Use No other...as...as
- **Comparative** Use ...than any other

For example

Superlative	Positive	Comparative
She is the tallest girl in the class.	No other girl in the class is as tall as her.	She is taller than any other girl in the class.
Russia is the largest country in the world.	No other country in the world is as large as Russia.	Russia is larger than any other country in the world.

Positive to Comparative Degree

The positive degree shows equality in comparison.

To transform it

- Begin with the second entity being compared.
- Change an affirmative sentence to negative and vice versa.

For example

Positive	Comparative
Radhika is as intelligent as Siya.	Siya is not more intelligent than Radhika.

Note

- When comparing only two persons or things, the adjective cannot be transformed into the superlative degree.
- Affirmative sentences become negative in transformation and vice versa

Interchanging the Types of Sentences

Change	Explanation	Example
Affirmative ⇌ Negative	• By using antonyms (not + antonym)	Apurva is an industrious girl. (Affirmative) Apurva is not a lazy girl. (Negative) I don't understand this. (Negative) I do understand this. (Affirmative)
Assertive ⇌ Interrogative	• By switching the position of the subject and the auxiliary verb and adding a question mark at the end. • If there is no auxiliary, add the appropriate form of 'do' in the beginning and question mark in the end.	You can wait for a minute. (Assertive) Can't you wait for a minute? (Interrogative) Who doesn't know Hindi in India? (Interrogative) Everybody knows Hindi in India. (Assertive)
Assertive ⇌ Exclamatory	• By adding exclamatory words such as what, how, or an interjection and adding an exclamation mark (!) at the end.	This is a very beautiful sight. (Assertive) What a beautiful sight this is! (Exclamatory) How wonderfully she has done it! (Exclamatory) She has done it wonderfully. (Assertive)
Simple ⇌ Compound	• To convert a simple sentence to a compound sentence, expand a phrase into a subordinate clause. • To convert a compound sentence to a simple one, reduce the independent clauses into a single clause using phrases or participles.	In spite of several attempts, he could not get the visa for Australia. (Simple) He attempted several times but he couldn't get the visa for Australia. (Compound) I will have lunch and come with you. (Compound) After having lunch, I will come with you. (Simple)

Simple ⇌ Complex	• To convert a simple sentence to a complex sentence, expand a phrase into a subordinate clause. • To convert a complex sentence to a simple sentence, reduce the subordinate clause to a phrase or modify it.	In spite of several attempts, he couldn't get the visa for Australia. (Simple) Though he attempted several times, he couldn't get the visa for Australia. (Complex) He carried an umbrella because he did not want to get drenched in the rain. (Complex) He carried an umbrella for not getting drenched in the rain. (Simple)

Synthesis of Sentences

Rules	Original Sentences	Combined Sentence
Using a Participle	He got up early. He went on a walk.	Getting up early, he went on a walk.
	She was irritated by her. She put on headphones.	Irritated by her, she put on headphones.
Using a Noun or Phrase in Apposition	This is my father. His name is Frank.	This is my father, Frank.
Using a Preposition with a Noun/Gerund	He performed so well. She was pleasantly surprised.	On seeing him perform so well, she was pleasantly surprised.
	He is quite sick. He went to work.	In spite of being quite sick, he went to work.
Using the Absolute Construction	The chair was broken. He threw it.	The chair being broken, he threw it.
	The exam was cancelled. He was elated.	The exam being cancelled, he was elated.
Using an Infinitive	Man works day and night. He has to support his family.	Man works day and night to support his family.
	She will go to Kanpur. She will see her father.	She will go to Kanpur to see her father.
Using an Adverb/Adverbial Clause	Great people serve their country. Their service is selfless.	Great people serve their country selflessly.

Interchange of Active and Passive Voice

Rules for Active-Passive Voice Conversions

1. Interchange the object and subject with each other, *i.e.* object of the active voice sentence become subject of the passive voice sentence.
2. Use preposition 'by' before the object of passive voice.
3. The IIIrd form of main verb is used in passive voice.
4. Pronouns can be changed in the following manner.

Subject	Object
I	me
we	us
you	you
he	him
she	her
they	them
Name (Jay/Mayur)	Name remains as it is (Jay/Mayur)

Change of Verb According to Tense

Tense or Modal + Base		Active Voice	Passive Voice
Simple	• Present • Past • Future	• beat/beats • beat • shall/will beat	• am/is/are beaten • was/were beaten • shall /will be beaten
Continuous	• Present • Past • Future	• am/is/are • beating • was/were beating • shall/will be beating	• am/is/are being beaten • was/were being • beaten Not applicable
Perfect	• Present • Past • Future	• have/has beaten • had beaten • shall/will • have beaten	• have/has been beaten • had been beaten • shall/will have been beaten
Perfect Continuous	• Present • Past • Future	Not applicable	Not applicable
	Can/may/must, etc. + base	can/may/must, etc. beat	can/may/must, etc. be beaten

Changes with Modals

- When a sentence in active voice has a modal auxiliary (can, could, may, might, etc.), the modal verb does not change its form and the sentence is changed into passive voice in the following manner
  Active Subject + modal + first form of verb + object
  Passive Object + modal + be + first form of verb + by + subject

e.g. (i) Shaurya <u>can</u> cook many international cuisines. *(Active)*

Many international cuisines <u>can be</u> cooked by Shaurya. *(Passive)*

(ii) My father could visit me in the evening today. *(Active)*

I could be visited by my father in the evening today. *(Passive)*

Changes in Interrogative Sentences

In interrogative sentences, the 'auxiliary' or the 'wh-word' that forms the question remains at its place, the question mark also remains at the end of the sentence. The rest of the changes (like interchange of places of subject and object) take place the same way as in the case of assertive sentences.

Note The word **'who'** changes to 'by whom' since it acts as the subject itself.

1. Yes-No Type Questions

e.g. (i) Do you like apples? *(Active Voice)*

Are apples liked by you? *(Passive Voice)*

(ii) Has she done her homework? *(Active Voice)*

Has her homework been done by her? *(Passive Voice)*

2. Wh-Type Questions

e.g. (i) What do you need? (*Active voice*)

What is needed by you? (*Passive voice*)

(ii) I need a phone. (*Active voice*)

A phone is needed by me. (*Passive voice*)

(iii) Where did she purchase this bag from? (*Active voice*)

From where was this bag purchased by her? *(Passive voice)*

Changes in Imperative Sentences

1. To convert orders into Passive voice, 'let' is used followed by 'be + past participle'.

   e.g. Open the door. *(Active voice)*
   Let the door be opened. *(Passive voice)*

2. To convert requests/advice/suggestions into Passive voice, the sentence is started with 'you'.

   e.g. (i) Please pass the book. *(Active voice)*
   You are requested to pass the book. *(Passive voice)*
   (ii) Help the ones in need. *(Active voice)*
   You should help the ones in need. *(Passive voice)*

Interchange of Direct and Indirect Speech

Rules for Changing Simple Direct Speech into Indirect Speech

Rules	Direct Speech	Indirect Speech
• Remove separating comma, inverted commas and use the connector 'that'.	He said, "I do not like pasta."	He said that he did not like pasta.
• When there is an object in Reporting verb, change 'said to' into 'told' and 'says to' into 'tells'.	He said to me, "You have been a great help." He says to me, "My teacher is highly educated."	He told me that I had been a great help. He tells me that his teacher is highly educated.
• When there is no object in Reporting verb, 'said' and 'says' remain the same.	Sheeba said, "I work in an MNC." Kamya says, "I will go to the party."	Sheeba said that she worked in an MNC. Kamya says that she will go to the party.

Changes in Reported Speech when Reporting Verb is in Past Tense

Change of Verb Forms	Change of Pronouns	Time, Place Expressions and Other Changes
is, am, are — was, were	1st person → according to the subject	now — then
has, have — had	2nd person → according to the object	ago — before
$V_3 - V_2$	3rd person → unchanged	today — that day
did — had + IIIrd form of the verb	2nd person → changed to 3rd person if the reporting verb has no object	last night—the previous night or the night before
was, were — had been will — would		next week — the following week here — there
shall — should		hither — thither
can — could		this — that
		thus — so
		come — go

Tensewise Conversion of Direct into Indirect Speech

Direct Speech	Indirect Speech
Simple Present Tense	Simple Past Tense
Present Continuous Tense	Past Continuous Tense
Present Perfect Tense	Past Perfect Tense
Present Perfect Continuous Tense	Past Perfect Continuous Tense
Simple Past Tense	Past Perfect Tense
Past Continuous Tense	Past Perfect Continuous Tense
Past Perfect Tense	Past Perfect Tense
Simple Future Tense (Will/Shall)	Should/Would
Future Continuous Tense (Shall Be/Will Be)	Should Be/Would Be
Future Perfect Tense (Shall/Will + Have)	Would + Have

Rules for Changing Interrogative Sentences into Indirect Speech

Interrogative sentences are of two types

1. Yes-No Type Questions

When the reported speech is a yes-no type question, the conjunction 'if' or 'whether' is used and the interrogative sentence (or question) is converted into an assertive sentence.

The other changes (tense, pronouns, etc.) are made as usual and the question mark is removed.

Most importantly, the reporting verb is changed from 'says' and 'said' to 'asks' and 'asked', respectively.

e.g. She said to me, "Do you want to play?" *(Direct)*

She asked me if I wanted to play. *(Indirect)*

2. Wh-Type Questions

No conjunction is used as the Wh-word itself works as a conjunction to join the reporting verb with the reported speech.

All other changes are made in the same manner as the yes-no type questions.

e.g. Mother said to him, "What do you want for dinner?" *(Direct)*

Mother asked him what he wanted for dinner. *(Indirect)*

Rules for Changing Imperative Sentences into Indirect Speech

- In case of imperative sentences, the preposition 'to' is used in place of conjunction after the reporting verb.
- Depending upon the type of imperative sentence (i.e. order, suggestion, advice, request, etc.), the reporting verb is changed into ordered, suggested, advised, requested, etc.
- In case of negative imperative sentences (such as don't play there), 'to' is put after 'not' that follows reporting verb.

In case of sentences beginning with 'Let's', the reporting verb is changed to proposed or suggested.

e.g. The officer said to her, "Please vacate this area." *(Direct)*

The officer requested her to vacate that area. *(Indirect)*

Rules for Changing Exclamatory Sentences into Indirect Speech

We replace the reporting verb with 'exclaimed with joy', 'exclaimed with sorrow', 'exclaimed with surprise', etc. according to the sense of the reported speech.

e.g. Rima said, "Yay! We won the competition." *(Direct)*

Rima exclaimed with joy that we had won the competition. *(Indirect)*

Nominalisation

Nominalisation is a type of word formation in which a verb, an adjective or a common noun is used as or transformed into a noun generally, abstract noun.

e.g. guide (Verb) → guidance (Abstract noun)

smart (Adjective) → smartness (Abstract noun)

child (Common noun) → childhood (Abstract noun)

Transforming a Verb in a Sentence into its Noun Form

A noun can be a subject or an object in a sentence. Therefore, when we are changing the 'verb' in a sentence into its 'noun' form, we need to provide another verb that may suit the context of the sentence and that does not harm its syntax or its meaning.

e.g.
- You need to justify your answer. *(Verb)*
- You need to give justification for your answer. *(Noun)*

Or

- Your answer needs justification.

You can understand that both the sentences have the same meaning as the original sentence. But the syntax of both is different.

Therefore, if you comprehend the sentence with the context with which the words are used, you will be able to change their construction using different parts of speech.

Transforming an Adjective in a Sentence into its Noun Form

Consider the following example

- The little boy gave a brave performance. *(Adjective)*
- The little boy exhibited bravery in his performance. *(Noun)*

Or

The little boy's performance exhibited bravery.

EXAM ORIENTED QUESTIONS

Q.1 Choose the correct option and rewrite the sentence according to the instruction given after each. **(ICSE 2025, 8 M)**

(i) **The teacher said, "Come early tomorrow, the examination begins at eight o'clock."**

(Begin: The teacher told us to.........)

(a) The teacher told us to come early the next day as the examination would begin at eight o'clock.

(b) The teacher told us to come early tomorrow as the examination begins at eight o'clock.

(c) The teacher told us the examination will begin at eight o'clock so come early tomorrow.

(d) The teacher told us to come by eight o'clock as the examination will begin early the next day.

(ii) **Rahul not only plays the guitar but also the drums.**

(Use: 'as well as')

(a) Rahul plays the guitar as well as the drums.

(b) Rahul plays the guitar as well the drums.

(c) Rahul plays the guitar as well as he does the drums.

(d) Rahul play's the guitar and the drums as well.

(iii) **She said she would not be available.**

(Add a question tag)

(a) Didn't she say that she would not be available?

(b) She said she would not be available, did she?

(c) She said she would not be available, didn't she?

(d) She said she would not be available, wouldn't she?

(iv) **This is the most beautiful painting in the exhibition.**

(Begin: No other......)

(a) No other painting is as beautiful as this exhibition.

(b) No other painting in this exhibition is beautiful.

(c) No other painting is beautiful as this painting in the exhibition.

(d) No other painting in the exhibition is as beautiful as this one.

(v) **I prefer aerobics to yoga.**

(Use: 'rather')

(a) I would rather do aerobics to yoga.

(b) I would rather do aerobics than yoga.

(c) I would rather prefer aerobics than yoga.

(d) I would rather do yoga than aerobics.

(vi) **The coach taught the children' the rules of the game.**

(Begin: The rules.........)

(a) The rules have being taught by the coach to the children.

(b) The rules of the game have been taught by the children to the coach.

(c) The rules of the game is taught by the coach to the children.

(d) The rules of the game were taught by the coach to the children.

(vii) **No sooner did the film star arrive than the crowd cheered.**

(Begin: As soon as.........)

(a) As soon as the film star arrived then the crowd cheered.

(b) As soon as the film star arrives the crowd starts cheering.

(c) As soon as the crowd cheers the film star arrives.

(d) As soon as the film star arrived the crowd cheered.

(viii) **School bags are often too heavy for students to carry.**

(Use: 'so')

(a) School bags are so heavy students cannot carry them.

(b) School bags are often so heavy that students cannot carry them.

(c) School bags are often so heavy for students to carry.

(d) School bags are heavy so students cannot carry them.

Ans. (i) (b) (ii) (a)
(iii) (c) (iv) (d)
(v) (b) (vi) (d)
(vii) (d) (viii) (b)

Q.2 Choose the correct option to rewrite the following according to the instructions given after each sentence. **(ICSE Specimen 2025)**

(i) The audience broke into loud applause as soon as he finished speaking.

(Begin with: No sooner...)

(a) No sooner he finished speaking that the audience broke into loud applause.

(b) No sooner had he finish speaking when the audience broke into loud applause.

(c) No sooner did he finish speaking than the audience broke into loud applause.

(d) No sooner the audience broke into loud applause than he finished speaking.

(ii) The news surprised everyone in my family.

(Begin with: The news took...)

(a) The news took everyone in my family by surprise.

(b) The news took everyone in my family with surprise.

(c) The news took with surprise everyone in my family.

(d) The news took everyone in my family for a surprise.

(iii) Yesterday was so much fun.

(End with a question tag)

(a) Yesterday was so much fun, would you say?

(b) Was yesterday much fun?

(c) Yesterday was so much fun, isn't it?

(d) Yesterday was so much fun, wasn't it?

(iv) I wouldn't eat that food if I was not really hungry.

(Use: 'unless')

(a) Unless I eat that food I will remain really hungry.

(b) I wouldn't be really hungry unless I ate that food.

(c) I wouldn't eat that food unless I was not really hungry.

(v) It is so hot and humid that I cannot sleep.

(Use: 'too')

(a) It is hot and humid too sleep.

(b) It is too hot and humid to sleep.

(c) It is hot and humid too, so I cannot sleep.

(d) It is too hot and humid such that I cannot sleep.

(vi) I prefer going out with friends to staying alone at home.

(Begin with: I would rather...)

(a) I would rather go out with friends than stay alone at home.

(b) I would rather prefer going out with friends than staying alone at home.

(c) I would rather prefer to go out with friends than stay alone at home.

(d) I would rather go out with friends to staying alone at home.

(vii) "Why were you absent yesterday?" the teacher asked me.

(Begin with: The teacher asked me why...)

(a) The teacher asked me why was I absent yesterday.

(b) The teacher asked me why I had been absent yesterday.

(c) The teacher asked me why I had been absent the day before.

(d) The teacher asked me why was I absent the day before.

(viii) Very few dancers are as graceful as she is.

(Begin with: She is...)

(a) She is one of the most graceful dancers.

(b) She is the most graceful dancer.

(c) She is more graceful than all the other dancers.

(d) She is more graceful than a few other dancers.

Ans. (i) (c) (ii) (a) (iii) (d) (iv) (c)
(v) (b) (vi) (a) (vii) (c) (viii) (a)

Q.3 For questions 1-20, choose the correct option to rewrite the sentences according to the instructions given after each sentence. **(Competency Based Que.)**

(i) As soon as Matthew reached the school, the bell rang.

(Begin with: No sooner...)

(a) No sooner did Matthew reached the school when the bell rang.

(b) No sooner does Matthew reach the school that the bell rang.

(c) No sooner did Matthew reach the school than the bell rang.

(d) No sooner did Matthew reach the school then the bell rang.

(ii) "Will you help me carry the books?" the teacher asked me.

(Begin with: The teacher asked me ...)

(a) The teacher told me to help her carry the books.

(b) The teacher told me to carry the books.

(c) The teacher asked me for carrying the books.

(d) The teacher asked me if I would help her carry the books.

(iii) **You love school. (End with a question tag)**
(a) You love school, do you?
(b) You love school, don't you?
(c) Do you love school?
(d) You love school, isn't it?

(iv) **He succeeded in his efforts to win the competition.**
(Begin with: His efforts to win the competition ......)
(a) His efforts to win the competition were successful.
(b) His efforts to win the competition were met with succeeded.
(c) His efforts to win the competition were a grand success.
(d) His efforts to win the competition are succeeding.

(v) **He is not a singer. He is not a dancer.**
(Use: 'neither')
(a) He is neither a singer nor a dancer.
(b) He is neither a singer nor is he a dancer.
(c) He is neither a singer or a dancer.
(d) He is neither a singer nor dancer.

(vi) **The shelf is so high that I cannot reach it.**
(Use : 'too' in place of 'so')
(a) This shelf is too high that I cannot reach it.
(b) This shelf is too high for me to reach.
(c) This shelf is too high to reach me.
(d) This shelf is too much high to reach.

(vii) **The donkey is more industrious than all other creatures.**
(Use: 'most industrious')
(a) The donkey is most industrious than any other creature.
(b) No other creature is most industrious than the donkey.
(c) The donkey is the most industrious than any other creature on earth.
(d) The donkey is the most industrious creature.

(viii) **These books need dusting again.**
(Begin: These books will...)
(a) These books will require dusting.
(b) These books will be dusted.
(c) These books will have to be dusted again.
(d) These books will be needing dusting again.

(ix) **No sooner did the plane take off than the child started wailing.**
(Begin: As soon as.....)
(a) As soon as the plane took off than the child started wailing.
(b) As soon as the plane took off, the child started wailing.
(c) As soon as the child started wailing, the plane took off.
(d) As soon as the child wailed, the plane took off.

(x) **Adopting a dog was the best thing I have ever done in my life.**
(Begin: No other.....)
(a) No other dog I have ever adopted was the best thing I have done in my life.
(b) No other best thing I have ever done in my life was adopting a dog.
(c) No other thing I have ever done in my life was as good as adopting a dog.
(d) No other thing I have ever done was as good as adopting a dog in my life.

(xi) **He was away from home, yet he remembered his parents' birthdays.**
(Use: 'although...')
(a) He remembered his parent's birthday although he was away from home.
(b) He was away from home although he remembered his parents' birthdays.
(c) Although he was away from home, he remembers his parents' birthdays.
(d) Although he was away from home, he remembered his parents' birthdays.

(xii) **The manager said to the clerk, "I hope you remembered to lock up the office."**
(Begin: The manager said ......)
(a) The manager said to the clerk that he hoped that he had remembered to lock up the office.
(b) The manager said the clerk that he hoped that he had remembered to lock up the office.
(c) The manager said to the clerk that he hoped that he remembered to lock up the office.
(d) The manager said to the clerk that he had hoped that he remembered to lock up the office.

(xiii) **As soon as the rain stopped, the children went out to play.**
(Begin: Hardly......)
(a) Hardly did the rain stop than the children went out to play.
(b) Hardly did the rain stopped when the children went out to play.

(c) Hardly had the rain stopped when the children went out to play.

(d) Hardly had the rain stopped than the children went out to play.

(xiv) Ishaan's team had scored the winning goal in the final match.

(Begin: The winning goal.....)

(a) The winning goal has been scored by Ishaan's team in the final match.

(b) The winning goal have been scored by Ishaan's team in the final match.

(c) The winning goal in the final match has been scored by Ishaan's team.

(d) The winning goal in the final match had been scored by Ishaan's team.

(xv) Suhani has gone to Sweden to visit her aunt.

(End with a question tag)

(a) Suhani has gone to Sweden to visit her aunt, isn't it?

(b) Suhani has gone to Sweden to visit her aunt, didn't she?

(c) Suhani has gone to Sweden to visit her aunt, hadn't she?

(d) Suhani has gone to Sweden to visit her aunt, hasn't she?

(xvi) I made the bed and changed the linen.

(Use: 'not only')

(a) Not only did I make the bed but also changed the linen.

(b) Not only did I made the bed but also changed the linen.

(c) Not only I made the bed and also changed the linen.

(d) Not only had I made the bed but also changed the linen.

(xvii) The baby played all day and was exhausted.

(Begin: Having......)

(a) Having played all day, the baby was exhausted.

(b) Having played on the day, the baby was exhausted.

(c) Having played during the day, the baby was exhausted.

(d) Having played in the day, the baby was exhausted.

(xviii) Mother said to Rohan, "Pack your books before going to bed."

(Begin: Mother instructed Rohan......)

(a) Mother instructed Rohan to pack the books before going to bed.

(b) Mother instructed Rohan to pack your books before going to bed.

(c) Mother instructed Rohan to pack his books before going to bed.

(d) Mother instructed Rohan to pack a book before going to bed.

(xix) If I had a chance, I would have saved the goal.

(Begin: Had.....)

(a) Had I a chance, I would have saved the goal.

(b) Had I saved the goal with a chance.

(c) Had I the chance, I would have saved the goal.

(d) Had a chance, I would have saved the goal.

(xx) He decided to sleep instead of watching a movie.

(Begin: Rather than....)

(a) Rather to sleep, he did not watch a movie.

(b) Rather than decide to sleep, he watched a movie.

(c) Rather than watching a movie, he decided to sleep.

(d) Rather than sleeping, he decided to watch a movie.

Ans.

(i) (c)	(ii) (d)	(iii) (b)	(iv) (a)
(v) (a)	(vi) (b)	(vii) (d)	(viii) (c)
(ix) (b)	(x) (c)	(xi) (d)	(xii) (a)
(xiii) (c)	(xiv) (d)	(xv) (d)	(xvi) (a)
(xvii) (a)	(xviii) (c)	(xix) (a)	(xx) (c)

Q.4 Choose the correct option to rewrite the following according to the instructions given after each sentence. **(ICSE 2024)**

(i) Arun and Nikhil had climbed the mountain.

(End with a question tag)

(a) Arun and Nikhil had climbed the mountain, didn't they?

(b) Arun and Nikhil had climbed the mountain, had they?

(c) Arun and Nikhil had climbed the mountain, hadn't they?

(d) Arun and Nikhil had climbed the mountain, did they?

(ii) The children have broken the window pane.

(Begin: The window pane............)

(a) The window pane had been broken by the children.

(b) The window pane has been broken by the children.

(c) The window pane has not been broken by the children.

(d) The window pane had not been broken by the children.

(iii) The apples are so cheap that they cannot be good. (Use: 'too')

(a) The apples are too cheap and good.

(b) The apples are too cheap as well as good.

(c) The apples are too good to be cheap.

(d) The apples are too cheap to be good.

(iv) She is very clever and beautiful. (Use: 'not only')

(a) Not only is she very clever but also beautiful.

(b) Not only was she beautiful and she was also clever.

(c) Not only is she clever she was also very beautiful.

(d) Not only was she very beautiful but is also clever.

(v) I prefer a simple vanilla ice cream to fancy desserts. (Begin: I would rather......)

(a) I would rather have a simple vanilla ice cream to fancy desserts.

(b) I would rather have a simple vanilla ice cream than fancy desserts.

(c) I would rather prefer a simple vanilla ice cream than fancy desserts.

(d) I would rather have a vanilla ice cream than a fancy dessert.

(vi) He asked, "When do you intend to make the payment?" (Begin: He asked ......)

(a) He asked when he did intend to make the payment.

(b) He asked when she is intending to make the payment.

(c) He asked when I intended to make the payment.

(d) He asked when they are intending to make the payment.

(vii) If the rain does not stop, Mariam will not be able to do the laundry. (Begin: Unless....)

(a) Unless the rain does not stop, Mariam will not be able to do the laundry.

(b) Unless Mariam does the laundry, the rain will not stop.

(c) Unless the rain stop, Mariam will not be able to do the laundry.

(d) Unless the rain stops, Mariam will not be able to do the laundry.

(viii) This is the best movie I have ever seen. (Begin: Never....)

(a) Never had I seen a good movie than this.

(b) Never I have seen a better movie than this.

(c) Never have I seen a better movie than this.

(d) I have never seen a good movie as this.

Ans. (i) (c) (ii) (a) (iii) (d) (iv) (a)
(v) (b) (vi) (c) (vii) (a) (viii) (c)

Q.5 Choose the correct option to rewrite the following according to the instructions given after each sentence. **(ICSE Specimen 2024)**

(i) The burglar ran away the moment he saw the guard. (Begin with: No sooner...)

(a) No sooner has the burglar seen the guard, he ran away.

(b) No sooner than the burglar saw the guard, he ran away.

(c) No sooner did the burglar see the guard when he ran away.

(d) No sooner had the burglar seen the guard than he ran away.

(ii) The parents have trained their children well. (Begin with: The children ...)

(a) The children were trained well by their parents.

(b) The children is being trained well by their parents.

(c) The children had been trained well by their parents.

(d) The children have been trained well by their parents.

(iii) My cousins returned home one month ago. (Begin with: 'It has'...)

(a) It has been one month for my cousins' return home.

(b) It has been one month since my cousins returned home.

(c) It has been one month when my cousins returned home.

(d) It has been one month ago that my cousins returned home.

(iv) Your form will be accepted if it is submitted on time. (Use: 'unless')

(a) Your form will be accepted unless it is submitted on time.

(b) Unless your form is submitted on time, it will not be accepted.

(c) Unless the form is accepted, it should be submitted on time.

(d) Your form will be accepted unless it is not submitted on time.

(v) **The house needs a thorough cleaning again.**
(Use: 'thoroughly')
(a) The house needs a thoroughly cleaning again.
(b) The house needed a cleaning thoroughly again.
(c) The house needs to be cleaned thoroughly again.
(d) The house needed to be thoroughly clean yet again.

(vi) **My sister offered me a new job in her company.**
(Begin with: A new job...)
(a) A new job was offered to me by my sister in her company.
(b) A new job has been offered to me by my sister in her company.
(c) A new job had been offered to me by my sister in her company.
(d) A new job was being offered to me by my sister in her company.

(vii) **"I am going to watch my friend's play tomorrow," she said. (Begin with: She said...)**
(a) She said that she is going to watch her friend's play tomorrow.
(b) She said that she will be going to watch her friend's play tomorrow.
(c) She said that she was going to watch my friend's play the following day.
(d) She said that she was going to watch her friend's play the following day.

(viii) **Nithin is more talented than most of the professional musicians I know. (Use: 'few')**
(a) Professional musicians I know have few talents as Nithin.
(b) Few professional musicians I know are as talented as Nithin.
(c) Few professional musicians I know are not as talented as Nithin.
(d) Professional musicians I know do not have as few talents as Nithin.

Ans. (i) (c) (ii) (d) (iii) (b) (iv) (b)
(v) (c) (vi) (a) (vii) (d) (viii) (b)

Q.6 Re-write the following sentences according to the instructions given after each. Make other changes that may be necessary, but do not change the meaning of each sentence. Choose the correct options. **(ICSE 2023)**

(i) **He said to me, "I don't believe you."**
(Begin: He said ....)
(a) He said he doesn't want to believe in me.
(b) He said that he didn't believe me.
(c) He said that he didn't believe in me.
(d) He said I don't believe you.

(ii) **Some boys were helping the wounded man.**
(Begin: The wounded ....)
(a) The wounded man was helping some boys.
(b) The wounded man were helping some boys.
(c) The wounded man was being helped by some boys.
(d) The wounded boys were helping the man.

(iii) **He is as wise as Solomon.**
(Use: 'wiser')
(a) Solomon was wiser than he is.
(b) He and Solomon are wiser.
(c) Solomon was the wisest.
(d) Solomon was not wiser than he is.

(iv) **She is weak but she is courageous.**
(Begin: Despite ......)
(a) Despite of being weak she is courageous.
(b) Despite being weak, she is courageous.
(c) Despite being courageous, she is not weak.
(d) Despite weak, she is courageous.

(v) **We will never forget what we saw.**
(Begin: Never......)
(a) Never forget what we see.
(b) Never will we forget what we had seen.
(c) Never will we see what we forget.
(d) Never will we forget what we saw.

(vi) **Jaswant's grandfather is too old to take up this job. (Use: ....so.........that)**
(a) Jaswant's grandfather is so old that he could not take up his job.
(b) Jaswant's grandfather is so old that he cannot take up this job.
(c) Jaswant's grandfather is so old that he could take up this job.
(d) Jaswant's grandfather is so old that he can take up this job.

Ans. (i) (b) (ii) (c) (iii) (d) (iv) (b)
(v) (d) (vi) (b)

Q.7 Re-write the following sentences according to the instructions given after each. Make other changes that may be necessary but do not change the meaning of each sentence. Choose the correct options. **(ICSE Specimen 2023)**

(i) **The captain said, "It gives me great pleasure to be here this evening."**

(Begin: The captain......)

(a) The captain said that it was giving him great pleasure to be there that evening.

(b) The captain said that it gives me great pleasure to be there this evening.

(c) The captain said that it gave him great pleasure to be here this evening.

(d) The captain said that it gave him great pleasure to be there that evening.

(ii) **He has applied many times. He has never been selected.**

(Begin: In spite......)

(a) In spite of applying many times, he had never been selected.

(b) In spite applying many times, he has never been selected.

(c) In spite of applying many times, he has never been selected.

(d) In spite never being selected, he has applied many times.

(iii) **Very few managers are as honest as James.**

(End: ....managers)

(a) James is more honest than other managers.

(b) James is more honest than most other managers.

(c) James is honest than many other managers.

(d) James is most honest among other managers.

(iv) **I accept your offer. (Use: 'acceptable')**

(a) Your offer is acceptable to me.

(b) Your offer was acceptable to me.

(c) Your offer is acceptable.

(d) Your acceptable offer came to me.

(v) **As soon as he finishes his work, he starts playing.**

(Begin: Hardly......)

(a) Hardly his work is finished, he starts playing.

(b) Hardly he finishes his work, he starts playing.

(c) Hardly he has finished his work and he starts playing.

(d) Hardly does he finish his work, when he starts playing.

(vi) **I have never seen Mr. Joe lose his temper.**

(Begin: Never......)

(a) Never I have seen Mr. Joe lose his temper.

(b) Never did I see Mr. Joe lose his temper.

(c) Never have I seen Mr. Joe losing his temper.

(d) Never ever did I see Mr. Joe lose his temper.

Ans. (i) (d) (ii) (c) (iii) (b) (iv) (a) (v) (d) (vi) (b)

Q.8 **Read each sentence with its instructions. Choose the correct answer from the options provided beneath each.** **(ICSE Specimen 2022 Sem II)**

(i) **He came to the party. (End with a question tag)**

(a) Isn't it? (b) Didn't he?

(c) Wasn't it? (d) Wasn't he?

(ii) **The teacher said, "Akhtar, why were you absent yesterday?"**

(Begin: The teacher asked Akhtar...)

(a) The teacher asked Akhtar why he was absent yesterday.

(b) The teacher asked Akhtar why were you absent yesterday.

(c) The teacher asked Akhtar why are you absent yesterday.

(d) The teacher asked Akhtar why he had been absent the previous day.

(iii) **In spite of the water logging, the traffic was heavy.**

(Begin: Despite...)

(a) Despite the water logging, the traffic was heavy.

(b) Despite of the water logging, the traffic was heavy.

(c) Despite the traffic being heavy, there was water logging.

(d) Despite of water logging, there was heavy traffic.

(iv) **Mother was too angry to argue with the shop keeper.**

(Remove 'too'.)

(a) Mother was too angry so that she could not argue with the shopkeeper.

(b) Mother was so angry to argue with the shop keeper.

(c) Mother was so angry that she could not argue with the shopkeeper.

(d) Mother was so angry not to argue with the shop keeper.

(v) **Everybody put up their hands.**

(Begin: There was nobody...)

(a) There was nobody who put up their hands.

(b) There was nobody who did not put up their hands.

(c) There was nobody whom put up their hands.

(d) There was nobody who should put up their hands.

(vi) We celebrated grandfather's hundredth birthday.

(Begin: Grandfather...)

(a) Grandfather's hundredth birthday was celebrated by us.

(b) Grandfather celebrated his hundredth birthday.

(c) Grandfather was celebrated on his hundredth birthday.

(d) Grandfather celebration was on his hundredth birthday.

(vii) Kaushik has the best handwriting in the class.

(Begin: No one...)

(a) No one has the better handwriting than Kaushik in the class.

(b) No one has the better handwriting in the class than Kaushik.

(c) No one in the class has better handwriting than Kaushik.

(d) No one's handwriting in the class is better than Kaushik.

Ans. (i) (b) (ii) (d) (iii) (a) (iv) (c) (v) (b) (vi) (a) (vii) (d)

Q.9 Read each sentence with its instructions. Choose the correct answer from the options provided beneath each: **(ICSE 2021 Sem I)**

(i) The news had been brought to us by him.

(Begin: He....)

(a) He brought us the news.

(b) He was brought the news to us.

(c) He has brought us the news.

(d) He bought us the news.

(ii) The National Anthem began when I reached school.

(Begin: No sooner....)

(a) No sooner had the National Anthem began then I reached school.

(b) No sooner had I reached school than the National Anthem began.

(c) No sooner does the National Anthem begin than I reached school.

(d) No sooner had I reached school then the National Anthem began.

(iii) Rajiv is too weak to walk. (Begin: Rajiv is so....)

(a) Rajiv is so weak so he cannot walk.

(b) Rajiv is so weak to walk.

(c) Rajiv is so weak that he cannot walk.

(d) Rajiv is so weak that he can walk.

(iv) It is dangerous as well as illegal to ride a motorcycle without a helmet. (Begin: It is not...)

(a) It is not dangerous but illegal to ride a motorcycle without a helmet.

(b) It is not only dangerous but also illegal to ride a motorcycle without a helmet.

(c) It is not only dangerous and also illegal to ride a motorcycle without a helmet.

(d) It is not only dangerous and illegal to ride a motorcycle without a helmet.

(v) Nima would rather read a book than watch a movie. (Rewrite using: 'prefer')

(a) Nima would rather prefer the movie to the book.

(b) Nima would prefer reading a book to watching a movie.

(c) Nima would prefer watched a movie to reading a book.

(d) Nima would prefer the book to watching a movie.

(vi) He said, "Will you listen to such a man?"

(Begin: He asked...)

(a) He asked them to listen to such a man.

(b) He asked them would you listen to such a man.

(c) He asked them not to listen to such a man.

(d) He asked them not to listen to such a man.

(vii) If you tell me the truth, I shall not punish you.

(Use: 'unless')

(a) Unless you tell me the truth, I shall punish you.

(b) Unless I punish you, you shall not tell me the truth.

(c) Unless I punish you, you shall tell the truth.

(d) Unless you tell me the truth, I shall not punish you.

(viii) In spite of repeated warnings Anshul paid no heed. (Use: 'despite)

(a) Despite paying repeated warning Anshul does not heed.

(b) Despite repeated warning Anshul paid no heed.

(c) Despite paying no heed Anshul has been repeatedly warned.

(d) Despite of repeated warning Anshul.

Ans. (i) (c) (ii) (b) (iii) (c) (iv) (b) (v) (b) (vi) (c) (vii) (a) (viii) (b)

Q.10 Re-write the following sentences according to the instructions given after each. Make other changes that may be necessary, but do not change the meaning of each sentence. **(ICSE 2020 Modified)**

(i) **The librarian orders books for the school library every year. (Begin: Books...)**
(a) Books are ordered every year by the librarian for the school library.
(b) Books are ordered for the school library every year by the librarian.
(c) Books order for the school library by the librarian every year.
(d) Books are ordered every year by the librarian in the school library.

(ii) **No one will deny that the children have worked very hard this year. (Begin: Everyone...)**
(a) Everyone will deny that the children have worked very hard this year.
(b) Everyone will agree that the children have worked very hard this year.
(c) Everyone will acknowledge that the children have worked very hard this year.
(d) Everyone will refuse that the children have worked very hard this year.

(iii) **As soon as the teacher enters, she is greeted by her students. (Begin: No sooner...)**
(a) No sooner the teacher enters than she is greeted by her students.
(b) No sooner has the teacher entered than she is greeted by her students.
(c) No sooner does the teacher enter than she is greeted by her students.
(d) No sooner will the teacher enter than she is greeted by her students.

(iv) **She is so busy that she finds no time to entertain her friends. (Rewrite using: 'too')**
(a) She is too busy to entertain her friends.
(b) She is too busy that she finds no time to entertain her friends.
(c) She is too busy to find time for her friends.
(d) She is too busy to entertain her friends, that's why.

(v) **In spite of the very hot weather, Kevin stepped out to buy some bread. (Begin: Despite...)**
(a) Despite the very hot weather, Kevin stayed inside to buy some bread.
(b) Despite the very hot weather, Kevin stepped out to buy some bread.
(c) Despite very hot weather, Kevin was stepping out to buy some bread.
(d) Despite of the very hot weather, Kevin stepped out for some bread.

(vi) **Sheela will be selected for the competition only if she goes for the auditions.**
(Begin: Unless...)
(a) Unless Sheela goes for the auditions, she will be selected for the competition.
(b) Unless Sheela goes for the auditions, she will not be selected for the competition.
(c) Unless Sheela goes for the competition, she will be selected for the auditions.
(d) Unless Sheela goes for the competition, she will be selected for the auditions.

(vii) **I would rather eat fruit than a lot of unhealthy junk food. (Begin: I prefer...)**
(a) I prefer eating fruit to eating a lot of unhealthy junk food.
(b) I prefer eating junk food to eating a lot of healthy fruit.
(c) I prefer eating fruit than eating a lot of unhealthy junk food.
(d) I prefer fruit over unhealthy junk food.

(viii) **The tree was cut down ruthlessly.**
(Begin: They...)
(a) They cut down the tree ruthlessly.
(b) They were cutting down the tree ruthlessly.
(c) They had cut the tree down ruthlessly.
(d) They ruthlessly cut the tree down.

Ans. (i) (b) (ii) (b) (iii) (c) (iv) (a)
(v) (b) (vi) (b) (vii) (a) (viii) (a)

Q.11 Re-write the following sentences according to the instructions given after each. Make other changes that may be necessary, but do not change the meaning of each sentence. **(ICSE 2019 Modified)**

(i) **The old woman said to Arun, "Can you help me to cross the street?"**
(Begin: The old woman asked Arun...)
(a) The old woman asked Arun if he can help her to cross the street.
(b) The old woman asked Arun whether he could help her to cross the street.
(c) The old woman asked Arun if he could help her in crossing the street.
(d) The old woman asked Arun can he help her to cross the street.

(ii) As soon as the Sun rose over the hills, the fog disappeared. (Begin: No sooner...)

(a) No sooner did the sun rise over the hills than the fog disappeared.

(b) No sooner has the sun risen over the hills, the fog disappeared.

(c) No sooner the sun rose over the hills, than the fog disappeared.

(d) No sooner does the sun rise over the hills than the fog disappears.

(iii) It rained so heavily that they could not go for the picnic. (Rewrite using: 'too...to')

(a) It rained too heavily for them to go for the picnic.

(b) It was too heavy to rain, so they could not go for the picnic.

(c) They were too heavy to go for the picnic because it rained.

(d) It rained too heavily that they could not go for the picnic.

(iv) If your friends get here before 7 o'clock we can take them out for dinner. (Rewrite using: 'unless')

(a) Unless your friends get here before 7 o'clock, we can take them out for dinner.

(b) Unless your friends don't get here before 7 o'clock, we can take them out for dinner.

(c) Unless your friends get here after 7 o'clock, we can take them out for dinner.

(d) Unless your friends get here by 7 o'clock, we can take them out for dinner.

(v) The school captain was elected by the students of Classes XI and XII. (Begin: The students...)

(a) The students of Classes XI and XII elected the school captain.

(b) The students of Classes XI and XII were elected as the school captain.

(c) The students of Classes XI and XII were electing the school captain.

(d) The students of Classes XI and XII had elected the school captain.

(vi) Greenland is the largest island in the world.

(Rewrite using: 'larger')

(a) Greenland is larger than any island in the world.

(b) Greenland is the larger island in the world.

(c) Greenland is larger than any other island in the world.

(d) Greenland is larger than the world's largest island.

(vii) How cruel Shylock was to demand his pound of flesh! (Begin: It was cruel...)

(a) It was cruel of Shylock to demand his pound of flesh.

(b) It was cruel to Shylock demanding his pound of flesh.

(c) It was cruel for Shylock to demand his pound of flesh.

(d) It was cruel that Shylock demanded his pound of flesh.

(viii) Arun was asked by his mother to explain the missing buttons on his shirt.

(Rewrite using: 'explanation')

(a) Arun was asked by his mother for an explanation of the missing buttons on his shirt.

(b) Arun was asked by his mother to explain about the missing buttons on his shirt.

(c) Arun was asked by his mother to give an explanation for the missing buttons on his shirt.

(d) Arun was asked by his mother for an explanation to the missing buttons on his shirt.

Ans. (i) (b) (ii) (a)
(iii) (a) (iv) (a)
(v) (a) (vi) (c)
(vii) (a) (viii) (a)

Q.12 Re-write the following sentences according to the instructions given after each. Make other changes that may be necessary, but do not change the meaning of each sentence. **(ICSE 2019 Modified)**

(i) "Will you lend me the book tomorrow?" Priya asked her classmate.

(Begin: Priya asked her classmate if...)

(a) Priya asked her classmate if she could lend her the book tomorrow.

(b) Priya asked her classmate if she will lend her the book tomorrow.

(c) Priya asked her classmate if he could lend her the book tomorrow.

(d) Priya asked her classmate if he would lend her the book tomorrow.

(ii) The teacher scolded him for coming late.

(Begin: He...)

(a) He was scolded by the teacher for coming late.

(b) He was scolding by the teacher for coming late.

(c) He has been scolded by the teacher for coming late.

(d) He was scolded by the teacher for his lateness.

(iii) **It was so hot that the P.T. period could not be held. (Begin: It was too...)**

(a) It was too hot to hold the P.T. period.

(b) It was too hot for the P.T. period to be held.

(c) It was too hot that the P.T. period was canceled.

(d) It was too hot for the P.T. period to have been held.

(iv) **As soon as her song was over, I knew that she had won the competition. (Begin: No sooner...)**

(a) No sooner had her song been over than I knew that she had won the competition.

(b) No sooner did her song finish than I knew she had won the competition.

(c) No sooner was her song over than I knew that she had won the competition.

(d) No sooner had her song finished than I knew that she had won the competition.

(v) **Our school sent up the best exhibit to the Town Hall. (Rewrite using: 'better')**

(a) Our school sent a better exhibit to the Town Hall.

(b) Our school sent the better exhibit to the Town Hall.

(c) Our school sent up a better exhibit to the Town Hall.

(d) Our school sent the best exhibit to the Town Hall than others.

(vi) **Visitors under eighteen were not allowed into the hall. (Begin: Only visitors...)**

(a) Only visitors under eighteen were allowed into the hall.

(b) Only visitors above eighteen were allowed into the hall.

(c) Only visitors below eighteen were allowed into the hall.

(d) Only visitors under eighteen were not allowed into the hall.

(vii) **As soon as the bell rang the children ran out. (Begin: No sooner...)**

(a) No sooner had the bell rung than the children ran out.

(b) No sooner did the bell ring than the children ran out.

(c) No sooner the bell rang than the children ran out.

(d) No sooner the bell rings than the children ran out.

(viii) **They were asked to combine all their ideas into one document. (Rewrite using: 'combination')**

(a) They were asked to combine all their ideas as a combination into one document.

(b) They were asked for a combination of all their ideas into one document.

(c) They were asked to make a combination of all their ideas into one document.

(d) They were asked to combine all their ideas into a combination in one document.

Ans. (i) (d) (ii) (a)
(iii) (a) (iv) (d)
(v) (a) (vi) (b)
(vii) (a) (viii) (b)

Q.13 Re-write the following sentences according to the instructions given after each. Make other changes that may be necessary, but do not change the meaning of each sentence. **(ICSE 2018 Modified)**

(i) **She laid the table after she had finished cooking. (Begin: When...)**

(a) When she finished cooking, she laid the table.

(b) When she had finished cooking, she laid the table.

(c) When she was finished with cooking, she laid the table.

(d) When finishing cooking, she laid the table.

(ii) **He is old but still he works hard. (Begin: Despite...)**

(a) Despite his old age, he still works hard.

(b) Despite being old, he works hard still.

(c) Despite he is old, he works hard.

(d) Despite of his old age, he works hard.

(iii) **The delivery boy was requested to bring the parcel the next day. (Rewrite using direct speech)**

(a) "Please bring the parcel the next day," the delivery boy was requested.

(b) "Bring the parcel the next day," he was asked the delivery boy.

(c) "Can you bring the parcel the next day?" the delivery boy was asked.

(d) "Please bring the parcel tomorrow," he was asked the delivery boy.

(iv) **I prefer playing a game to watching television. (Begin: I would rather...)**

(a) I would rather play a game than watch television.

(b) I would rather playing a game to watching television.

(c) I would rather watch television than play a game.

(d) I would rather playing a game over watching television.

(v) **Every family has a black sheep.**

(Begin: There is no...)

(a) There is no black sheep in every family.

(b) There is no family without a black sheep.

(c) There is no such thing as a black sheep in the family.

(d) There is no family that has a black sheep.

(vi) **I have never worn a more ill-fitting suit.**

(Begin: This is the ...)

(a) This is the most ill-fitting suit I have ever worn.

(b) I have ever worn a suit that was more ill-fitting than this.

(c) I have ever worn a more ill-fitting suit than this.

(d) This is the worst suit I have ever worn.

(vii) **Anil is too fast a runner not to come first in the race. (Begin: Anil is so...)**

(a) Anil is so fast a runner that he cannot come first in the race.

(b) Anil is so fast a runner that he is sure to come first in the race.

(c) Anil is so fast that he is not a runner to come first in the race.

(d) Anil is so fast a runner that he might come first in the race.

(viii) **As soon as the sports meet ended, the children ran on the field. (Begin: Hardly...)**

(a) Hardly did the sports meet end when the children ran on the field.

(b) Hardly the sports meet ended when the children ran on the field.

(c) Hardly the sports meet had ended, the children ran on the field.

(d) Hardly had the sports meet ended when the children ran on the field.

Ans. (i) (b) (ii) (a)
(iii) (c) (iv) (a)
(v) (b) (vi) (a)
(vii) (b) (viii) (d)

Q.14 Re-write the following sentences according to the instructions given after each. Make other changes that may be necessary, but do not change the meaning of each sentence. **(ICSE 2017 Modified)**

(i) **Not many people read for pleasure these days.**

(Begin: Few...)

(a) Few people are reading for pleasure these days.

(b) Few people read for pleasure these days.

(c) Few people read pleasure these days.

(d) Few people have read for pleasure these days.

(ii) **Since her childhood Meera has been good at Mathematics. (End: ...childhood.)**

(a) Meera has been good at Mathematics since her childhood.

(b) Meera was good at Mathematics since her childhood.

(c) Meera is good at Mathematics since her childhood.

(d) Meera had been good at Mathematics since her childhood.

(iii) **"We have had no rain since January," Ramu said.**

(Begin: Ramu said that they...)

(a) Ramu said that they have had no rain since January.

(b) Ramu said that they had no rain since January.

(c) Ramu said that they have had no rain since January.

(d) Ramu said that they had had no rain since January.

(iv) **It is dangerous as well as illegal to drive a motorcycle without a helmet. (Begin: It is not...)**

(a) It is not dangerous and illegal to drive a motorcycle without a helmet.

(b) It is not safe nor legal to drive a motorcycle without a helmet.

(c) It is not safe and legal to drive a motorcycle without a helmet.

(d) It is not only dangerous but illegal to drive a motorcycle without a helmet.

(v) **He had plenty of wealth but he was not happy.**

(Begin: In spite...)

(a) In spite of having plenty of wealth, he was not happy.

(b) In spite of plenty of wealth, he was not happy.

(c) In spite he had plenty of wealth, he was not happy.

(d) In spite of he had plenty of wealth, he was not happy.

(vi) **He was so tired that he could not stand.**

(Use: too)

(a) He was too tired to stand.

(b) He was too tired that he could not stand.

(c) He was too tired that he could stand.

(d) He was tired too much to stand.

(vii) **Every one of them was an experienced mountaineer. (Begin: There was no...)**

(a) There was no experienced mountaineer among them.

(b) There was no one among them who was not an experienced mountaineer.

(c) There was no mountaineer among them who was not experienced.

(d) There was no one among them who was an experienced mountaineer.

(viii) I have never seen a film as bad as this. (Begin: This is....)

(a) This is the worst film I have ever seen.

(b) This is worse than any film I have ever seen.

(c) This is a bad film I have ever seen.

(d) This is the worst film I have seen.

Ans. (i) (b) (ii) (a) (iii) (d) (iv) (d) (v) (a) (vi) (a) (vii) (b) (viii) (a)

Q.15 Re-write the following sentences according to the instructions given after each. Make other changes that may be necessary, but do not change the meaning of each sentence. **(ICSE Specimen 2017 Modified)**

(i) We had not even walked one kilometre when they stopped us. (Begin: Hardly...)

(a) Hardly we had walked one kilometre when they stopped us.

(b) Hardly had we walked one kilometre when they stopped us.

(c) Hardly did we walk one kilometre when they stopped us.

(d) Hardly had walked we one kilometre when they stopped us.

(ii) The memory is so vivid that I will never forget it. (Use: 'too' in place of 'so')

(a) The memory is too vivid for me to forget it.

(b) The memory is too vivid that I will never forget it.

(c) The memory is too vivid to forget.

(d) The memory is too vivid I will never forget it.

(iii) That need not happen. (Rewrite using: 'does')

(a) That does not need to happen.

(b) That does need not to happen.

(c) That does happen not need.

(d) That does need happen.

(iv) Food and sleep were all we cared about. (Begin: All...)

(a) All that we cared about were food and sleep.

(b) All we cared about was food and sleep.

(c) All that we cared about is food and sleep.

(d) All we cared about was food and sleeping.

(v) We sat there face to face with our accuser. (Begin: There...)

(a) There we sat face to face with our accuser.

(b) There was us sitting face to face with our accuser.

(c) There we sat, face to face with our accuser.

(d) There we were, sitting face to face with our accuser.

(vi) Herbert consulted his parents before accepting the job offer. (Begin: Herbert did not...)

(a) Herbert did not consult his parents before accepting the job offer.

(b) Herbert did not accept the job offer before consulting his parents.

(c) Herbert did not accept the job offer before he consulted his parents.

(d) Herbert did not consult before accepting the job offer.

(vii) Put your tools away, the children may fall over them. (Use: 'lest')

(a) Put your tools away, lest the children may fall over them.

(b) Put your tools away, lest the children fall over them.

(c) Put your tools away, lest falling over them the children may.

(d) Put your tools away, lest the children fall over.

(viii) It was the last time he saw his wife. (Begin: Never...)

(a) Never he saw his wife again.

(b) Never had he seen his wife again.

(c) Never will he see his wife again.

(d) Never would he see his wife again.

Ans. (i) (b) (ii) (a) (iii) (a) (iv) (b) (v) (a) (vi) (b) (vii) (b) (viii) (b)

Q.16 Rewrite the following sentences according to the instructions given after each. Make other changes that may be necessary but do not change the meaning of each sentence. Choose the correct option.

(i) There have been people who have already written about this earlier. (Begin: You are not the ....)

(a) You are not the only person to write about this.

(b) You are not the last person to write about this.

(c) You are not the former person to write about this.

(d) You are not the first person to write about this.

(ii) **I am listening to such a miraculous and enchanting music for the first time. (Begin: I have not ....)**

(a) I have not listened to such a miraculous and enchanting music before.

(b) I have not listen to such a miraculous and enchanting music before.

(c) I have not been listening to such a miraculous and enchanting music before.

(d) All of the above

(iii) **Can you imagine how the people at places having – 24°C temperature survive? (Begin: You .....)**

(a) You can imagine how people at places having – 24 °C temperature survive.

(b) You can imagine how people at places not having – 24 °C temperature survive.

(c) You cannot imagine how people at places having – 24 °C temperature survive.

(d) None of the above

(iv) **He never expected to receive such a nice gift from his friends. (Begin: It was ....)**

(a) It was beyond him to receive such a nice gift from his friends.

(b) It was beyond his expectation to receive such a nice gift from his friends.

(c) It was beside his expected to receive such a nice gift from his friends.

(d) It was beside his expectation to receive such a nice gift from his friends.

(v) **Radhika is unable to accept this shocking news. (Use: 'cannot')**

(a) Radhika cannot accept this shocking news.

(b) Radhika cannot deny this shocking news.

(c) Radhika cannot reject this shocking news.

(d) Radhika cannot criticise this shocking news.

Ans. (i) (d) (ii) (a) (iii) (c) (iv) (b) (v) (a)

Q.17 **Rewrite the following sentences according to the instructions given after each. Make other changes that may be necessary but do not change the meaning of each sentence. Choose the correct option.**

(i) **Only a foolish person would be taken in by this trick. (Begin: None ....)**

(a) None but than a foolish person would be taken in by this trick.

(b) None but a foolish person will be taken in by this trick.

(c) None other than a foolish person will be taken in by this trick.

(d) None other than a foolish person would be taken in by this trick.

(ii) **The children will sit out in the garden, if the weather is cool.**

(Begin: The children won't ....)

(a) The children won't sit out in the garden, unless the weather is cool.

(b) The children won't sit out in the garden, if the weather is hot.

(c) The children won't sit out in the garden, if the weather is cool.

(d) All of the above

(iii) **I've never seen so many people in this building before.**

(Begin: This is ....)

(a) This is last time when I see so many people in this building.

(b) This is the first time when I have seen so many people in this building.

(c) This is the last time that I have seen so many people in this building.

(d) This is first time that I see so many people in this building.

(iv) **There is no success without effort.**

(Begin: You will ....)

(a) You will get success unless you make an effort.

(b) You will get success if you make an effort.

(c) You will not get success unless you make an effort.

(d) Both (b) and (c)

(v) **If you are not a member, you cannot borrow books.**

(Begin: Only ....)

(a) Only members could borrow books.

(b) Only members can borrow books.

(c) Only members cannot borrow books.

(d) Only members could not borrow books.

Ans. (i) (d) (ii) (b) (iii) (b) (iv) (d) (v) (b)

ICSE Specimen Paper 2025

Question Paper 2025

Sample Question Paper

ICSE SPECIMEN PAPER 2025

FULLY SOLVED

(ENGLISH LANGUAGE - 1)

General Instructions

Maximum Marks : 80

Time allowed : Two hours

Answers to this paper must be written on the paper provided separately.

You will **not** be allowed to write during the first **15** minutes.

This time is to be spent in reading the question paper.

The time given at the head of this paper is the time allowed for writing the answers.

Attempt **all five** questions.

The intended marks for questions or parts of questions are given brackets ().

You are advised to spend not more than 30 minutes in answering **Question 1** and 20 minutes in answering **Question 2**.

Question 1

Write a composition (300-350 words) on any one of the following. **(20)**

(Do not spend more than 30 minutes on this question.)

(i) Write an original short story in which a woman, her strange neighbour and a police officer form the main characters.

(ii) Your teacher has asked you to form a group and work on a particular project. Write an account of how you worked together and what each of you learned from the experience.

(iii) *'Peer pressure is a force for good.'*

Express your views either **for** or **against** this statement.

(iv) Describe the locality in which you live. Give details of the things you see and hear as you walk around your locality. What do you especially like about the place?

(v) Study the picture given below. Write a story or a description on an account of what it suggests to you. Your composition may be about the subject of the picture or you may take suggestions from it; however, there must be a clear connection between the picture and your composition.

Question 2

Select any one of the following.

(Do not spend more than 20 minutes on this question.) **(10)**

(i) Your uncle was unable to attend your birthday celebration but has sent you one thousand rupees as a gift. Write a letter thanking him, tell him how you will spend the money and why you have made that particular choice.

(ii) The garbage bins in your locality have not been cleared regularly resulting in the overflow of garbage in the area. Write a letter to the Municipal Commissioner of your city/town complaining about the problem. Offer suggestions for the removal of the garbage and cleaning up of the place.

Question 3

(i) Your school is hosting an Art and Craft exhibition. Write a notice informing the pupils at your school about the event. **(5)**

(ii) Write an e-mail to a local artist inviting him/her to inaugurate the exhibition and be the Chief Guest on the occasion. **(5)**

Question 4

Read the following passage carefully and answer the questions that follow.

One day, I found the pond occupied by several buffaloes. Their keeper, a boy a little older than me, was swimming about in the middle. Instead of climbing out on the bank, he would pull himself up on the back of one of his buffaloes, stretch his naked brown body out on the animal's glistening ***hide***, and start singing to himself.

When he saw me staring at him from across the pond, he smiled, showing gleaming white teeth on a dark face. He invited me to join him in a swim. I told him I couldn't swim, and he offered to teach me.

His name was Ramu, and he promised to give me swimming lessons every afternoon, and so it was during the afternoons - especially summer afternoons when everyone was asleep-that we usually met. Before long, I was able to swim across the pond to sit with Ramu astride a ***contented*** buffalo.

Sometimes, I would slip into the water. Emerging in shades of green and khaki, I would sneak into the house through the bathroom and bathe under the tap before getting into my clothes.

One afternoon, Ramu and I found a small tortoise in the mud sitting over a hole in which it had laid several eggs. I presented the tortoise to Grandfather. He had a weakness for tortoises, and was pleased with this addition to his menagerie, giving it a large tub of water all to itself, with an island of rocks in the middle. If one of the dogs bothered it too much, it would draw its head and legs into its shell and defy all its attempts at rough play.

Ramu came from a family of bonded labourers and had received no schooling. But he was well-versed in folklore and knew a great deal about birds and animals.

'Many birds are sacred,' said Ramu, as we watched a blue jay swoop down from a peepul tree and carry off a grasshopper.

Both Ramu and Grandfather were of the opinion that we should be more gentle with birds and animals and should not kill so many of them.

"It is also important that we respect them", said Grandfather. "We must acknowledge their rights. Birds and animals are finding it more difficult to survive, because we are trying to destroy both them and their forests."

Ramu and I spent long summer afternoons at the pond. I still remember him with affection, though we never saw each other again after I left Dehra.

— *Rusty, the Boy from the Hills, Ruskin Bond*

(i) For each word given below, choose the correct meaning (as used in the passage) from the options provided. **(2)**

1. Hide *(line 3)*

   (a) blanket (b) fur (c) undisclosed (d) skin

2. Contented *(line 9)*

   (a) cheerful (b) lazy (c) satisfied (d) container

(ii) Which word in the passage is the opposite of 'easy'? **(1)**

(a) Sneak (b) Difficult (c) Labourer (d) Survive

(iii) Answer the following questions briefly in your own words.

(a) What did Ramu like to do once he had climbed on the back of a buffalo? **(2)**

(b) What offer did Ramu make to the narrator? **(2)**

(c) Why do you think the narrator would bathe before entering the house? **(2)**

(d) Who was the large tub of water for? **(1)**

(e) How would the tortoise protect itself from the dogs? **(2)**

(iv) Despite the lack of schooling, what did Ramu know? How, according to Ramu and Grandfather, should we treat birds and animals? Answer in not more than fifty words. **(8)**

Question 5

(i) Fill in each of the numbered blanks with the correct form of the word given in brackets. Do not copy the passage but write in correct serial order the word or phrase appropriate to the blank space. **(4)**

Example:

(0) The Sun .... (shine) bright outside.

Answer: shone

It was hot in the railway compartment and the fan .... (1) (not work).

The elderly lady .... (2) (use) up all her water because she had cheerfully shared it with her fellow passengers. She knew that the train .... (3) (halt) at the station for only three minutes. Calling a shoeshine boy, she said, 'Will you help me? I .... (4) (need) a bottle of cold water and here is the money,' and she put a twenty rupee note in his hand. The boy snatched the money and .... (5) (disappear) into the crowd on the platform. A fellow passenger .... (6) (cannot believe) what he had witnessed. 'What .... (7) (you do)?" He said, 'You .... (8) (never see) your money again. Just then, the whistle was heard and the train began to move. At that moment, the child appeared at the window with the water. 'Your water,' he gasped, out of breath. 'And the change.'

(ii) Fill in the blanks with appropriate words. **[4]**

(a) We can cut ...... this field instead of taking the main road.

(b) Passengers are advised ...... standing on the footboard of a moving bus.

(c) They have been working on the project ...... years now.

(d) Ever ...... the accident, he has been afraid of boarding buses.

(e) It is a hard climb ...... the hill.

(f) She turned ...... the offer because she did not like the terms and conditions.

(g) I will need to speak ...... my parents before I sign up for the school trip.

(h) The sports teacher was taken ...... when he heard how enthusiastic the team was.

(iii) Join the following sentences to make one complete sentence **without using *and, but*** or ***so***. Choose the correct option. **[4]**

1. Stay still. We cannot take your photograph otherwise.

(a) Stay still, else we cannot take your photograph otherwise.

(b) Stay still because we can take your photograph otherwise.

(c) Unless you stay still, we cannot take your photograph.

(d) If you stay still, we cannot take your photograph.

2. Roy's mother rang up the school office. She wanted to enquire about the swimming classes at the summer camp.

(a) Roy's mother rang up the school office as she want to enquire about the swimming classes at the summer camp.

(b) Roy's mother rang up the school office to enquire about the swimming classes at the summer camp.

(c) Roy's mother has rung up the school office to enquire about the swimming classes at the summer camp.

(d) Roy's mother rang up the school office wanting enquiry about the swimming classes at the summer camp.

3. I left my keys somewhere. Do you know where they are?

(a) Do you know where I had left my keys?

(b) Do you know where my keys were left behind?

(c) Do you know where I left my keys?

(d) Do you know where I would have left my keys?

4. The captain should not be blamed for the team's defeat. The players should not be blamed for the team's defeat.

(a) The captain should neither be blamed nor the players should be blamed for the team's defeat.

(b) Neither the captain nor the players should be blamed for the team's defeat.

(c) The captain should not be blamed for the team's defeat as the players should not be blamed for the team's defeat.

(d) The captain should not be blamed for the team's defeat but the players too should not be blamed for the team's defeat.

(iv) Choose the correct option to rewrite the following according to the instructions given after each sentence. **(8)**

1. The audience broke into loud applause as soon as he finished speaking. *(Begin with: No sooner...)*
   (a) No sooner he finished speaking that the audience broke into loud applause.
   (b) No sooner had he finish speaking when the audience broke into loud applause.
   (c) No sooner did he finish speaking than the audience broke into loud applause.
   (d) No sooner the audience broke into loud applause than he finished speaking.

2. The news surprised everyone in my family. *(Begin with: The news took ...)*
   (a) The news took everyone in my family by surprise.
   (b) The news took everyone in my family with surprise.
   (c) The news took with surprise everyone in my family.
   (d) The news took everyone in my family for a surprise.

3. Yesterday was so much fun. *(End with a question tag)*
   (a) Yesterday was so much fun, would you say?
   (b) Was yesterday much fun?
   (c) Yesterday was so much fun, isn't it?
   (d) Yesterday was so much fun, wasn't it?

4. I wouldn't eat that food if I was not really hungry. *(Use: 'unless')*
   (a) Unless I eat that food I will remain really hungry.
   (b) I wouldn't be really hungry unless I ate that food.
   (c) I wouldn't eat that food unless I was not really hungry.
   (d) I wouldn't eat that food unless I was really hungry.

5. It is so hot and humid that I cannot sleep. *(Use: too)*
   (a) It is hot and humid too sleep.
   (b) It is too hot and humid to sleep.
   (c) It is hot and humid too so I cannot sleep.
   (d) It is too hot and humid such that I cannot sleep.

6. I prefer going out with friends to staying alone at home. *(Begin with: I would rather...)*
   (a) I would rather go out with friends than stay alone at home.
   (b) I would rather prefer going out with friends than staying alone at home.
   (c) I would rather prefer to go out with friends than stay alone at home.
   (d) I would rather go out with friends to staying alone at home.

7. "Why were you absent yesterday?", the teacher asked me. *(Begin with: The teacher asked me why...)*
   (a) The teacher asked me why was I absent yesterday.
   (b) The teacher asked me why I had been absent yesterday.
   (c) The teacher asked me why I had been absent the day before.
   (d) The teacher asked me why was I absent the day before.

8. Very few dancers are as graceful as she is. *(Begin with: She is...)*
   (a) She is one of the most graceful dancers.
   (b) She is the most graceful dancer.
   (c) She is more graceful than all the other dancers.
   (d) She is more graceful than a few other dancers.

Answers

1. (i) For answer refer to page no. 44 question no. 2.

(ii) For answer refer to page no. 15 question no. 16.

(iii) **For the Motion**

The pressure to conform to do what others are doing can be powerful and hard to resist. A person might feel pressured to do something just because others are doing it. The pressure becomes even more powerful when it comes from one's peers or friends. Peer pressure is a phenomenon that can influence a person to do something because one's peers are doing it.

Peer pressure is often painted in a negative light evoking images of young individuals being coerced into harmful behaviours or adopting unhealthy habits. However, when channelled positively, peer pressure can be a powerful force for good. It can encourage individuals to strive for a better performance and adopt healthier lifestyles, thereby fostering personal growth and development.

One of the most significant benefits of positive peer pressure is its ability to motivate individuals towards excellence. In educational settings, the influence of peers who prioritise their studies can be contagious. For instance, students who see their friends dedicating time to homework and preparing diligently for exams are likely to feel motivated to mirror these productive behaviours. This form of peer pressure can create a supportive environment where students push each other to achieve their best, ultimately raising the academic standards of the entire group.

Moreover, peer pressure can promote healthy social behaviours and ethical standards. Young people learn a great deal about social interactions from their peers. When surrounded by friends who respect others, engage in community service and uphold integrity, individuals adopt these positive traits. This leads to a more compassionate and responsible community.

Additionally, peer pressure can be a pivotal force in discouraging negative habits. For example, a group of friends can influence a member to stop smoking or reduce alcohol consumption. The desire to fit in and be accepted can motivate individuals to make healthier lifestyle choices which might be difficult to undertake alone.

However, the positive outcomes of peer pressure depend significantly on the group dynamics and the prevailing attitudes within a peer group. It is crucial for individuals, especially young people, to choose their friends wisely. Being part of a group that values positive and constructive behaviours can transform peer pressure into a beneficial force that enhances one's life.

In conclusion, peer pressure undoubtedly has the potential to be a force for good. It encourages excellence, promotes ethical behaviour and supports healthy lifestyle choices. Like any tool, the impact of peer pressure depends on how it is used. If leveraged positively, it can lead to personal and communal improvement.

Against the Motion

We all share the need to connect with others, no matter our age. We want a sense of belonging at home and within the community. Being accepted by peers is an important part of adolescence. Teens yearn to fit in and to be seen in a favourable light. As a result, peers often have a strong influence on teen behaviours, choices and actions. More often than not, peer pressure takes a negative turn. Hence, I do not agree with the statement—'Peer pressure is a force for good'.

The impact and scope of influence of peer pressure is so adverse that it has a negative impact on an individual. Friends or peers may encourage engaging in risky things such as doing drugs, reckless driving, alcoholic habit, bunking classes, etc. As a result, one could get distracted and go on a path that ruins one's future.

The impact of peers can be easily found in the age of social media wherein individuals participate in reckless acts to fit in with peers. They try to follow the standard and, in doing so, go against their values and belief systems. Often, children, enticed with what their friends have, become entitled and show immature behaviour. They even participate in illegal activities to fulfill their need to fit in.

If an individual does not fit in and give in to peer pressure, he/she is often bullied to the point that the person develops mental health problems and even causes self-harm. Now and then, the effect of peer tension on young teenagers is disrupting to the point that they can barely remain in their skin, are separated from loved ones and become discouraged and restless.

Thus, peer pressure is not a force for good.

(iv) Locality refers to the specific geographical area or neighbourhood in which a community of people live and work. It is a fundamental concept that helps define the character, culture and identity of a particular place. The term is often used to describe the unique features of a specific region as well as the social connections and shared experiences of its residents.

One of the most important aspects of locality is the sense of community that it fosters. Whether it is a small town, a large city neighbourhood or a rural area, a locality can create a strong sense of belonging and shared identity among its residents. This sense of community is often built around common interests, traditions and values which are strengthened by the interactions and relationships between people in the area.

I live in a great residential locality in Delhi. It is society with multiple complexes. There is a huge park nearby with lush greenery and many different kinds of birds. Multiple amenities are easily accessible in my locality. We have three malls which are 10 minutes ride away with many big brands and eateries. There are also many famous street food stalls which offer a diverse range of food options. From vegetarian delights to international cuisines, you'll find it all here. The nearby market is bustling with a variety of snacks, chaat, candies and cuisines. And, the best part? You can enjoy all this in one place from hotdogs and momos to hot and cold beverages like coffees, teas, milkshakes and juices.

Another gem is the local market. From 10:30 a.m. until 8:30 p.m., it's a bustling market with hundreds of retailers selling anything and everything. But, as evening descends, this place undergoes a magical transformation into a foodie's paradise. The aroma of Gulab jamun, Dahi vada, Samosa, Dosa, Pav bhaji, Pani puri, Chinese food and Soft beverages fills the air. You'll also find mobile food vendors here. This market focuses on traditional Indori food. Poha Jalebi merits special mention, as it is the city's king of street food. Poha is available at all times, 24 hours a day, 365 days a year.

Overall, it is a fantastic and well-known street market in my city where people enjoy shopping.

(v) He was the funniest boy I had ever met. He would make everyone laugh even in the most trying times. Blessed with a funny nature, Varun would make everyone forget his/her worries in his company. No amount of sadness could dampen his spirit.

I remember once three of us friends including Roshni and Varun and I had failed the chemistry exam badly. Our parents had been called and we were told that we would have to repeat a year. That was a very hard time but, even then, no look of worry could be spotted on Varun's face or in his behaviour. His cheer remained undiminished even when his father suffered a major financial loss in business. Even during that time, Varun was known to spread cheer around. He always pushed his worries to the backseat and dedicated himself towards making others happy.

However, the loss of Varun's pet Munch, a few months ago, immersed him in grief. That was the only time that robbed him of his smiling face. For days, he did not speak to anyone and shut himself up in his room. We could not see him like that so Roshni and I decided to do something to dispel his gloom.

One day, we all went to his place and rang the doorbell of his house. There, we kept a little box, slightly open from one side and hid ourselves so that he could not see us. When he opened the door, he was surprised to find no one. He picked up the box with a look of amazement on his face. He took the lid off and out came a puppy, quite like Munch. He held it in his hands and started to play with it. It brought his smile back. Then, we all came into the sight and shouted with excitement, 'Surprise!'

Indeed, that little effort from our end helped Varun come out of his sorrow. Later, we played with the puppy and, then, went to the park. We played till late in the evening and enjoyed as our friend was back again.

2. (i) XYZ Apartments

PQR City

14th July, 20XX

Dear Uncle,

I hope this letter finds you in the best of health and spirits. I am well and happy here. I have written to tell you that it upset me that you couldn't attend my birthday party. At the same time, I want to thank you for the money (1000 rupees) that you sent me as a birthday gift. I can't tell you how much I appreciate it. It really means a lot to me that you remembered my special day. I've already put your gift to good use. I have given it as fee for an educational tour that our school is organising to Amritsar. We will be going to the Wagah border, the Jallianwallah Bagh, the Golden temple and many other places.

I am grateful for your generosity and support. You've always been an amazing uncle to me and I feel truly blessed to have you in my life.

Thank you again for your kindness and thoughtfulness. I hope we can catch up soon and celebrate properly.

Yours loving,

XYZ

(ii) 202, M.G. Road,

Agra

27th July, 20XX

The Municipal Commissioner,

Municipal Corporation,

Agra

Subject Complaint regarding overflowing garbage and lack of cleanliness in locality

Dear Sir/Ma'am,

Through this letter, I would like to draw your attention to the overflowing garbage and lack of cleanliness in M.G. Road, Agra. It is a matter of great disappointment that in the times when the entire country is striving towards cleanliness and sanitation, our locality presents a picture of dirt. It is not the lack of garbage bins or cleaning staff, but the lack of action on the part of the staff that the bins are always overflowing. As a result, there is a bad odour in the locality and people are becoming prone to diseases.

Hence, I request you to solve this problem and ensure that the locality maintains its cleanliness. For the same, I suggest that garbage vans and staff should come regularly to clean the locality. Further, regular inspection can ensure that the system is effective in its implementation. With your aid, we would be able to move ahead in our path towards cleanliness.

Thanking you,

Yours faithfully,

ABC

3. (i) **SHOW YOUR SKILL!**

Art and Craft Exhibition

25th December, 20XX

9 a.m. to 12 p.m.

School Auditorium

All the students from Classes IX to XII are requested to register their names with the Head Girl by 20th December, 20XX.

(ii) **E-mail-id** xyz@gmail.com

Invite to inaugurate the Arts and Crafts exhibition as a Chief Guest

Respected Sir/Ma'am,

With great pleasure and pride, ABC School would like to inform in that it is organising an Arts and Crafts Exhibition on 3rd August, Friday from 10:00 a.m. to 3:00 p.m. in the Assembly Area, ABC School. For the same, we would be honoured if you could inaugurate and grace the exhibition as the Chief Guest.

With your valuable experience and knowledge, students would be motivated to participate in creative activities and take up art as a proper career. Hoping for a positive reply.

Anticipating a positive response,

Yours faithfully,

PQR

4. (i) 1. (d) skin 2. (c) satisfied

(ii) (b) Difficult

(iii) (a) Once he had climbed the back of the buffalo, Ramu liked to stretch his naked brown body out on the animal's glistening hide/back and start singing to himself.

(b) Ramu offered to teach the narrator to swim every afternoon.

(c) The narrator would bathe before entering the house to avoid being scolded for swimming in the village pond when everyone was asleep. He thought that his elders become angry so he would sneak into the house through the bathroom and bathe under the tap to get clean first.

(d) The large tub of water was for the tortoise presented by the narrator to his grandfather.

(e) To protect itself from the dogs, the tortoise would draw its head and legs into its shell and defy all the dogs' attempts at rough play.

(iv)

Ramu	came	from	a	family
of	bonded	labourers	and	received
no	schooling.	However,	he	was
well-versed	in	folklore	and	knew
a	great	deal	about	birds
and	animals.	We	should	be
gentle	with	birds	and	animals
and	should	not	kill	them.
It	is	also	important	to
acknowledge	and	respect	their	rights.

5. (i) 1. was not working
2. had used
3. halted/would halt
4. need
5. disappeared
6. could not believe
7. are you doing
8. will never see

(ii) a. across
b. against
c. for
d. since
e. up
f. down
g. to
h. aback

(iii) 1. (c) Unless you stay still, we cannot take your photograph.
2. (b) Roy's mother rang up the school office to enquire about the swimming classes at the summer camp.
3. (c) Do you know where I left my keys?
4. (b) Neither the captain nor the players should be blamed for the team's defeat.

(iv) 1. (c) No sooner did he finish speaking than the audience broke into loud applause.
2. (a) The news took everyone in my family by surprise.
3. (d) Yesterday was so much fun, wasn't it?
4. (d) I wouldn't eat that food unless I was really hungry.
5. (b) It is too hot and humid to sleep.
6. (a) I would rather go out with friends than stay alone at home.
7. (c) The teacher asked me why I had been absent the day before.
8. (a) She is one of the most graceful dancers.

QUESTION PAPER 2025
ENGLISH LANGUAGE
(PAPER - 1)

General Instructions

Maximum Marks : 80

Time allowed : Two hours

Answers to this paper must be written on the paper provided separately.

You will **not** be allowed to write during the first **15** minutes.

This time is to be spent in reading the question paper.

The time given at the head of this paper is the time allowed for writing the answers.

Attempt **all five** questions.

The intended marks for questions or parts of questions are given brackets ().

You are advised to spend not more than 30 minutes in answering **Question 1** and 20 minutes in answering **Question 2**.

Question 1

Write a composition (300-350 words) on any one of the following. **(20)**

(Do not spend more than 30 minutes on this question.)

(i) Write an original short story in which a poor tailor wins an award which changes his/her life.

(ii) Your friends once played a harmless prank on you. Give an account of what happened, your response to the prank and what you learnt from the experience.

(iii) Describe what you see and hear as you move about the corridors and compound during your school break time. How does the scene change after the bell rings?

(iv) 'More collaboration, less competition is the need of the hour'. Express your views either **for** or **against** this statement.

(v) Study the picture given below. Write a story or a description or an account of what it suggests to you. Your composition may be about the subject of the picture, or you may take suggestions from it; however, there must be a clear connection between the picture and your composition.

Question 2

Select any one of the following. **(10)**

(Do not spend more than 20 minutes on this question.)

(i) Your grandmother has taught you a special skill. Write a letter thanking her. Explain how you will use that skill and why it is important to you.

(ii) There is no bus stop in your locality. Write a letter to the Municipal Commissioner of your town/city complaining about the problem. Offer possible solutions.

Question 3

(i) Your school is hosting an Inter School Story Writing Competition. Write a notice informing the students about the event. **(5)**

(ii) Write an email to a famous person inviting him/her to be the Judge on the occasion. **(5)**

Question 4

Read the following passage carefully and answer the questions that follow.

A little later, when he went to the pump to wash, he saw the school children pouring by with their **satchels** across their shoulders. They all wore the same clothes - grey shorts or skirts and light blue shirts or blouses - faded and mended, and they all had their hair oiled and combed down very flat. Some went by in laughing, racing groups, others had to be led by their mothers or grandparents to the school building. This reminded him of his sisters in the village.

The boys in the kitchen now looked at him with less hostility. Jagu seemed pleased with Hari too and sometimes handed him a glass of tea in the middle of the day. When he had a few moments to **spare**, Jagu sat down at one of the long wooden tables, drummed loudly on it and sang a song in a dialect Hari did not know. When he caught Hari listening and smiling, he smiled back. Then Hari knew that he too had a village somewhere that he called home. It was just that he was a silent, hardworking, worried man and had no time and no gift for speech.

It was the watch mender, Mr. Panwallah, who was truly a benefactor, the kindest and most helpful of all. One afternoon, during those hot, still hours when there were no customers for a change, Hari was standing in front of the eating house, idly watching the traffic because he was too tired to do anything else, and Mr. Panwallah called to him to come and sit beside him on the bench behind the counter in his shop.

"Want to help?" he asked. "Want to learn how to make a clock tick? I'm just going to open this big grandfather clock sent to me for repair - you'll be able to see the workings plain. Don't often get a piece like this anymore – wall clocks, yes and electronic gadgets – but you don't often come upon a grandfather clock like this. It's a real piece of luck, being able to show you one of this size." Look, he said, swinging open the door at the back and revealing the machinery to a fascinated Hari who felt as if the door had opened into a new and strange house. Mr. Panwallah showed Hari what was wrong with it, what had made it stop. "Interesting, isn't it? How would you like to learn? Tell you what - I'll take you on as an apprentice. You don't have much to do between two and four, do you? Of course you will have to ask Jagu first. I can pay you a little, not much and you can help me for two hours a day. Perhaps I can make a watch mender of you."

– Village by the Sea, Anita Desai

(i) For each word given below choose the correct meaning (as used in the passage) from the options provided. **(2)**

1. Satchels *(line 2)*

(a) snatching (b) scarves (c) school bags (d) sweaters

2. Spare *(line 9)*

(a) share (b) offer (c) thin (d) extra

(ii) Which word in the passage is the opposite of 'closed'? **(1)**

(a) Behind (b) Fascinated (c) Opened (d) Revealing

(iii) Answer the following questions briefly in your own words.

(a) How were the school children dressed? **(2)**

(b) In what way was Jagu kind to Hari? **(2)**

(c) What did the song tell Hari about Jagu? **(2)**

(d) Which sentence in the passage tells us that Jagu was not a talkative man? **(2)**

(e) Why were there no customers at that time of the day? **(1)**

(iv) In not more than 50 words describe how Mr. Panwallah introduced Hari to watch mending. **(8)**

Question 5

(i) Fill in each of the numbered blanks with the correct form of the word given in brackets. Do not copy the passage but write in correct serial order the word or phrase appropriate to the blank space. **(4)**

Example :

One day we (0) .... (lift) the box up.

Answer : (0) lifted

We (1) .... (find) a dead mouse (2) ....(lie) among our treasures. It (3) .... (be) an exciting discovery.

A boy took it up by its tail and (4) .... (wave) it in front of our faces.

"What shall we do with it?" he (5) .... (cry). "It stinks!" someone (6) .... (shout).

"Throw it out of the window quick!"

He (7) .... (hesitate). They all (8) .... (look) at me.

(ii) Fill in the blanks with an appropriate words. **(4)**

(a) My best friend, John is named .... his grandfather.

(b) A grey mist hung .... the fields.

(c) The little girl spoke .... against the bully.

(d) They accused him .... theft.

(e) The police got the fire .... control.

(f) There is a bridge .... the river.

(g) The driver jumped .... the car.

(h) I have not seen my uncle......... last summer.

(iii) Choose the correct option to make one complete sentence **without using *and*, *but*** or **so**. **(4)**

1. These are fresh mangoes. I bought them yesterday.
   (a) These are fresh mangoes which I bought yesterday.
   (b) These mangoes were fresher when I bought them yesterday.
   (c) These are fresh mangoes which were bought yesterday.
   (d) These are fresh mangoes brought by me yesterday.
2. The debating teams were very happy. They were declared joint champions.
   (a) The debating teams were very happy as they have been declared joint champions.
   (b) The debating teams are very happy as they are declared joint champions.
   (c) The debating teams were very happy as they had been declared joint champions.
   (d) The debating teams will be very happy as they will be declared joint champions.
3. The rain came down. All the people ran away.
   (a) When the rain came down, all the people ran away.
   (b) When it rained, the people ran away.
   (c) The rain had come down all the people ran away.
   (d) The The rain having come, all the people ran away.
4. The disciple was wise. The teacher did not trust him.
   (a) Although the disciple was wise yet the teacher trusted him.
   (b) Although the disciple was not wise the teacher trusted him.
   (c) Although the disciple is wise, the teacher trusted him.
   (d) Although the disciple was wise, the teacher did not trust him.

(iv) Choose the correct option and rewrite the sentence according to the instruction given after each. **(8)**

1. The teacher said, "Come early tomorrow, the examination begins at eight o'clock."
   (Begin: The teacher told us to.........)
   (a) The teacher told us to come early the next day as the examination would begin at eight o'clock.
   (b) The teacher told us to come early tomorrow as the examination begins at eight o'clock.
   (c) The teacher told us the examination will begin at eight o'clock so come early tomorrow.
   (d) The teacher told us to come by eight o'clock as the examination will begin early the next day.
2. Rahul not only plays the guitar but also the drums.
   (Use: 'as well as')
   (a) Rahul plays the guitar as well as the drums.
   (b) Rahul plays the guitar as well the drums.
   (c) Rahul plays the guitar as well as he does the drums.
   (d) Rahul play's the guitar and the drums as well.
3. She said she would not be available.
   (Add a question tag)
   (a) Didn't she say that she would not be available?
   (b) She said she would not be available, did she?
   (c) She said she would not be available, didn't she?
   (d) She said she would not be available, wouldn't she?

4. **This is the most beautiful painting in the exhibition.**

(Begin: No other......)

(a) No other painting is as beautiful as this exhibition.
(b) No other painting in this exhibition is beautiful.
(c) No other painting is beautiful as this painting in the exhibition.
(d) No other painting in the exhibition is as beautiful as this one.

5. **I prefer aerobics to yoga.**

(Use: 'rather')

(a) I would rather do aerobics to yoga.
(b) I would rather do aerobics than yoga.
(c) I would rather prefer aerobics than yoga.
(d) I would rather do yoga than aerobics.

6. **The coach taught the children' the rules of the game.**

(Begin: The rules.........)

(a) The rules have being taught by the coach to the children.
(b) The rules of the game have been taught by the children to the coach.
(c) The rules of the game is taught by the coach to the children.
(d) The rules of the game were taught by the coach to the children.

7. **No sooner did the film star arrive than the crowd cheered.**

(Begin: As soon as.........)

(a) As soon as the film star arrived then the crowd cheered.
(b) As soon as the film star arrives the crowd starts cheering.
(c) As soon as the crowd cheers the film star arrives.
(d) As soon as the film star arrived the crowd cheered.

8. **School bags are often too heavy for students to carry.**

(Use: 'so')

(a) School bags are so heavy students cannot carry them.
(b) School bags are often so heavy that students cannot carry them.
(c) School bags are often so heavy for students to carry.
(d) School bags are heavy so students cannot carry them.

Answers

1. (i) For answer refer to page no. 44 question no. 1.

(ii) For answer refer to page no. 15 question no. 1.

(iii) For answer refer to page no. 3 question no. 1.

(iv) For answer refer to page no. 26 question no. 1.

(v) In a small village, a mother and her children worked in their vegetable garden. Every morning, they stepped into their green fields, caring for their plants with love. Their hard work made the crops grow fresh and healthy. It was not just about growing food; it was about connecting with nature and learning patience.

One bright morning, the family was harvesting brinjals. The mother, dressed in a pink saree, smiled as she handed the vegetables to her children. The boy, wearing a vest, held a basket filled with colorful brinjals. His younger sister, in a blue dress, stood nearby, watching happily. Their faces glowed with joy and satisfaction. They knew that their efforts had borne fruit and their happiness was pure.

For them, farming was not just work-it was a way of life. They enjoyed growing their own food and felt proud of their efforts. The mother had taught her children that nature rewards those who care for it. With patience and dedication, their small garden provided enough vegetables for their daily meals. Sometimes, they even shared extra produce with neighbors. This created a strong bond among the villagers.

The village believed in working together. People helped each other during planting and harvesting seasons. They knew that unity made life easier and happier. Unlike cities, where people bought everything from markets, villagers valued the food they grew with their own hands. It was fresh, healthy and free from chemicals. Their connection with the land was deep and meaningful.

As they gathered the last batch of brinjals, the children laughed and played. The mother looked at them with love, knowing she was teaching them valuable lessons-hard work, teamwork and gratitude for nature.

The picture of this happy family in their green fields shows the beauty of simple living. It reminds us that joy comes not from wealth but from the satisfaction of honest effort, the love of family and the strength of a close-knit community.

2. (i) Mamura, Sector - 66

Noida - 201301

4th March, 2025

Dear Grandma,

I hope you are doing well. I am writing this letter to thank you for teaching me gardening. I really enjoyed learning how to plant seeds, water them and take care of the plants.

This skill is very special to me because it connects me to nature and reminds me of you. I will use it to grow my own flowers and vegetables. It will help me keep the environment green and beautiful. Gardening also teaches me patience and hard work.

I will always remember the time we spent together in the garden. Thank you for your love and guidance. I feel lucky to have you as my grandmother.

Take care and stay healthy.

With love,

Nilima

(ii) H.No. 45, Greenwood Colony

Rajgarh Road, Guwahati - 781003

4th March, 2025

The Municipal Commissioner

Guwahati Municipal Corporation

Guwahati - 781001

Subject Request for a Bus Stop in Our Locality

Respected Sir/Madam,

I am writing to bring to your attention the lack of a bus stop in our locality. Many people, including students, office workers and senior citizens, face great difficulty because of this. We have to walk a long distance to catch a bus, which is very inconvenient, especially during bad weather.

I request you to kindly arrange a bus stop in our area. A suitable place for it would be near Lachit Nagar Point on Rajgarh Road. This will help many people and make travel easier for everyone.

I hope you will consider our request and take action soon. Thank you for your time and support.

Yours sincerely,

Reshmi Saikia

3. (i) **Inter-School Story Writing Competition**

Our school is hosting an Inter-School Story Writing Competition. Students from all classes can participate. The event will be held on 6th March, 20XX, in the school auditorium. Interested students must register by 5th March, 20XX. For details, contact your class teacher.

(ii) abc@gmail.com

Invitation to Judge Our Public Speaking Competition

Dear Dr. Tharoor,

I hope you are doing well. We are organizing an Inter-School Public Speaking Competition on 28th March, 2025 at St. Xaviers College, Gurgaon. We would be honored if you could be the judge for the event. Your presence and guidance would inspire our students.

Please let us know your availability.

Best regards,

Ravi Shashank

St. Xaviers College

4. (i) 1. (c) school bags

2. (d) extra

(ii) (c) Opened

(iii) (a) The school children wore grey shorts or skirts and light blue shirts or blouses. Their clothes were faded and mended and their hair was oiled and combed flat.

(b) Jagu was kind to Hari by giving him a glass of tea during the day and smiling at him when he noticed Hari listening to his songs.

(c) The song made Hari realize that Jagu also had a village he called home.

(d) "It was just that he was a silent, hard-working, worried man and had no time and no gift for speech."

(e) There were no customers because it was a hot afternoon, a quiet time for business.

(iv)

Mr. Panwallah	called	Hari	to	sit
beside	him	and	showed	him
the	inside	of	a	big
grandfather	clock.	He	explained	what
was	wrong	with	it	and
how	to	fix	it.	He
then	offered	to	take	Hari
as	an	apprentice,	paying	him
a	little	and	patiently	training
him	for	two	hours	daily.

5. (i) 1. found 2. lying
3. was 4. waved
5. cried 6. shouted
7. hesitated 8. looked

(ii) (a) after (b) over
(c) out (d) of
(e) under (f) over
(g) out of (h) since

(iii) 1. (a) These are fresh mangoes which I bought yesterday.
2. (c) The debating teams were very happy as they had been declared joint champions.
3. (a) When the rain came down, all the people ran away.
4. (d) Although the disciple was wise, the teacher did not truest him.

(iv) 1. (b) The teacher told us to come early tomorrow as the examination begins at eight o'clock.
2. (a) Rahul plays the guitar as well as the drums.
3. (c) She said she would not be available, wouldn't she?
4. (d) No other painting in the exhibition is as beautiful as this one.
5. (b) I would rather do aerobics than yoga.
6. (d) The rules of the game were taught by the coach to the children.
7. (d) As soon as the film star arrived the crowd cheered.
8. (b) School bags are often so heavy that students cannot carry them.

SAMPLE QUESTION PAPER

ENGLISH LANGUAGE

(PAPER - 1)

General Instructions

Maximum Marks : 80

Time allowed : Two hours

Answers to this paper must be written on the paper provided separately.

You will **not** be allowed to write during the first **15** minutes.

This time is to be spent in reading the question paper.

The time given at the head of this paper is the time allowed for writing the answers.

Attempt **all five** questions.

The intended marks for questions or parts of questions are given brackets ().

You are advised to spend not more than 30 minutes in answering **Question 1** and 20 minutes in answering **Question 2**.

Question 1

Write a composition (300-350 words) on any one of the following. **(20)**

(Do not spend more than 30 minutes on this question.)

(i) Write an original short story entitled 'God helps those who help others.'

(ii) 'Online classes are the future of education.' Express your views **for** or **against** this statement.

(iii) Every year, the school holds a fair known as 'The Annual School Fete'. Describe what you see at the fete. Give details of the food, game and other stalls put up there.

(iv) You are a resident of London, England and are visiting India for the first time to attend a training course. Write an account of your experience and what you learnt on reaching there.

(v) Study the picture given below. Write a short story or a description or an account of what it suggests to you. Your composition may be about the subject of the picture or you may take suggestions from it; however, there must be a clear connection between the picture and your composition.

Question 2

Select any one of the following.

(Do not spend more than 20 minutes on it.) **(10)**

(i) Write a letter to the Editor of a newspaper about the insanitary conditions prevailing in your locality and the indifference of the Municipal authorities in spite of repeated letters of complaint.

(ii) Your friend, Suraj, has cleared the prestigeous CAT examination. Write a letter congratulating him for his success expressing how proud you are of him.

Question 3

(i) You are Manish/Mishita, the Secretary of Tours and Trips Society of Translam Academy International, Meerut. The school is organising a 20-day historical tour to some places inviting students interested in visiting those places. Write a notice in about 50 words to be put up on the school notice board. **(5)**

(ii) Write an email to your cousin Swinky with mail id swinky912@hotmail.com telling her about your recent 20-day historical tour. You are Kama. **(5)**

Question 4

Read the following passage carefully and answer the questions that follow.

Apollo Hospital group has installed the world's most advanced Cyberknife robotic radio surgery system at the Cancer Speciality Centre in Chennai, India. Although it meant a substantial cost for the hospital, Apollo decided to go ahead with the project due to the new-found enthusiasm for robotics in India.

From the Chandrayaan-I project for sending robots to the Moon to biomedical engineering and the auto industry, India has been using robotics on a wide scale.

In an increasingly technology-driven country, robotics has fast assumed significance not only for industrial applications but also for using in various day-to-day human activities. According to the Oxford Dictionary, robotics is the branch of technology that deals with the design, construction, operation, structural disposition, manufacture and application of robots.

The word robotics was derived from the word robot. It was first used in print by Isaac Asimov, in his science fiction story 'Liar!' published in May 1941, in the magazine Astounding Science Fiction. Today, it is a confluence of science using the continuing advancements of mechanical engineering, material science, sensor fabrication, manufacturing techniques and advanced algorithms.

Presently, robotics is at the **pinnacle** of technical development. Though robotics in India is at a nascent stage, industrial automation in India has opened up a huge potential for robotics. Innovation coupled with consolidated research and development has catapulted India's scientific position in robotic technology to a very high level. Analysts claim that the Indian manufacturing industry has been growing at an average rate of 10 percent to 12 percent per year and the global market for robots is projected to rise by an average of 4.2 percent, while in India, the industry is expected to grow at a rate 2.5 times that of the global average.

In medicine, the importance of robotics has been growing. Robotic surgery is a new and exciting emerging technology that holds significant promise. Robots are increasingly being used in a variety of clinical and surgical settings for increasing surgical accuracy and decreasing operating times. Often they create better healthcare outcomes than standard current approaches. Robotic technology will have a **tremendous** social and cultural impact on the future of healthcare. In providing healthcare, robots are expected to augment traditional treatment, resulting in humans and robots working side by side. It has been proven that robotic systems have benefited our society in many ways. For instance, some robots have helped children with developmental disabilities, others have improved the health status of people where as with different deficiencies. People who have experienced therapy robots in their lives have commented that robots brought confidence in their lives as well as solved problems related to health.

The other fact is that in some industrial countries robots are helping children with deficiencies to develop faster and have positively influenced their behaviour.

Experts predict that by 2020, robots will become more intelligent and irreplaceable as they would perform most household chores such as laundry and home maintenance.

They would provide valuable services for children and elderly people. Thus, in the future, robots promise to play an important role in our lives.

(i) For each word given below, choose the correct meaning (as used in the passage) from the options provided. **(2)**

1. Tremendous *(line 27)*

(a) trivial (b) notable (c) miniscule (d) infinitesimal

2. Pinnacle *(line 16)*

(a) nadir (b) trough (c) zenith (d) highest point

(ii) Which word in the passage means the opposite of the word 'surplus'? **(1)**

(a) Augment (b) Catapulted (c) Deficiencies (d) Disabilities

(iii) Answer the following questions briefly in your own words.

(a) In which sectors has India been using robotics? **(2)**

(b) What does 'robotics' mean? **(2)**

(c) Why are robots being increasingly used in clinical surgeries? **(2)**

(d) What is the current scientific position of India in robotic technology? **(2)**

(e) Which word or phrase in the passage denotes that setting up a radio surgery system was an expensive deal for Apollo Hospital group? **(1)**

(iv) Describe in your own words the present scenario of robotic technology in India and its growing influence in medicine. Do not exceed 50 words. **(8)**

Question 5

(i) **Fill in each of the numbered blanks with correct form of the words given in brackets. Do not copy the passage but write in correct serial order the word or phrase appropriate to the blank space.** **(8)**

Example Ritika ....(0).........(talk) to her grandfather yesterday.

Answer : (0) talked

Single combat has been known to exist ever since man first (1)......... (appear) on Earth. Early man had to (2)......... (hunt) for his food and he (3)......... (use) the same weapons in single combat as he did for (4)......... (hunt). The development of weapons from the early clubs to the sword (5)......... (vary) from country to country.

In the sixteenth century, fencing (6)......... (bring) to England by the Italians. Junior fencers gained their qualifications by (7)......... (fight) for a prize before their peers.

Fencing has since (8)......... (become) a popular sport appealing to both men and women alike.

(ii) **Fill in each blank with an appropriate words.** **(4)**

(a) .... Peter and John, there were three other boys present.

(b) He was stabbed .... a lunatic with a dagger.

(c) She dislikes being looked ....

(d) Don't throw food .... the dog.

(e) I'm going for lunch and will be back .... 30 minutes.

(f) You have .... Thursday noon to submit your assignment.

(g) Michael Phelps won eight gold medals .... Beijing in 2008.

(h) I see a spider .... the door.

(iii) **Join the following sentences to make one complete sentence without using and, but or so. Choose the correct option.** **(4)**

1. **He is not educated. He possesses practical wisdom.**
   - (a) Though he is not educated but he possesses practical wisdom.
   - (b) Though he is not educated yet he possesses practical wisdom.
   - (c) Though he is not educated, he possesses practical wisdom.
   - (d) None of the above

2. **They gave her the best treatment. They could not save her.**
   - (a) Although they gave her the best treatment, they could not save her.
   - (b) Although they gave her the best treatment, yet they could not save her.
   - (c) They gave her the best treatment in spite they could not save her.
   - (d) None of the above

3. **God made small things. God made great things.**
   - (a) God made both small and great things.
   - (b) God made small, great things.
   - (c) Small things were made by God, so were great things.
   - (d) God made small as well as great things.

4. **Martin is not tall. His father is also not tall.**
   - (a) Either Martin or his father is tall.
   - (b) Either Martin or his father is not tall.
   - (c) Neither Martin nor his father is not tall.
   - (d) Neither Martin nor his father is tall.

(iv) Choose the correct option to rewrite the following according to instructions given after each sentence. **(8)**

1. I saw Paul three years back. It's been a long time.

   (Rewrite using : for)

   (a) I haven't seen Paul for three years, long time.
   (b) I haven't seen Paul for a long time.
   (c) I have seen Paul for three years.
   (d) I have seen Paul for three years, which is a long time.

2. It's not necessary to take a lot of luggage when going on holiday.

   (Use : much)

   (a) You needn't take much luggage when going on holiday.
   (b) You don't have to take much luggage when going on holiday.
   (c) You don't need much luggage when going on holiday.
   (d) All of the above

3. Perhaps, he hasn't received the doctor's results yet.

   (Use : may)

   (a) You may not have received the doctor's results yet.
   (b) He may not have received the doctor's results yet.
   (c) He may have received the doctor's results yet.
   (d) You may have received the doctor's results yet.

4. The doorbell rang in the middle of her phone conversation.

   (Rewrite using : while)

   (a) The doorbell rang while she was speak on the phone.
   (b) The doorbell was ringing while she was talking on the phone.
   (c) The doorbell rang while she was talking on the phone.
   (d) None of the above

5. That letter arrived only a few minutes ago.

   (Rewrite using : just)

   (a) The letter arrived just.
   (b) The letter has just arrived.
   (c) Just the letter arrived.
   (d) The letter has arrived just.

6. Kerrie has paid the bill.

   (Begin with : The bill...)

   (a) The bill was paid by Kerrie.
   (b) The bill has been paid by Kerrie.
   (c) The bill had been paid by Kerrie.
   (d) The bill is paid by Kerrie.

7. Does the police officer catch the thief?

   (Begin with : Is...)

   (a) Is the thief being caught by the police officer?
   (b) Is the thief being catch by the police officer?
   (c) Is the thief catch by the police officer?
   (d) Is the thief caught by the police officer?

8. She said, 'I have finished the work.'

   (Begin with : She said that...)

   (a) She said that she finished the work.
   (b) She said that she has finished the work.
   (c) She said that she had finished the work.
   (d) She said that the work was finished by her.

Answers

1. *(i)*

God Helps those Who Help Others

Smriti got up late that day as her college was closed. Both her parents were working in different offices so they had left for the day. As she was preparing breakfast for herself, she suddenly remembered that she had promised to look after her sick uncle that day as her aunt had to visit a government office to get some work done. Smriti had promised her aunt that she would reach their home by 10 a.m. so that her aunt could go for her work.

So, Smriti finished her breakfast quickly and was ready to go. Taking an auto-rickshaw, she went to her uncle's house. After her aunt left for work, Smriti sat and conversed with her uncle who was lying in bed. Then, she prepared a cup of ginger tea for him and brought it for him. As she started cooking khichri for his lunch, her phone rang. It was her mother who was yelling at her. Smriti could not understand what her mother was shouting about. The only thing she understood was that her mother was telling her to come home immediately.

Smriti left for home soon after cooking the khichri and giving it to her uncle. She had already made a call to her aunt and explained why she had to leave. On reaching home, to her horror, she was told by her mother, who had returned from office, that the house had been burgled. Apparently, in her hurry to reach her uncle's home, Smriti had left the front door unlocked. Thus, the burglar had an easy time stealing all their valuable items. The police were already there and were dusting various locations for fingerprints of the burglar.

The next day, they were pleasantly surprised to receive a phone call from the police station that informed them that the burglar had been caught due to his fingerprints. He had been in jail three times earlier for burglaries so the police knew where they could find him. The stolen valuables were also recovered from the burglar. Thus, Smriti realised that the saying 'God helps those who help others' is true.

(ii)

For the Motion

I strongly support the statement that online classes are the future of education.

In today's fast-changing world, technology, has become an integral part of our lives and education is no exception. Online learning provides students with the flexibility to study at their own pace and convenience. Unlike traditional classrooms, where learning is bound by fixed schedules, online education allows students to access lessons anytime, anywhere. This is especially beneficial for students in remote areas who might not have access to quality schools and teachers.

Another key advantage of online learning is that it caters to different learning styles. Some students understand concepts better through videos, while others prefer reading notes or participating in interactive discussions. Online classes offer recorded lectures, quizzes and AI-based personalised learning tools, making lessons more engaging and effective.

Furthermore, online education reduces financial burdens. Schools and universities save on infrastructure costs, while students save on transportation and accommodation expenses. The availability of digital resources also eliminates the need for costly textbooks, making education more affordable for many.

The COVID-19 pandemic demonstrated how online education can ensure uninterrupted learning even in challenging times. Even today, many schools and universities continue to integrate digital learning, proving that online education is not just a temporary solution but a long-term necessity. With further advancements in artificial intelligence and virtual reality, online learning will only become more immersive and interactive, solidifying its place as the future of education.

Against the Motion

I respectfully disagree with the motion that online classes are the future of education.

Education is not just about acquiring knowledge-it is about interaction, discipline, and holistic development. In physical classrooms, students engage in discussions, clear doubts instantly, and develop essential social skills. Teachers do more than just deliver lessons; they guide, mentor, and inspire students. The warmth of a teacher's encouragement or the motivation of peer competition cannot be replaced by a screen.

Another significant concern is accessibility. Not all students have access to stable internet connections, advanced devices, or a quiet environment for studying. Many children, especially those from economically weaker backgrounds, struggle with online learning, widening the educational divide. A system that benefits only the privileged cannot be considered the future of education.

Health issues also cannot be ignored. Spending long hours in front of a screen leads to eye strain, headaches, and fatigue. Additionally, reduced physical activity affects students' overall well-being. In online classes, students are often easily distracted and lack the discipline that a structured school environment provides.

Moreover, real-life classrooms teach students teamwork, leadership, and confidence-qualities that are difficult to develop in a virtual setting. Schools provide opportunities for extracurricular activities, sports, and social interactions, all of which play a crucial role in shaping a well-rounded individual. No digital platform can truly replicate these experiences.

Thus, while online classes can be a helpful supplement to education, they cannot replace the traditional classroom. The ideal way forward is a blended learning approach that integrates technology with classroom teaching to create a balanced and effective education system.

(iii) **The Annual School Fete**

The school fete is an occasion looked forward to by all of us. In my school, it was held on 10th October this year. Feverish preparations began two weeks prior. Each class was asked to set up a stall of their choice. Contributions from the students were collected and invitations were sent to the parents, VIPs of the city and other prominent people.

The day arrived too soon and turned out to be cloudy. By mid-day, the Sun peeped through the clouds that hung heavy in the sky. The clouds threatened to ruin everything but thankfully a westerly breeze blew them steadily away, bringing much cheer to our dampened spirits.

It was exciting to see students manning the stalls, selling assorted items from raffle tickets to 'ring a gift', hoopla, target practice, etc. A giant wheel was running for small children who were shouting with delight as the wheel went round. There were also stalls of eatables selling snacks, chowmein, cakes, chocolates and cold beverages. There was even a tea stall for those who wanted to drink something warm.

The students were working as if they were true businessmen, accounting for cash and stocks. The stalls selling eatables were the most crowded. The occasional crackle of the loudspeaker broke the revelry to make an announcement.

A friendly tap on my shoulder made me turn around. "Hi, Mohit", said Devesh as he took my hand and escorted me to his stall selling raffle tickets. He persuaded me to buy one. I reluctantly parted with a ten rupee note in exchange for the ticket which I carelessly shoved in my back pocket. Thereafter, I had a gala time with my friends eating chowmein and ice cream till we had run out of money.

Just as I was about to depart, the microphone crackled to life to announce the number of the first prize winner in the lucky draw. I pulled out the crumbled ticket from my pocket. And lo and behold! I had struck the jackpot! In a trance, I walked up to the podium, to collect my prize which was a wonderful new tablet computer. I will never forget this day when I was introduced to the digital world in such a delightful manner.

(iv) As a resident of London, England, I had always been curious about India-its history, its people and its way of life. So when I had the chance to visit for a training course, I was both excited and a little nervous. No amount of reading or research could truly prepare me for what I was about to experience.

From the moment I arrived, India felt like a world of contrasts-modern and traditional, fast-paced yet deeply rooted in culture. The streets were lively, filled with people going about their day and there was a certain rhythm to the chaos that was strangely fascinating. It didn't take long for me to realise that India was not just one experience but a collection of many, woven together in a way that was both complex and beautiful.

The training course was held at a well-established institution and I was fortunate to interact with professionals from different parts of the country. What stood out to me was how passionate and driven everyone was, yet there was an ease and warmth in their interactions. Discussions often extended beyond the classroom, with people sharing insights about their industries, their cities and even their personal experiences. The learning was not just academic-it was an exchange of perspectives that broadened my understanding of both my field and the people I was working with.

Outside of the training, I took time to explore. Walking through the streets, visiting local markets, and trying different foods, I began to appreciate the layers of everyday life here. I wasn't just a visitor; I was a learner, observing and absorbing. Conversations with locals, whether it was a shopkeeper or a fellow commuter, added depth to my experience.

By the time I left, I realised that this trip had given me much more than professional knowledge. It challenged me to step out of my comfort zone, to see things from new perspectives, and to embrace the unknown with an open mind. India was not just a destination, it was an experience that had left a lasting impression on me, one that I would carry long after I returned home.

(v) This given picture shows a part of the Wagah Border Ceremony, also called 'the Beating Retreat Ceremony', which is a daily military practice conducted at the border outpost of Wagah in Punjab. The security forces of both India and Pakistan take part in this exercise conducted at sunset every day. From the Indian side, soldiers of the Border Security Force (BSF) participate in this exercise. From the Pakistani side, the Pakistan Rangers carry out this exercise. The drill comprises elaborate and rapid colourful movements by soldiers of both sides. Thousands of people gather on either side of the border gates every evening to witness the ceremony. The event has many international viewers too.

Security guards man the borders on both sides. As the Sun sets, the iron gates at the border are opened and the two flags are lowered at the same time. The flags are folded and the ceremony ends with a retreat that involves a handshake between soldiers from either side, followed by the closing of the gates again. The ceremony is symbolic of the rivalry between the two nations. In addition, it is also a reflection of the goodwill and cooperation between India and Pakistan, two nations divided by politics but united by sentiments.

The Wagah border bears historical and political significance for people of both the countries and stands testimony to the Partition of 1947. It remains a cause for tension on the Indian subcontinent even today due to the mass killings that took place at that time. Some people are of the opinion that partition should have never happened. Others strongly favour partition and say that it was suitable for colonial India at that time. The ceremony at the Wagah border may be conducted by two nations but, in reality, the people on the Pakistan side are no different than the people on the Indian side. Citizens of both the nations still wish to cross the border without any fear or hatred and greet each other without any weapons and security.

2. (i) 102, Gumti No. 5,

Kanpur

4th April, 20XX

The Editor,

The Times of India,

Kanpur, Uttar Pradesh

Insanitary conditions in Gokul Dham Colony

Dear Sir/Ma'am,

Through the columns of your prestigious daily, I wish to draw the attention of the concerned authorities towards the extremely pitiable conditions in Gokul Dham Colony. Sanitation is the cornerstone of public health and our colony drastically lacks it. Improper disposal of domestic waste and open sewages have been causing catastrophic effects on the health of the children as well as the adults in our colony.

This, in turn, is giving rise to serious diseases like diarrhea, cholera, etc. Water-logging and open manholes are other sources of diseases like malaria. They have also posed a risk before parents who are scared of sending their children out for playing. Yet, the local authorities are indifferent to such a grave concern. This is not only astonishing but also shameful on their part.

I would like to request the civil authorities to show their concern in this regard and take necessary steps immediately.

Thanking you,

Yours sincerely,

Sima Kushwaha

(ii) 14/3 Ashok Vihar,

New Delhi

1st October, 20XX

Dear Suraj,

It was indeed a pleasure to hear from Dinesh that you have passed the CAT examination with 99 percentile and are expecting to get admission in one of the IIMs. Please accept my heartiest congratulations on this achievement. You really deserved it. Your hardwork and perseverance have paid you dividends. Your excellent result is owed to the immense hardwork and dedicated effort put in. Studying systematically and sacrificing your leisure has helped you crack the much dreaded CAT examination with flying colours!

I am sure both uncle and aunt are extremely proud of you. Please pay my sincere regards to them. However, the interview is a hard nut to crack too. Please prepare thoroughly well for it leaving no stone unturned.

Wishing you all the very best and hoping for complete success!

Tell me about your counselling and good luck for your interview. Congratulations!

Yours lovingly,

Ravi

3. (i) **Time for Tour!**

20-day Tour to Historical Places

From 24th December, 20XX to 14th January, 20XX

for students of Classes IX – XII

Interested students must submit their parents' acceptance letter and deposit ₹ 2500 by 15th November, 20XX.

(ii) **E-mail-id** swinky912@hotmail.com

20-day historical trip

Dear Swinky,

How are you? I am doing good here. It's been a long time and I desperately wanted to tell you about the 20-day tour organised by the Tours and Trips society of our school.

The trip organised was an amazing learning experience for us. We travelled across 7 states—Tamil Nadu, Kerala, Delhi, Assam, Maharashtra, Punjab and Gujarat. We visited various religious as well as historically important places like Rameshwaram Temple, Jallianwala Bagh, Kartavya Path, etc.

The glory of our past, our culture and our struggles to reach where our nation stands today were deeply imbibed in us throughout our trip.

There are many more things that I want share with you when I visit you over the weekend.

Meeting you soon,

Yours lovingly

Kama

4. (i) (1) (b) notable (2) (d) highest point

(ii) (c) deficiencies

(iii) (a) India has been using robotics in the sectors of space exploration, biomedical engineering and the automobile industry. Recently, Apollo Hospital Group has installed world's most advanced Cyberknife robotic radio surgery system in a Cancer Speciality Centre in Chennai.

(b) 'Robotics' refers to the branch of technology that deals with the design, construction, operation, structural disposition, manufacture and application of robots.

(c) Robots are being increasingly used in clinical surgeries due to their higher surgical accuracy, reduced operating time and creation of better healthcare outcomes when compared with the currently standard approach to surgeries.

(d) The current scientific position of India in robotic technology is that it is at a very high level as Indian manufacturing industry has been growing at an average rate of 10% to 12% which is 2.5 times that of the global average.

(e) The phrase in the passage that denotes that it was an expensive deal is 'substantial cost' in the first paragraph. Apollo Hospital group has installed the world's most advanced Cyberknife robotic radio surgery system at the Cancer Speciality Centre in Chennai, India.

(iv)

Robotic	technology	in	India	Is
advancing	rapidly,	influencing	Industries,	space
research	and	healthcare.	Robotic	surgery
enhances	precision,	reduces	recovery	time
and	improves	patient	outcomes.	Robots
assist	in	therapy	and	elderly
care.	With	ongoing	research	and
innovation,	robotics	is	set	to
transform	India's	medical	and	industrial
sectors,	making	processes	more	efficient.

5. (i) (1) appeared (2) hunt (3) used (4) hunting
(5) varied (6) was brought (7) fighting (8) become

(ii) (a) Besides (b) by (c) at (d) to
(e) in (f) until (g) in (h) on

(iii) (1) (c) Though he is not educated, he possesses practical wisdom.

(2) (a) Although they gave her the best treatment, they could not save her.

(3) (d) God made small as well as great things.

(4) (d) Neither Martin nor his father is tall.

(iv) (1) (b) I haven't seen Paul for a long time.

(2) (d) All of the above

(3) (b) He may not have received the doctor's results yet.

(4) (c) The doorbell rang while she was talking on the phone.

(5) (b) The letter has just arrived.

(6) (b) The bill has been paid by Kerrie.

(7) (d) Is the thief caught by the police officer?

(8) (c) She said that she had finished the work.